Time Bomb 2000

ISBN
9 780130 952844

Selected Titles from the
YOURDON PRESS COMPUTING SERIES
Ed Yourdon, *Advisor*

ANDREWS AND STALICK Business Reengineering: The Survival Guide

BASSETT Framing Software Reuse: Lessons From the Real World

COAD AND NICOLA Object-Oriented Programming

COAD AND YOURDON Object-Oriented Analysis, 2/E

COAD AND YOURDON Object-Oriented Design

COAD AND MAYFIED Java Design: Building Better Apps and Applets

COAD WITH NORTH AND MAYFIELD Object Models: Strategies,
    Patterns, and Applications, 2/E

CONNELL AND SHAFER Object-Oriented Rapid Prototyping

CONSTANTINE Constantine on Peopleware

CONSTANTINE AND YOURDON Structured Design

DEGRACE AND STAHL Wicked Problems, Righteous Solutions

DeMARCO Controlling Software Projects

DeMARCO Structured Analysis and System Specification

EMBLEY, KURTZ, AND WOODFIELD Object-Oriented Systems Analysis

FLAVIN Fundamental Concepts in Information Modeling

GARMUS AND HERRON Measuring the Software Process:
    A Practical Guide to Functional Measurements

GROCHOW Information Overload:
    Creating Value with the New Information Systems Technology

JONES Assessment and Control of Software Risks

KING Project Management Made Simple

PAGE-JONES Practical Guide to Structured Systems Design, 2/E

PINSON Designing Screen Interfaces in C

PUTMAN AND MYERS Measures for Excellence:
    Reliable Software on Time within Budget

RODGERS Oracle: A Database Developer's Guide

RUBLE Practical Analysis and Design for Client/Server and GUI Systems

RUHL Programmer's Survival Guide: Career Strategies for Computer

SHLAER AND MELLOR Object Lifecycles: Modeling the World in States

SHLAER AND MELLOR Object-Oriented Systems Analysis:
    Modeling the World in Data

STARR How to Build Shlaer-Mellor Object Models

THOMSETT Third Wave Project Management

ULRICH AND HAYES The Year 2000 Software Crisis: Challenge of the Century

YOURDON Death March: The Complete Software Developer's Guide to Surviving
    "Mission Impossible" Projects

YOURDON Decline and Fall of the American Programmer

YOURDON Rise and Resurrection of the American Programmer

YOURDON Modern Structured Analysis

YOURDON Object-Oriented Systems Design

YOURDON Structured Walkthroughs, 4/E

YOURDON AND ARGILA Case Studies in Object-Oriented Analysis and Design

YOURDON, WHITEHEAD, THOMANN, OPPEL, AND NEVERMANN
    Mainstream Objects: An Analysis and Design Approach for Business

YOURDON INC. Yourdon Systems Method: Model-Driven Systems Development

Time Bomb 2000

What the Year 2000 Computer Crisis Means to You!

Edward Yourdon
and
Jennifer Yourdon

Prentice Hall PTR
Upper Saddle River, New Jersey 07458
http://www.phptr.com

Library of Congress Cataloging-in-Publication Data

```
Yourdon, Edward.
     Time bomb 2000: what the year 2000 computer crisis means to you!
  / Edward Yourdon, Jennifer Yourdon.
     p.  cm.
  Includes bibliographical references and index.
  ISBN 0-13-095284-2
  1. Year 2000 date conversion (Computer systems)  2. Software
  maintenence. I. Jennifer Yourdon.  II. Title.
QA76.76.S64Y68  1997
363.34'97--dc21                                        97-36590
                                                          CIP
```

Editorial/production supervision: *Kathleen M. Caren*
Production Team Extraordinaire: *Joanne Anzalone, Lisa Iarkowski,*
    Patti Guerrieri, Camille Trentacoste
Cover design director: *Jerry Votta*
Cover design: *Scott Weiss*
Back cover photo: *Charlie Samuels*
Manufacturing manager: *Alexis R. Heydt*
Acquisitions editor: *Stephen Solomon*
Marketing manager: *Dan Rush*
Editorial assistant: *Bart Blanken*

© 1998 Prentice Hall PTR
Prentice-Hall, Inc.
A Simon & Schuster Company
Upper Saddle River, New Jersey 07458

Prentice Hall books are widely used by corporations and government agencies for training, marketing, and resale.

The publisher offers discounts on this book when ordered in bulk quantities. For more information, contact Corporate Sales Department, Phone: 800-382-3419;
FAX: 201-236-7141; E-mail: corpsales@prenhall.ocm

Printed in the United States of America
10 9 8 7 6

ISBN: 0-13-095284-2

Prentice-Hall International (UK) Limited, *London*
Prentice-Hall of Australia Pty. Limited, *Sydney*
Prentice-Hall Canada Inc., *Toronto*
Prentice-Hall Hispanoamericana, S.A., *Mexico*
Prentice-Hall of India Private Limited, *New Delhi*
Prentice-Hall of Japan, Inc., *Tokyo*
Simon & Schuster Asia Pte. Ltd., *Singapore*
Editora Prentice-Hall do Brasil, Ltda., *Rio de Janeiro*

To my family, in the hope that this book will help us muddle through the Year-2000 problem together. And most of all, to my wife, Toni, whose love and support make it possible for me to face the Year-2000 problem with strength and hope for the future.

Ed Yourdon

To the people I feel so lucky to call my family and friends.

Jennifer Yourdon

Contents

Preface

The day the world ends, no one will be there, just as no one was there when it began. This is a scandal. Such a scandal for the human race that it is indeed capable collectively, out of spite, of hastening the end of the world by all means just so it can enjoy the show.

Jean Baudrillard, Cool Memories, *Chapter 5 (1987)*

Saturday morning, 11:00 AM

Your head throbs as you roll out of bed. It was quite a celebration last night—the celebration of a lifetime—and you've slept through your alarm clock. But now it's Saturday morning, and you always call your dear old mom in North Carolina every Saturday morning. So you shuffle past the kitchen, pause briefly to snarl at the coffee machine that failed to brew your morning coffee as usual, and slump into the living room sofa to conduct the weekly hi-Mom-howya-doin' ritual. You pick up the phone, and after a moment, snarl again—there is no dial tone.

Shuffling back to the bedroom, it becomes obvious why you didn't hear the alarm clock—there's no electricity. And, when you step into the shower to wash away the headache, there is no hot water. You're in a worse mood when you step out again. Snarls have given way to soft curses, but you realize that you need to sound pleasant and cheerful when you talk to Mom, so you force a smile onto your face as you head for the living room again. You pick up the phone again, and after another moment of silence, all attempts at civility vanish—still no dial tone. You hold the phone in front of your face and curse in loud, angry terms at the telephone company.

There's still no dial tone at 1 PM, and the coffee maker still won't work. To make matters worse, the refrigerator has stopped too, and the freezer is now leaking water onto the floor. You've gotten dressed in the interim, and even though you've frequently criticized the coffee at the corner deli, you now decide that it's better than no coffee at all. As you reach the front door of the apartment building, you remember that you ran out of cash during the celebrations last night, so you stop at the bank on the corner to get a few dollars out of the ATM machine—but the machine gobbles up your bank card and refuses to give you any cash at all. When you reach the deli on the corner, you find it even more curious that *their* phone is also out of service, and that they're operating without electricity. And when you return to your apartment, you still find silence rather than a dial tone when you pick up the phone.

More silence on Sunday, and again on Monday. It's now been three days since you've had working telephone service, and it's no longer funny. Not only have you been unable to reach Mom in North Carolina, but you haven't been able to communicate with any of your friends and business associates. Indeed, the whole point of staying home on Monday (January 3) was that you were expecting a *very* important call from a prospective employer who had been trying to lure you away from your current job with a possibility of a 50 percent salary increase—but only if the negotiations could be finalized by January 3.

We won't continue the vignette any further—you get the point. If your phone was out of service for three days, it would be somewhat annoying, and there could possibly be some important consequences. But suppose that it wasn't just your phone that was inoperable, but every phone in your building ... in your neighborhood ... in your city ... in your state ... in the entire country? Suppose that nobody could call anybody else for three days? Would civilization come to a screeching halt? Not likely—but there would be a lot of grumpy people, and there would inevitably be some financial consequences.

Let's make this vignette more serious: suppose the phone outage persisted not just for three days, but for a full month. No phone calls for the entire month of January; nobody has a dial tone. Don't just nod your head when you read this sentence: *think about it.* Suppose you couldn't call anyone, and no one could call you because nobody in your city had a working phone, and as far as you could tell, nobody in North America, Europe, or anywhere else where phones were taken for granted had viable telephone service. (It's worth noting, by the way, that approximately 50% of the human race, particularly in large sections of China and Africa, has *never* made a phone call, so not everyone would be affected!)

Obviously, a month without telephone service would be pretty serious—but what if it was a full year? Could your employer survive for a full year, let alone a month, without phone service? Could your city? Could the national government of whatever country you live in? And if you think a year is bad, what about a decade? A century ago, *all* of what was then considered "modern society" functioned quite well without telephones—but would that be possible today?

Lest you think that we're concocting stories to pick on the phone company, remember the other events in the vignette above: your bank's ATM machine doesn't work and the lights are out. And, let's expand our vignette a bit: What about your car? Suppose you turned the key in the ignition and nothing happened? Or, to put things into the proper perspective: Suppose you were driving home a little early from the New Year's Eve festivities, and just at the stroke of midnight, all the red lights and alarm signals on the dashboard begun to flash and beep at you? Now what?

Welcome to the Year-2000 problem. No, this is not a joke, and it's probably not an exaggeration. It won't happen to you on *this* New Year's Eve ... but the next New Year's Eve that falls on a Friday will be December 31, 1999. And when the clock strikes midnight on that very special Friday night, every computer system in the world will encounter a "rollover" phenomenon that may or may not be fatal. In the best of cases, your phone will still work on Saturday morning, January 1, 2000 (indeed, the major telephone companies assure us this will be the case), and so will your car, the electric utility company, and all of the other machines and devices that you've come to depend on, often without even realizing that there's a computer inside.

But in the worst of all cases, the rollover phenomenon that occurs when 1999 changes to 2000 could cause consequences that make the vignettes above seem quite tame by comparison. The computer industry is planning to spend between $300-600 *billion* over the next two to three years in an attempt to avoid this problem, and some experts are already warning that this estimate is too low.[1] But as we write this book in late 1997, it's becoming increasingly clear that the vast complex of computer systems will *not* be completely modified and upgraded to deal with what has come to be known as the as "Year-2000" or "Y2K" software problem.

Because of the magnitude of the Year-2000 problem, hundreds of technical articles have already been published in computer journals, and dozens of computer conferences have been held to offer advice to computer professionals and managers. Numerous articles have appeared in *Fortune, Forbes,* the *Wall Street Journal,* the *Economist,* and other business publications to warn senior managers of the impact of the problem. Articles have even appeared on the front pages of the *New York Times,* the *Boston Globe,* and *Newsweek.* And, several technically-oriented Year-2000 books have been published—with more on the way.[2]

But this is not a book aimed at computer professionals, even though that's the area in which one of the authors makes his living. This book is aimed at computer users, including our family, our neighbors, our friends, and all the millions of people who *use* computers without really understanding or caring about how they work. The technical books and articles warn the computer professionals: "The Year-2000 problem could be really serious if we don't do something about it. We need to get started right now in order to avoid a major disaster!" But this book asks the question: *What if the computer industry doesn't manage to fix the Year-2000 problem successfully?* How serious a problem could it be, and what should your fallback plan be? What would be the economic consequences of a telephone outage for a day, or a month, or a year, or a decade? The telephone, of course, is only one form of communication; what if we didn't have FedEx, the Post Office, or the Internet available? What if the Year-2000 problem knocks out electricity for three days, or the water supply for a month, or access to your bank account for a year, or regular Social Security checks for a decade? Then there's the field of transportation: What are the *personal* consequences of failures with cars, buses, trains, and airplanes? What about credit cards and the stock market? What about newspapers, radio, and television? Hospitals, access to medicine, access to doctors? Food supplies? Welfare? The Internal Revenue Service? The Defense Department? Schools and universities? Oh yes, one last question: What about your job?

If you've never heard of the Year-2000 problem before, the notion that every aspect of our social infrastructure could shut down for even a single day seems preposterous. And when it's presented in such simplistic terms, it *is* preposterous; Year-2000 problems won't happen in the same way, at the same time, in all of these areas. It's highly likely, for example, that when you pick up the phone on January 1, 2000, you *will* get a dial tone—because it's one of the most fundamental, obvious, high-priority aspects of telephone service that AT&T, MCI, Sprint, and the regional Bell operating companies are working on. However, we're far less confident about all of the tiny telephone companies that have sprung up since the tele-communications industry decentralized; indeed, we're not even sure that the larger phone companies will succeed in converting the other aspects of their operational systems. What happens, for example, if you get a phone bill on January 31, 2000 for $325,914,166.14? What happens if every telephone customer in your city gets an equally preposterous bill? What happens when every customer tries to call the phone company's Customer Service department, on the same day, to complain about his or her bill? What happens when the phone company's computer systems decide to cancel everyone's service because of non-payment of his or her bill?

Why do we think something like this could happen? Not because we think the phone company is incompetent, but because the effort to fix the software is a massive job with a very immovable deadline. Most of the large telephone companies have a "portfolio" of computer programs and systems with a total of some 300-400 *million* program instructions that need to be examined for possible corrections for proper operation after January 1, 2000. Banks are dealing with equally large numbers, and as we'll see later in the book, the federal government is dealing with an even larger software portfolio. Unfortunately, the computer industry has been notorious for being substantially behind schedule and over budget, even on projects that are a hundred times smaller than the Year-2000 project. Not only that, programmers have a notorious record for innocently injecting "bugs" into the complex software systems they create. If the statistics about the error-prone nature of "normal" software development is any indication, Year-2000 project teams will still be fixing their mistakes in 2005.

For those who are curious about the details, we explain in Appendix A how this problem came about and what kind of corrections are necessary for Year-2000 projects. In Appendix B, we discuss the "domino effect" problem that can occur if a relatively simple error in, say, the computer systems of banks "ripple" into the credit card systems, and then into the Wall Street stock market systems, etc. This is a variation on the "chaos theory" argument that says a butterfly flapping its wings in Tokyo could cause a tornado in Wichita, Kansas.

If you're not interested in the technical computer details, or if you've already heard the basic explanations of the Year-2000 software problem, feel free to skip the appendices. The "meat" of this book is a discussion of the consequences of Year-2000 failures in our personal lives, and the contingency plans we should be making. As we'll discuss in Chapter 1, one aspect of this contingency planning is to assign reasonable levels of probability to different levels of "severity" of Year-2000 problems. Do you think the most likely scenario is a rash of Year-2000 problems that will last for two or three days? Or, do you think the most likely scenario is a massive decade-long collapse reminiscent of the Great Depression of the 1930s? We personally believe that a majority of the Year-2000 problems will be of the minor variety, though there could well be some "minor" problems that render such critical systems as banking, telecommunications, and utilities inoperable for a few days. We also believe that a significant minority of the Year-2000 problems—perhaps as great as 25-35%—will be of the "moderate" variety, causing failures that will take a month to solve; invoicing and billing systems within business organizations are a prime example of this category.

Unfortunately, we also think that a small percentage—perhaps in the range of 5-10%—of the Year-2000 problems could be of the "serious" variety, i.e., requiring a year to repair. In many cases, this will occur because the "cleanup" process can be time-consuming and tedious. A hurricane usually lasts for only a day, but the hurricane *recovery* can easily take a year if the damage is extensive; we believe the same situation will occur with a small percentage of the Year-2000 software bugs.

Here's an example: Your local bank runs afoul of the Year-2000 problem and begins generating wildly incorrect banking statements. Panicked customers begin withdrawing their cash, and after a few days of attempting to cope with the crisis, the bank has to shut down operations. Assuming that you have a standard bank account (as opposed to uninsured certificates of deposits), and assuming your balance is less than $100,000, your account is insured by the Federal Deposit Insurance

Company (FDIC). Assuming that several banks have the same problem, and that all of their banking records are corrupted by Year-2000 bugs, how long do you think it will be before the FDIC gives you your money? Many of us would be grateful indeed if it only took a year—but attempting to carry out our day-to-day business without the funds in that frozen account could be a problem indeed.

Finally, we think that a very small percentage of Year-2000 problems could be sufficiently devastating that it could take a decade to recover. A decade, by the way, is approximately the length of the Great Depression; we won't try to draw any parallels between the events of 1929 and 1999 at this point, but we do want to emphasize that not all problems can be fixed or forgotten overnight. Our primary concerns in this area are the massive government agencies and systems that are in shaky condition already. Two that come to mind are the Internal Revenue Service (IRS) and Social Security Agency (SSA), though several other federal agencies were experiencing Year-2000 difficulties as this book went to press in late 1997. We'll discuss in Chapter 10 why we think it's possible that the political fallout of the Year-2000 problem could lead to both the IRS and SSA being abolished in their present form, and being replaced by something fundamentally different. For those who have based their life's plans on the assumption that income and savings would be taxed in a certain way, or that retirement funds would be available at a certain age, it could well take a decade to recover from such a shock.

With this kind of framework—minor, moderate, serious, and devastating failures—we'll begin examining each of the major aspects of society mentioned up to this point: communications, utilities, transportation, banking and finance, news broadcasting, travel, medicine, social services, education, government, and employment. Chances are that you'll ignore certain categories. Parents of school-age children, for example, might be thrilled at the prospect of television disappearing from their lives for a year. But, there are likely to be a few categories that represent life-and-death risks. If you're a diabetes patient, the notion that insulin might be unavailable for a month is not a joking matter.

Of course, a far more pleasant Year-2000 scenario would be to assume that nothing will go wrong at all. In the best of all worlds, $300-600 billion will be spent by the world's government agencies and private corporations, the computer problems will be quietly taken care of, and we'll all enjoy New Year's Eve in 1999 with nary a hiccup. Another scenario you're likely to hear is: "Well, it may be a problem for a few of the big companies with those old-fashioned mainframe computers, but it won't be a problem for small companies with their modern PCs; and in any case, most individuals don't depend very much on computers for their day-to-day lives." Perhaps this will turn out to be true, in which case we'll be justifiably criticized for needless scare-mongering. But even though both authors are optimists in our day-to-day lives, our investigation of the Year-2000 situation leads us to believe that it's *very* unlikely that we'll escape serious problems so easily.

Thus, one of our tasks in the chapters ahead is to explain some of the reasons why the Year-2000 rollover could cause significant problems in the various aspects of society that affect all of us. If nothing else, the issues raised in this book may lead you to ask the appropriate officials—i.e., the spokespeople and managers of the various organizations that provide critical services—whether they can confidently promise that their organizations *will* be Year-2000-compliant. When Senator Alphonse D'Amato asked this question of the Federal Reserve

Bank, in his capacity as head of the Senate Banking and Finance Committee, the answer he got was, "No comment." A common variation, which we received from several large organizations while researching this book, was, "We don't know what you're talking about, but whatever it is, don't worry about it." What will you do if you get that answer from *your* bank ... or *your* phone company ... or *your* automobile manufacturer ... or *your* local doctor and hospital?

What most people will do, in the final analysis, is *nothing*. After all, the prospect of a moderate, serious, or devastating collapse of the nation's socio-economic system is too awful for many people to accept. And the actions that would be required to protect oneself from such a disaster would require too much of a sacrifice for most people to accept in advance. This is rather puzzling, because our society has long accepted the notion of paying for insurance associated with crises it hopes will never occur. We pay hundreds of dollars per year for automobile insurance, but nobody wants an auto accident. We pay for medical insurance, and then hope that we won't have to use it for operations or serious illness. And even though each of us must accept the inevitability of our eventual death, we certainly don't expect it to happen next month or next year—yet most of us realize that it's important to plan for it by purchasing life insurance. The Year-2000 planning that we discuss in this book is, in a sense, just another form of insurance; unfortunately, we aren't very optimistic that most people will see it that way.

As we wrote this book during the summer and fall of 1997, we posted draft chapters on our Internet Web site. As a result, we received feedback and comments via e-mail from literally hundreds of people around the world. In addition to pointing out factual errors and making numerous suggestions for improvements, we found a wide range of opinions about the ultimate impact of the Year-2000 problem. Some of our readers and reviewers pleaded with us to take a stand: "If you really think it's going to cause another Great Depression, put yourself on the line and say so." And a few readers criticized us for alarmist exaggerations, implying that perhaps we were doing it in an attempt to generate more sales of the book. Especially when communicating with non-computer-savvy readers, we consider scare-mongering to be the moral equivalent of shouting "Fire!" in a crowded theater—and we did our best to avoid it. But if an occupant of such a theater smells smoke, there's a moral obligation to say so. And if the theater is constructed of wood and other flammable materials, we also think it's appropriate to shout, "There are no smoke detectors or fire sprinklers in this building!" and then let people draw their own conclusions.

We don't *know* what's going to happen when the clock strikes midnight on December 31, 1999; nobody else does either. Some have suggested to us that by making the decision to write a book, we have created an obligation for ourselves to find out, so that we could state the future with certainty. Instead, we've tried to describe plausible scenarios to allow you to evaluate the likelihood of their occurrence, and then we offer some suggestions for responding to those scenarios. We don't have the "answer" to the Year-2000 problem, and given the complexity of the problem, we think it's pretentious for anyone to suggest that he or she does. Instead of presenting answers, we've focused on raising what we think are responsible questions that you should be asking yourselves.

Ultimately, what we think, and what other people think or do, is not your problem. What *you* do is the real issue—in the final analysis, you're responsible for your own actions and for the health and happiness of your family and loved ones. The issues we're writing about in this book are of direct concern to our family, and it forms the basis for our own plans for the Year-2000. We can only hope that we've made a modest contribution to society by articulating the issues for your consideration.

Edward Yourdon
Jennifer Yourdon
New York City, 1997

Endnotes

1. Paul A. Strassmann, "Numbers Add Up to a Bigger Year 2000 Disaster," *Computerworld*, June 13, 1997.
2. See, for example, William M. Ulrich and Ian S. Hayes, *The Year 2000 Software Crisis: Challenge of the Century* (Prentice Hall, 1997).

Year-2000 Fallback Planning Overview

Planning ahead is a measure of class. The rich and even the middle class plan for future generations, but the poor can plan ahead only a few weeks or days.
Gloria Steinem, *"The Time Factor,"* Outrageous Acts and Everyday Rebellions, *1983.*

Introduction

"So what?"

That's the question you should be ready to ask by now. If you've read the brief vignettes in the preface, you should have some awareness that the Year-2000 phenomenon *might* be a problem for you. Indeed, you may have been aware of the problem already, for it's been widely discussed in magazines and newspapers for the past couple of years.

When informed of the Year-2000 problem, most people—including (ironically) many computer professionals—shrug their shoulders and say, "Well, I guess it *could* be a problem. I sure hope they're working on it..." *They* are the computer programmers who are methodically scanning through hundreds of millions of program instructions, replacing two-digit representations of the year with four-digit years in computer systems. We've convinced many of our friends and colleagues that there aren't enough programmers available, and that this massive task probably won't be finished in time—there's simply too much to do, it's an error-prone process, and most companies have gotten started far too late. Our friends shrug their shoulders again, and refer to a different category of "they": politicians, corporate managers, disaster relief agencies, and other civic leaders, who will be expected to organize and plan an appropriate response to whatever goes wrong.

If you're willing to put your fate in the hands of "they," you can skip the remainder of this book. But keep in mind that the Year-2000 problem is unlike normal hurricanes and blizzards, which can be anticipated days or weeks in advance, so that citizens can be warned to take shelter, board up their windows, or evacuate. With Y2000, we can anticipate *when* the problem will begin occurring, but we don't know whether it will be the equivalent of a Force-5 hurricane or a mild spring breeze. It's never happened before, and there are no well-practiced contingency plans to draw upon.

Even with the "familiar" forms of disaster, there are agonizing delays before recovery and relief operations spring into action. As the residents of Florida can testify from repeated experience, it often takes two to three days for state and federal relief agencies to respond to a massive hurricane. And as the residents of Grand Forks, North Dakota can testify with some bitterness after the disastrous spring flood of 1997, it can take well over a month for Congress to stop bickering about allocating relief funds and actually take action. Situations like these involve *one* hurricane or *one* flood; what happens if something of this magnitude hits every part of the country (including the government itself!) at the same time?

It's comforting to think that the government will take care of things when there's a problem, and that organizations like the Red Cross will help with real emergencies. Government's ability to deal with even familiar disasters is certainly less than perfect, though perhaps it's the best that can be expected. But when it comes to Y2000, we're far less impressed. As we'll see in Chapter 10, state and federal government agencies are generally much farther behind in converting their own computer systems than private industry. Directly or indirectly, the actions, operations, and policies of dozens of government agencies at the city, county, state, and federal levels affect every citizen of this country. If a substantial number of these agencies fail or go into a tailspin because of Year-2000 bugs, government becomes part of the problem, not part of the solution.

Obviously, this is not a black-and-white issue; we're not trying to suggest that government is evil or malicious, nor that it's hopelessly and utterly incompetent. Assuming that our leaders are concerned about the welfare of the country, and assuming that they'll respond to serious disasters, then it's reasonable to expect that government will eventually help organize and direct the appropriate recovery process from Year-2000 failures. But, there's ample evidence from governmental responses to crises over the past century to suggest that it could be sluggish, disorganized, misguided, and downright harmful to some individual members of society.

Back to the question posed at the beginning of this chapter: *So what?* We have some detailed answers to that question in the next several chapters, for the "So what?" question depends on whether you're concerned about the loss of basic utilities (electricity, water), food supplies, communication (phone, fax, and mail), or your job. Before we plunge into the details, though, we want to set a framework for developing your own fallback plan. This involves the notion of "risk management," and it also requires you to think about the *duration* of a Year-2000 problem.

Risk Management

Though the Year-2000 problem itself is unique, the notion of planning and preparing for future problems is not. Engineers, planners, and (ironically) managers of computer projects routinely practice *risk management* prior to, and throughout the conduct of, any important and/or expensive project in which something might conceivably go wrong.

We don't have room in this book to provide you with a comprehensive treatment of the subject of risk management; if the idea appeals to you, there are numerous textbooks available.[1] But the basic concepts are straightforward, and we've summarized them below:

- *Identification of risks:* It's hard to anticipate or plan for a risk if you don't have any idea of what it might be. It might not have occurred to you, before you glanced at the table of contents of this book, that your bank account or your job were at risk because of Y2000; but once you've identified the risk, you can begin making plans to deal with it. Risk identification is one of the primary objectives of this book. We may not have covered everything that could possibly go wrong, but we'll discuss the major Year-2000 risk areas in the next several chapters, and this should be enough to help you begin thinking about any others that might be relevant.

- *Evaluation and assessment of risk likelihood and risk impact:* You probably don't spend much time worrying about the risk of being struck by a bolt of lightning, because the odds are infinitesimally small; on the other hand, if such an event were to occur, the consequences would probably be fatal. You manage your day-to-day affairs in this fashion, developing both offensive and defensive plans based on your assessment of the likelihood of unpleasant events (illness, unemployment, violent crime, etc.) and the impact of those events. You need to do the same thing for Year-2000 risks. How likely is it, for example, that the stock market will shut down—and what are the consequences if it does? We can make some general observations about this, based on our knowledge of both the computer situation and the overall economic impact of various Year-2000-related failures; however, this is something you'll need to assess very carefully on your own. Some people, for example, have no stock market investments and would not be impacted if Wall Street ground to a halt; other people have invested their life savings and their retirement portfolio in stocks and bonds, and would be devastated if the market crashed.

- *Regular monitoring of risks:* In most situations, risk is not static; it ebbs and flows, and it increases and decreases over a period of days, weeks, months, and years. The Year-2000 problem is *not* going to be a one-shot affair that occurs pre-

cisely at the stroke of midnight on December 31,
1999; ramifications of the problem will begin
occurring in 1999, and will last well into the
next decade. Depending on the efforts of the
computer programmers, the risk of Year-2000
problems within specific companies will hopefully decrease over the next two years; but depending on the tendency of corporate
management to procrastinate and delay a serious
commitment of resources to Year-2000 projects,
the risk of failure will increase sharply between
now and January 1, 2000. More important, the
"ripple effect" problem discussed in Appendix B
will cause Year-2000 problems to ebb and flow
throughout the entire socio-economic system of
the U.S., and all other countries around the
world. This is something you'll need to monitor
both before and after January 1, 2000, and it's
not something we can do for you in this book. If,
for example, your bank provides you with convincing evidence in 1999 that all of its computer
systems are Year-2000-compliant, then perhaps
you don't need to withdraw all your funds. But
if you learn in 2001 that your bank has made
massive loans to a large corporation that has just
defaulted on its repayments because of its own
Year-2000 problems, then perhaps you should
hustle down to the bank and transfer your money before the bank collapses.

- *Proactive planning to eliminate risks in advance:*
  In most cases, the best way to deal with a risk is

to "head it off at the pass" and eliminate it before it even occurs. Depending on your situation, as well as on your degree of involvement and dependency on computer systems, this may or may not be practical. If you believe, for example, that the Year-2000 problem will create a severe disruption of social services within your metropolitan area, perhaps you should move to a smaller community now, while it's still relatively easy. If you believe that your company or industry will be severely affected, then you have a couple years to begin finding a fallback job or a new career.

• *Reactive planning to minimize the impact of risks that materialize:* Proactive planning is sometimes expensive, and it may involve some unpleasant sacrifices. Not everyone is willing to change jobs or move out of the city. Indeed, it may be utterly impractical in some situations (it's hard to imagine spending the next few years trying to learn to live without the telephone, just because we think the Year-2000 problem might cause a disruption). Similarly, many people are unable or unwilling to take the proactive step of moving out of geographic regions with a frequent occurrence of hurricanes; but they *do* have a reactive plan that essentially says, "If a big storm hits, get into the basement as quickly as possible, because that's the best way to minimize the likelihood of being seriously injured—and get some candles in case we have a power failure for a couple days."

There are two additional items to keep in mind: first, because of the unique, unfamiliar nature of the Year-2000 problem, none of us will be able to fully anticipate all of the risks. To some extent, this is the same situation we face in other aspects of our life: We don't really know whether, at some point, we're going to be faced with a serious illness, long-term unemployment, or a massive fire that burns our home to the ground. That's why most people try to set aside a "nest egg" or "rainy day fund"; that's why most of us have insurance policies. The more of a buffer and reserve that we have, the more we're able to absorb the impact of an unexpected problem.

Ironically, the institutions that we've depended on to help us in this area may be among those at risk. We tend to keep our nest egg account in a bank or brokerage company; we tend to establish insurance policies with trusted, stable insurance companies. As we've already implied in this book, institutions like these are heavily dependent on computer systems that will fail on January 1, 2000 unless they're fixed. So, one of the aspects of risk management that you'll need to worry about is whether your bank, insurance agent, and/or stock broker are part of the problem or part of the solution.

The larger problem is that many American families have no nest egg at all. This is particularly true of young adults, especially those with new families and savings that consist of equity in their home. As numerous books and magazine articles have informed us over the past few decades, ours is a consumption-oriented society with a very low savings rate. To put it more bluntly, many families live from paycheck to paycheck, with a substantial amount of credit card debt. They may have a positive net worth, from an accounting perspective, but only because of the contribution of the equity in their home. A home is a highly illiquid asset, unless one considers home-equity loans that are readily available today. But in a Year-2000 crisis, such loans may be much more difficult to obtain. Not only that, the amount of equity in a home is largely a function of the market value of the home; if that drops substantially because of a Year-2000-induced recession, many American families would find that they have a negative net worth.

The lack of a liquid, fungible nest egg is the bad news. The good news is that some people will be able to profit from the Year-2000 crisis because they'll be better prepared and better able to take advantage of risks that others are trying to avoid. By analogy, not everyone went bankrupt during the Great Depression, and a few people actually prospered. We offer no specific stock market advice in this book, but we note that a Year-2000-induced stock market crash is certainly a possibility. If you believed that was likely, and if you liquidated your stock-market investments during the record-high levels of 1997, you might be in a very good position to pick up bargain-priced stocks in the early years of the next decade.

We won't pursue this notion of aggressive, opportunistic planning for profits or advantages that might be achieved as a result of the Year-2000 problem. It's easy enough to talk about it now, but if a serious Year-2000 crisis does occur, such behavior will generally be described as profiteering, hoarding, or scalping. In any case, we think that most people will have enough trouble surviving the Year-2000 problem without even thinking about how to profit from it.

Severity of the Problem (Day, Month, Year, Decade)

Assessing the impact of a Year-2000 risk involves (among other things) an assessment of the pervasiveness of the risk, and also the duration of the risk. By pervasiveness, we mean is the problem localized within your neighborhood or town, or is everyone facing the same problem throughout the country? If your town is serviced by a small, independent phone company that collapses because of a Year-2000 problem, it will be very inconvenient for you and your neighbors. But if the major metropolitan areas survive with uninterrupted phone service because of the successful Year-2000 conversion efforts of AT&T, then your town's plight will get nothing more than a few minutes' sympathetic coverage on the evening news. On the other hand, if the IRS collapses and a new tax collection scheme is imposed, it will affect everyone. The same is likely to be true if we experience massive Year-2000 failure in several other federal government agencies.

Regarding duration, we have found it useful to identify four distinct time periods: 2-3 days, a month, a year, and a decade. Each of the time periods we've chosen is approximately ten times longer than the one before; because of that, each time duration is likely to require a *qualitatively* different risk management approach. Also, each "level" of time duration has a different degree of likelihood. You might decide, for example, that your local phone company is so well-organized that if something does go wrong, they'll surely have it fixed within 2-3 days. But your personal risk management assessment might lead you to conclude that your bank is so screwed up, even under normal circumstances, that if it encounters a Year-2000 problem, it will be at least a month before things are back to normal.

To see the impact of these different durations of time, consider a non-computer metaphor: Think back to when you were a kid, and your friends and siblings had a tendency to "dunk" one another underwater in the neighborhood swimming pool. If you knew that you were about to be dunked for 2-3 minutes, what would you do? Assuming that you couldn't avoid the experience by swimming away quickly, the answer is simple—hold your breath. The best you can hope for is that you have a moment to prepare, so that you can take a deep breath before your head goes underwater.

But, what would happen if you knew that you were going to be held underwater for 2-3 hours by the neighborhood bully? Unless you had superhuman powers, there is no way that you could hold your breath for three hours; the three-minute risk management strategy simply cannot be "extended" to deal with this new situation. Admittedly, the possibility of being subjected to this kind of treatment is pretty small, but if you *did* have to plan for it, the answer might be to get some scuba gear and make sure the compressed-air tanks are full. If you had more time to prepare, it might even be worth taking some scuba diving lessons. You might also take a proactive risk avoidance strategy—leaving the swimming pool when the bully jumps in, or advising your parents of the imminent danger you face.

What if the underwater dunking lasted for 2-3 days? Obviously, a completely different risk management strategy would be required because any commercially available scuba gear is going to run out of air in a few hours. In addition, you've got to figure out how to sleep and how to get the required food and liquid nutrition to keep you going for three days.

What if the situation persisted for a year, or a decade? We won't try to imagine possible solutions, but you see the point. And while you might argue that the example is ridiculously unlikely beyond the three-minute dunking, we can assure you that it's not so unlikely with regard to the Year-2000 problem. You shouldn't have too much trouble imagining a scenario in which the effects of a Year-2000-related problem last for a few days or a month; and, your risk management strategy should take that into account.

Is a one-year timeframe unrealistic? If the Year-2000 problem does lead to a nationwide (or worldwide) recession, then unemployment will go up sharply. And if the Year-2000 problem causes your employer to go bankrupt, then you may not be able to find a replacement job in 2-3 days or a month. Those who were laid off during the recession of the early 1990s will tell you that it can easily take 6-12 months, or more, to find a job.

As for the prospect of a decade-long Year-2000 impact—as we noted in the Preface, it's not beyond the realm of possibility that major federal agencies like the IRS or SSA could go belly-up because of the political repercussions of a massive Year-2000 failure. Not only would this have long-term repercussions for taxpayers and retired citizens, it would also have serious consequences for those whose jobs and careers have depended on the *existing* IRS/SSA environment. If you're a tax attorney whose past 20 years of employment have depended on your expertise at deciphering arcane IRS rulings, how long will it take you to readjust your life in a world where the IRS tax labyrinth has been replaced with a simple flat tax?

Of course, there's one other Year-2000 scenario: Maybe there won't be any Year-2000 problems at all. Maybe every company and every government agency around the world will finish repairing all of their mission-critical computer systems in time, and maybe they won't make any mistakes. Maybe we'll all wake up on January 1, 2000 and find that aside from a few niggling, insignificant problems, all the computers continue humming along as usual. Maybe we authors will be accused of behaving like the boy who cried "Wolf!" in the fairy tale. If so, it will be deeply embarrassing to us—but that's a small price to pay! Like everyone else in American society, we authors have jobs, bank accounts, telephones, and credit cards. Our lives will be considerably less complicated if we don't have to face disruptions in these areas, even if it does mean spending the first year of the new millennium apologizing to everyone for a problem that never occurred.

Even in the unhappy event that we're correct about the severity of Year-2000 problems, it won't be the end of Western civilization. We're *not* suggesting that Americans will wake up on January 1 and collectively say, "Oh my goodness, our computers have stopped working! Let's all commit suicide!" Nor do we suggest that the entire population will passively sit in their homes, waiting for legions of programmers to belatedly fix the computer problems and save the day. Life will go on, one way or another; many of the computer systems *will* work on January 1, and people will eventually find a way to compensate for the failures of the other ones. As one computer scientist remarked to us, World War II was fought without computers—and all of world society survived in a more-or-less reasonable fashion prior to the advent of computers in the early 1950s. We could do it again, if necessary, especially because it would be only a matter of days, weeks, or months before most of the Year-2000 bugs were fixed, and the computers restored to their normal operation.

One could make the same kind of upbeat, rosy assessment of the Crash of 1929 and the decade-long Great Depression that followed. It wasn't the end of the world; life went on. The banking system didn't disappear, the U.S. government didn't fall, and 75% of the workforce continued to hold jobs. But on the other hand, 25% of the workforce was unemployed, some 9000 banks failed, many people lost their life savings, and some other governments (including Germany) did fall. It may not have been the end of the world, but it was a very unpleasant period of time for a number of individuals. Obviously, the Year-2000 situation is quite different than the events that led to the Depression; and just as obviously, we hope that the consequences will be far less significant. But just as a few prescient individuals anticipated the Crash of 1929 and thus avoided some of the subsequent problems, we believe that some early planning could reduce the impact of whatever Year-2000 problems might occur.

"Bottom Line" Advice

Chances are that 90% of the population of the U.S. will never hear about this book, and 99% will never read it. Even if 1% do read the book (which would make it a phenomenal bestseller!), the majority won't take any action. They may worry about some of the scenarios we've outlined, and perhaps even lose a couple nights' sleep. And while it's understandable that very few people will have the determination and stamina to prepare for a year-long or decade-long disaster, it's sad to realize that the relatively easy preparation for 2-3 days or a month of disruption will also be ignored.

What you *should* do, in our opinion, is read through each of the remaining chapters in this book and make your own assessment of the likely impact of Year-2000 problems in the various areas that could affect you. As you do this, you may find yourself frustrated that our descriptions of possible Year-2000 scenarios are not more precise. Even if we were capable of confidently stating, "There is a 75% chance that Bank XYZ will fail because of Year-2000 problems, and a 90% chance that the IRS will be unable to *ever* get its computer systems working correctly," our assessment would be based on the information available to us in late 1997, when this book was being written. We expect the situation to change dramati-

cally—hopefully for the better, but possibly for the worse—
during 1998 and 1999, as private-sector and public-sector
organizations stop talking about the Year-2000 problem and
start *doing* the repair work. By mid-1999, if not earlier, it
should be abundantly clear to you and everyone else whether
the IRS and Bank XYZ will be ready or not. However, it will
be crucial for you to have made your own contingency plans
in advance, so that you can take whatever action is appropriate
without any further delays.

If you need to boil it all down to a few simple guidelines,
consider the following recommendations:

- *The majority of Year-2000 problems are likely to
  be of the kind that will last 2-3 days.* This scenario
  is the bare minimum of risk management contingency planning you should be doing—indeed, it's so simple and inexpensive that it's
  extremely short-sighted *not* to do so. You should
  prepare in much the way you would prepare for
  a major blizzard or hurricane that knocks out all
  public services for a few days. That means a few
  days' worth of spare food, water, candles, and
  cash. It means that your office might close down
  for a few days, and you might lose your salary for
  that period. It means that you might lose access
  to the convenience of phone, television, and
  ATM machines for a few days. Preparing for this
  is not a difficult task at all, and the financial investment is modest indeed. People who live in
  areas of the country subject to extreme weather
  conditions do this already. But, people who live

in major urban areas like New York, Chicago, and Los Angeles generally don't.

- *A significant percentage of the Year-2000 problems will be serious enough to last for a month.* You'll have to decide whether you're cautious enough to prepare for such a contingency, but in our opinion, this is where you should be doing most of your planning and serious thinking. One of us, for example, is a self-employed consultant who has already concluded that the Year-2000 disruptions probably means there will be no clients and no revenue for at least the month of January 2000, and perhaps for much of the ensuing year. Planning for this in mid-1997 is not a problem; coping with it unexpectedly in January 2000, when our family was counting on that month's income, would have been a problem. Stockpiling a month's worth of cash, in anticipation of a bank failure, is difficult but not impossible; stockpiling a month's worth of food, if you're an urban dweller in a cramped apartment, may turn out to be far more difficult. In the unlikely but nevertheless possible occurrences of situations like this—e.g., food shortages in urban centers—you should plan for a temporary escape, such as a month-long vacation to visit relatives in the countryside.

- *A minority of the Year-2000 problems will have year-long consequences.* The primary things we're worried about here are loss of employment and long-term disruption of banks, public institutions, and social services. People raised during the Great Depression advised their children to amass a nest egg that would last them for at least six months of unemployment, but few of today's families are in that position. At this point, there may not be enough time left before January 1, 2000 for the average middle-class family to save a year's living expenses. If you're in such a position, the one thing you *can* do is begin cutting back on your level of spending, and begin preparing yourself psychologically for the possibility of a *major* reduction in lifestyle. Don't take on any long-term financial commitments; do try to eliminate as much short-term, credit-card-oriented debt as possible. If you have friends or colleagues who were downsized, outsourced, or laid off during the recession of the early 1990s, ask them what strategies they used to get themselves through a year or two of difficult times.

• *Finally, there is the possibility of a few Year-2000-induced disasters that could take a decade to resolve.* One example of such a disaster would be a complete collapse of the nation's financial system, and its replacement with a new financial system (and new currency) that would effectively wipe out the accumulated wealth of the nation's citizens. It's important to emphasize that the nation's banks, financial institutions, and appropriate government agencies are working quite hard to ensure such a nightmare won't occur—but if it did, the consequences would be felt for a number of years.

A more likely disaster scenario is a collapse of one
or more of the major federal government agencies, such as the IRS, Medicare, or Social Security.
If the political reaction to such a collapse was to
eliminate the social services provided by those
agencies, or to change the nation's taxation system
entirely, it could well take a decade to adapt and
adjust. Since we have no idea exactly how the
Year-2000 situation will unfold, there's no way
that we can make any plausible, detailed predictions about the situation in 2005 or 2010; all we
can say is that whatever long-term assumptions
you've made (many of which are implicit and sub-
conscious) may turn out to be invalid.

If you think such a situation is entirely impossible, consider
the citizens of the former Soviet Union. How many of them
would have predicted the complete collapse of the Communist
economic system prior to Gorbachev's resignation in 1991?
And, how many of them are coping adequately with a transi-
tion period that will last far more than a single decade before a
new equilibrium emerges? The only thing we can advise for a
situation like this is an emphasis on flexibility and adaptabil-
ity; beyond that, any semblance of traditional planning is
likely to be futile. If the Year-2000 problem leads to something
equivalent to the collapse of the Soviet Union—*extremely*
unlikely, perhaps, but not impossible—then all bets are off. It
will be a whole new ball game.

Endnotes

1. See, for example, Robert N. Charette, *Software Engineering Risk Analysis and
   Management* (McGraw-Hill, 1989) or Capers Jones, *Assessment and Control of
   Software Risks* (Prentice Hall, 1994).

Year-2000 Impact on Jobs

A tremendous number of people in America work very hard at something that bores them. Even a rich man thinks he has to go down to the office everyday. Not because he likes it but because he can't think of anything else to do.

W. H. Auden, The Table Talk of W. H. Auden, *"November 16, 1946".*

The greatest analgesic, soporific, stimulant, tranquilizer, narcotic, and to some extent even antibiotic—in short, the closest thing to a genuine panacea—known to medical science is work.

Thomas Szasz, The Second Sin, *"Medicine" (1973).*

Introduction

Capers Jones, a software expert in the Year-2000 field, estimates that 5-7% of U.S. businesses will go bankrupt as a result of Year-2000 failures.[1] If those companies happen to be somewhere else—a remote region of the Appalachians or a manufacturing plant on the other side of the country—then you're likely to shake your head sympathetically and carry on with your own life. But what if it's *your* company? What if *several* of the companies in your industry, or in your region of the country, go bankrupt as a result of the Year-2000 crisis?

As with other aspects of the Year-2000 phenomenon, it may be difficult to accept the possibility that such a thing could

happen. And indeed, it may not be a "permanent" phenomenon; maybe your office will only shut down for 2-3 days. But
it might be out of operation for a month, in a fashion analo-
gous to the aftermath of a major hurricane. And if your
employer *does* shut down permanently, it's conceivable that it
could take a year for you to find a replacement job.

The Year-2000 problem threatens three of the most important economic goals of politicians and economic policymakers:
full employment, price stability, and economic growth. Why
are these goals so important to politicians? Because they're also
the most important to *the voters*. Most of us want steady
employment so that we can feed our families, pay the rent,
buy necessities, and occasionally buy some treats for ourselves.
We want to be confident that the dollars we receive today will
be sufficient to cover our needs tomorrow; in other words, we
don't want to worry that inflation will erode the value of our
savings accounts. In the U.S., inflation has rarely been above
10% in this century, but we all have read and heard about
hyperinflation in countries like Germany and Brazil.[2] Such
inflation can lead to widespread social discontent, speculative
investments, and efforts to convert one's money into a more
stable currency.[3] As for the third goal, steady economic growth
leads to improved living standards, and usually greater labor
productivity, which is accompanied by increased income. Not
only is this desirable, it's something that we've come to expect
during our lifetimes, if only because we constantly hear our
leaders promising they can deliver it to us.

This chapter focuses on jobs and unemployment, and
exactly what happens when the latter rises—whether because
of a Year-2000-related problem or any other reason. If you're
in your 20s or early 30s, then you probably weren't in the
labor force when unemployment was last near 10%, during

the 1981-82 recession. Indeed, some of us have been in the labor force for only a few years, and have thus enjoyed the good fortune of experiencing a "tight" labor market during the current economic boom. Unemployment is one of the most widely followed economic indicators, most commonly expressed by the unemployment rate (the number of people unemployed divided by the number of people in the labor force, or people actively seeking work). High unemployment can cause severe social discontent; our parents and grandparents still remember the marches and strikes during the Great Depression, when the unemployment rate peaked near 25%. More recently, look to France where unemployment hovered near 13% as this book was being written, and where a sense of frustration led to the election of a Socialist government in the spring of 1997. The chart below shows how U.S. unemployment has varied over the past 50 years; it illustrates graphically that we have had very little experience with high unemployment rates since the end of World War II.

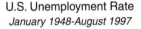

U.S. Unemployment Rate
January 1948-August 1997

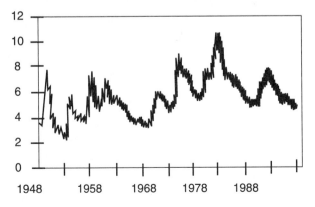

As we wrote this book in the summer and fall of 1997, the U.S. had an unemployment rate below 5%, inflation of less than 2%, and an economic expansion in its sixth year. The U.S. is currently at, or near, what economists call "full employment." Some minimal level of unemployment will always exist because in a dynamic economy, even in the best of times, workers change jobs and adapt to shifting market conditions, or are unemployed because of "seasonal" factors (the ski bum that looks for work in the summer), or because of "frictional" factors (the family that moves to the West Coast to enjoy nicer weather and then looks for new jobs). This minimal level of unemployment is called the "full employment level." So, what happens if circumstances—whether politics, international competition, or Year-2000 problems—cause unemployment to rise?

On the simplest level, when unemployment increases, people lose their "wage income." As the phrase suggests, wage income is what is earned on the job—and for most workers in the U.S., it is the only source of income. Non-wage income is income earned from sources outside the job, e.g., interest and investment income, or rental income. What would happen if wage income were lost for two or three days? Well honestly, not too much. Think of it from your own perspective—if you were to lose two or three days' pay, you probably wouldn't be thrilled, but you could survive and pay your rent—and you probably would enjoy your few days off.

But, what would happen if wage income was lost for a month? This could be a quite serious problem for many people. Many members of the labor force don't have enough savings to survive for a month without pay. Many young people, and many lower-income workers, would be forced to go on unemployment for a month, and/or look for another job, and/

or seek other benefits. Some would be lucky enough to be able to borrow from friends or family. Most young workers and low-income laborers, however, would change their lifestyle by cutting down on their consumption spending. These workers would eliminate any "luxury" items from their budget, perhaps substitute lower-cost items for higher-cost goods, and cut down on any entertainment expenses. This reduction in consumption spending would have a slight dampening effect on the economy, but if workers were only out of work for a month, the effect would probably be visible but relatively slight.

Things obviously become much more serious if people lose their jobs for a year. A very small percentage of these unfortunate workers would exit the labor force completely, based on their assessment that they didn't really need to work anyway. A much larger percentage would begin looking for another job, and would begin collecting unemployment. A small percentage would also begin collecting welfare. In this instance, the effect on consumption spending would be much more marked. A moment of personal introspection will confirm this: How would you change your spending habits if you were out of work for a year? All "frivolous" expenses—vacations, dinners out, movies, unnecessary clothing, etc.—would be eliminated.

When people lose their jobs, they begin depleting their savings by spending the money in their savings accounts. That can be quite a problem, because the U.S. is a nation that saves very little by international standards. The savings rate was currently less than 4% in August 1997. This issue got a lot of attention in the 1980s when the U.S. savings rate dipped to about 3%. A low savings rate can be an important political issue. When savings are low, there is less money in banks to be lent out for new plants and equipment, which can thus reduce the future potential output of the economy. When the saving rate is low, there are also less funds available for U.S. government borrowing, and the government is forced to borrow from abroad.

Why do Americans save so little? One reason is that interest rates are relatively low in the U.S., so people don't earn much when they just put money in the bank—and the stock market has performed very well in recent years, so there are attractive alternatives. Another reason is that in the U.S., interest income is taxed (unlike some other countries), creating yet another disincentive. A final possible explanation is that U.S. consumers are generally very confident about the future, and about their upcoming job prospects. American consumers feel that if they lose their jobs, they will be able to get another one relatively easily, so they do not have to save too much. This is somewhat borne out by the available economic data. Consumer confidence and the savings rate are negatively correlated, which means that when consumer confidence is high, savings is low. This correlation has become even more negative in recent years;[4] thus, during this decade, there has been even less of an inclination for Americans to save *as long as their confidence in the economy remains high.*

As shown in the chart below, consumer confidence can be a sensitive indicator of recessions and other macroeconomic shocks. Most recently, consumer confidence plunged during the Iraqi invasion of Kuwait, reflecting the concerns of consumers about the implications of the invasion. Consumer confidence may be an indicator to watch in the months immediately before and after January 1, 2000, to see how broad-based the effect on the economy will be. If consumer confidence drops sharply because of the various Year-2000 problems discussed in this book, the savings rate would be expected to increase—but this is only relevant if the majority of people have jobs that provide sufficient earnings with which to accomplish their savings activities.

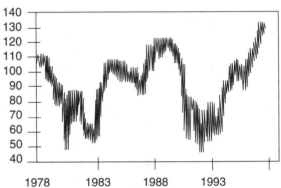

U.S. Consumer Confidence
January 1978-August 1997

This raises an interesting question: What *kind* of savings do Americans indulge in? It is difficult to pinpoint this precisely, but there are some data available. We can obtain data from the Federal Reserve, but reading that there is over $1 trillion in currency, demand deposits, NOW accounts, credit unions, and non-bank travelers checks is not very useful. We found it more useful to look at U.S. Census Bureau data: As of 1993, 11% of all households had a *zero or negative* household net worth, while 14% had a household net worth of between $1 and $4,999. So in total, 25% of U.S. households have a net worth of less than $5,000. Depending on monthly living expenses and the number of people in the household, 25% of U.S. households could be in serious trouble if income was lost for a month. It is also possible, of course, that this definition of "household net worth" includes some items which are not liquid, i.e., they can't be readily turned into cash.

What does all this mean? Well, if people are out of work for two or three days, it doesn't mean very much. If people are out of work for a month, however, some people's savings could be seriously depleted. Many young workers who have been in the labor force only a few years have very little savings, have started families, perhaps have taken on mortgages, have borrowed money for down payments on houses, and have credit card debt to boot! Related to the statistics detailed above, 15% of married-couple households under 35 years of age *have a zero to negative net household worth*. A further 19% of married-couple households in that same age group have a net worth of between $1 and $4,999. For these households, and many more, a month out of work would be extremely difficult. This month out of work will depress consumption for more than that month, however, because when workers do return to work, they will work on building up their savings in case they ever have to face the same problem again, and will keep consumption spending down for a period of time.

As the length of time out of work increases, the younger and older members of the labor force become more and more at risk. The youngest members of the labor force are at risk because they have the least amount of savings, and often have debt they need to pay off. Older workers are also at risk because they are at the end of their income-earning cycle, and have begun to decrease their budgets. They are also the least flexible members of the workforce, and will find it difficult to get new jobs. A year out of work for either of these groups would almost certainly be a very severe problem; those who have enough savings to last a year will do so, but will do so frugally. They will cut down on consumption spending, collect unemployment if possible, and try to limit the depletion of their savings account. The inevitable reduction in consumption spending will be a damper for the U.S. economy. And, those who don't have enough savings to last a year, and don't have any investments, will liquidate their savings and then be forced to rely on other sources of income.

If Year-2000 problems throw people out of work for a month, some may be forced to withdraw a portion of their mutual fund investments, or funds from their 401K retirement plans. This will be a drag on the stock market, and could cause a small correction, depending on the amount of money that is withdrawn. Obviously, a year's loss of employment could lead to significant withdrawals from stocks and mutual funds, as individuals liquidate investments to support themselves. Also, for that year, those same employees will no longer be contributing to their 401K plans, nor will they be contributing any money on their own to mutual funds or the stock market.

This could lead to a serious drop in the stock market, which could make matters worse. A decline in share prices can cause a "negative wealth effect." What does this mean? First, declines in share prices decrease the "paper" value of people's investments, or their wealth. Seasoned veterans of the stock market, with millions of dollars of disposable income, might be able to survive such a decline without losing much sleep; but, the great majority of middle-class investors will "feel poorer" and will cut back on their spending. This decrease in consumption demand, depending on its severity, will cause companies to cut back on production, and perhaps staff. This could lead to more layoffs, which will only make the cycle begin again. Second, a decline in the share price of some companies will reduce their net worth. Companies too feel poorer; it curtails their ability to make investments, acquire other companies, and it can lead to further layoffs.

A drop in the stock market could also have international ramifications, as the U.S. stock market is the benchmark and leader for global stock markets. In the financial community, it's often said that, "When the U.S. gets a sniffle, Europe gets a cold," which seems applicable both to the strength of the U.S. dollar and also the equity market. When the U.S. stock market fell by 29% in 1987, the Australian stock market fell by 25%, the Japanese stock market fell by 15%, and the stock market in the United Kingdom lost over 21% of its value. We stress these numbers because of their potential impact on the global job market, and the potential for a global recession.

An increase in unemployment will also reduce government revenues. As might be expected, this is a negligible factor if people are out of work for only a day or two (though there have been extraordinarily few cases when the entire population has been unemployed for a day or two, since the U.S. is not prone to the kind of national strikes one occasionally sees in Europe). But if people are out of work for a month, the loss in income tax revenue is more substantial, especially if large numbers of people are involved. Workers idle for a year will mean quite serious losses in income tax revenue. That, coupled with increased government spending on unemployment, welfare, and other benefits will increase the government deficit, if only temporarily.

It's useful to see what has actually happened in the past when the unemployment rate has risen. As the chart below indicates, there is a very high correlation between the unemployment rate and the average weeks spent unemployed. This makes sense: When jobs are harder to find (as evidenced by a higher unemployment rate), people tend to stay out of work longer. The strength of this relationship has deteriorated a bit over time, though even recently it still has some statistical significance. What it tells us, quite simply, is that if we see a doubling in the unemployment rate because of the Year-2000 problems (or any other problems, for that matter), average weeks of unemployment are likely to increase by approximately 50%. This means that if the unemployment rate increases from its current level of approximately 5% to a new level of 10% (a "doubling" phenomenon that was last experienced during the 1981-82 recession), people will, on average, be unemployed for 23 weeks. An average is, of course, an average, so unfortunately some people will be unemployed for longer than 23 weeks. That's an awfully long time to be without a paycheck.

Avg. Weeks Unemployed and Unemployment Rate
January 1950-August 1997

Unemployment (l.h.s.)

Duration Unemployed (r.h.s.)

Another consequence of an increase in the unemployment rate is a loss in employment tax revenues for the government. Obviously, if people are out of work for a day or two, the loss in tax revenues will be negligible—but if people are out of work for a month, the loss in income tax revenue is more substantial. Workers idle for a year will mean quite serious losses in income tax revenue. Since 1982, the correlation between government employment tax receipts and the unemployment rate has been -0.64—suggesting that if the unemployment rate were to double, the government should expect roughly 60% less in employment taxes. This is not an insignificant amount of money—the U.S. Treasury has averaged approximately $40 billion per month in employment taxes since the beginning of 1995. Consequently, a doubling in the unemployment rate could translate into a loss of roughly $24 billion *every* month. This means, of course, that the government will have less money to spend at the exact time when the U.S. economy would need an extra boost from government spending.

On a nationwide basis, an increase in unemployment will depress the economy. More people out of work will mean less demand. As demand decreases, manufacturers will cut their production, and this, by definition, will mean a decrease in the nation's economic output. Gross Domestic Product (GDP), which consists of all output produced *within* the U.S., is a common measure of economic output. It is not, however, a measure to watch carefully as the Year-2000 deadline approaches because the GDP figures are "old news" when they are released a month after the end of a financial quarter. Instead, you should watch more current indicators like unemployment, consumer confidence, industrial production, and retail sales (all of which are regularly reported in major newspapers throughout the U.S.) to gauge how the economy is being affected.

As in most of our examples, if people are out of work for a few days, there should be little impact on GDP. However, if even a small percentage of people are out of work for a month, there can be a noticeable impact on GDP. A good illustration of what could occur because of Year-2000 problems is the GM strike of 1996.

In late October of 1996, General Motors negotiators and laborers in the Canadian Auto Workers (CAW) finally resolved a 20-day strike. The strike, though it involved 26,000 auto workers in Canada, had forced production cuts and layoffs in 26 plants in the U.S. and Mexico, which either receive parts from, or ship parts to, GM plants in Canada. More than 20,000 workers in the rest of North America were laid off as a result of this Canadian strike. These workers were laid off for almost the whole duration of the strike (twenty days), plus several more days after the resolution of the strike as the inventories of the plants were being replenished. Analysts reported that GM lost over $200 million in profits during these twenty days.

No sooner had the Canadian GM strike ended when United Auto Workers (UAW) members in two GM plants in the U.S. walked off the job. The strikers included almost 5,000 workers in Janesville, Wisconsin, responsible for some of GM's very profitable sports utility vehicles, as well as 2,700 workers in Indianapolis responsible for the stamped metal parts (fenders, hoods, etc.) for eight of ten GM U.S. truck plants. The Wisconsin strike alone cost GM approximately $5.5 million *every* day it was shut down. The strike in Indianapolis lasted five days and forced the shutdown of four GM truck plants in Ohio, New Jersey, Louisiana, and Indiana because of a shortage of fenders, hoods, and other metal parts. These shortages in parts were almost immediate, and the resulting shutdowns idled almost 20,000 GM workers. When the two strikes were finished, it took a few extra days to get the plants up and running again, and to have the plants ready to open their doors to workers again. All told, GM lost *over* $1 billion in profits in 1996 because of walkouts. GM was not the only loser in this situation—the workers who did not receive their paychecks suffered, as did the auto dealers who relied on having inventory to make a living.

Our purpose here is not to pick on GM, the UAW, or the CAW. But, we believe these events bear striking similarities to the ripple effects Year-2000 problems could have, and they show how severe the economic consequences of a shutdown of a key U.S. industry can be. We can easily imagine a scenario in which Plant A in XYZ company cannot produce its goods because of a Year-2000 problem, and so Plants B, C, and D must temporarily shut down because they rely on the output of Plant A. Keep in mind that these are only *intra*-company problems. What if Plant E in 123 company relies on the output of Plant B of XYZ company?

If unemployment increases significantly and the economy begins a downturn, as we expect, what will the authorities do? If the decline, or *expected* decline, in GDP is significant enough, the Federal Reserve will lower interest rates to stimulate the economy. The Alan Greenspan-led Federal Reserve has been quite successful in taking a "forward-looking" approach to monetary policy. For example, in the beginning of 1994, the Fed raised interest rates before actual signs of inflation had emerged. This was quite different from U.S. central bank policy in the 1970s and 1980s, when the Fed typically voted to raise rates only *after* inflation indicators had become too high. Likewise, the Fed would vote to lower rates when the economy was already in a recession. This policy often caused what is known as "overshooting"—when the Fed would lower rates so much that the economy would overheat and begin a boom cycle with inflation; subsequently, the Fed would raise interest rates so much that the economy would turn down into a recession.

This overshooting occurred because of the lag of monetary policy. Economists believe that it takes six to eighteen months for the impact of interest rate changes to be felt on the economy. In the past, the Fed would continue lowering rates as long as economic indicators remained weak, even though effects of past interest rate cuts were yet to be felt.[5] In 1994, a new era began, when Alan Greenspan decided that interest rate changes should be made based on forecasts of where the economy would be a year in the future. That way, if the economy was expected to be weak in twelve months, the Federal Reserve would begin cutting interest rates in the previous year.

While this may all sound rather academic to the average worker, there may be some very real consequences in the coming years. It will be very interesting, for example, to see whether the Fed will include the Year-2000 problem in its forecasts during its 1999 policy meetings. How will the Federal Reserve quantify those problems? Unless the potential economic ramifications of the Year-2000 problem become clearer by then, it would seem difficult for the Fed to quantify the magnitude of the Year-2000 problem in its forecasts. That being said, if in the beginning of the Year 2000 substantial jobs were lost and the economy contracted sharply, it's highly likely the Fed would begin lowering interest rates with little or no delay. Unfortunately, the economic impact of the lower interest rates wouldn't be felt until the year 2001 or later; indeed, some of the economists who have studied the government's economic policy in the years immediately following the Great Crash of 1929 argue that traditional tools of monetary policy (such as raising or lowering key interest rates) may not be sufficient to cope with a severe economic downturn.

We can look to Japan for a more recent example of how difficult it can be to revive an extremely depressed and structurally weak economy. The once-envied Japanese economy has been wallowing since 1990, despite official interest rates, which reached a historic low of 0.5%. The Japanese government has implemented numerous tax incentive schemes and fiscal stimulus plans, yet in the second quarter of 1997, the Japanese GDP fell by an annualized 11%! Sometimes, like in recent years in Japan, the bulk of economic problems are structural and will not be solved by simply lowering interest rates.

Lower interest rates, or borrowing costs, may not help companies who are grappling with Year-2000 problems—companies may not need to borrow money at low interest rates, and might instead prefer a large supply of Jolt Cola to encourage their computer programmers to work 72 hours per day. Similarly, if lower interest rates are introduced at the same time that consumer confidence is eroding because of pervasive Year-2000 difficulties, then as we noted above, consumers are likely to spend less and save more, to the extent they are able to do so. The lack of a classical response to lower interest rates could extend the slowdown.

Another impact of a downturn in the U.S. economy would be the ripple effects on other countries, especially our neighbors and biggest trading partners, Canada and Mexico. Canada, for example, relies on the U.S. for roughly 75% of its exports. If the U.S. economy slows down, there will be less domestic demand for Canadian goods, and this will have a negative impact on international economies. In addition to our closest trading partners, the economies of western Europe and Japan will also be affected negatively; meanwhile, these same countries will be dealing with their own Year-2000-induced unemployment problems.

How Could the Year-2000 Problem
Cause All of This?

Our fundamental argument should be familiar to you by now: Any business that's highly dependent on computer systems, which in turn are highly dependent upon the ability to calculate dates correctly, may be vulnerable to serious problems after December 31, 1999. If Year-2000-sensitive computers control the electronic locks, lights, phone systems, or other control equipment, it may not be possible for employees to function at all. If computers are essential for entering orders, scheduling the activities of people and manufacturing equipment, generating invoices, and performing other "mission-critical" operations, a Year-2000 failure could make it impossible to carry on "business as usual" until the problem is fixed.

While these kinds of "direct" consequences are probably fairly easy to understand if you look closely at the activities within your company, the "indirect" consequences of Year-2000 failures may be more subtle and surprising. As we explain in more detail in Appendix B, every individual, and also every company, depends to a greater or lesser extent on a complex web of services and products provided by other individuals and organizations. Even if your company has worked diligently to ensure that all of its computers are Year-2000-compliant, it will be hard to carry on business if the lights go out and the phones don't work. If your critical subcontractors or suppliers disappear, it may be difficult to manufacture your products; if your distributors, wholesalers, and independent sales agents can't contact you, you can't sell your product. And for a retail business, it may be even more obvious—what if your customers can't contact you because of failures in the communication system or the transportation system?

In some cases, the situation could be deceptively simple. Your cousin Vinnie, for example, operates a small pizza stand with two part-time high school kids and *no* computer. Why should he (or, for that matter, his high school assistants) worry about the Year-2000 problem? Very simple: The pizza stand is located in the Wall Street area, and 95% of its business consists of serving a slice-and-a-Coke to busy stock brokers. If Wall Street is closed for a month, it's highly unlikely that the stock brokers will make a special trip to enjoy Vinnie's pepperoni pizza.

A variation on this theme occurred in 1987 after the famous stock market crash. A number of limousine drivers found that their fat-cat customers weren't so fat any more, and had been reduced in status (particularly in the area of expense account perks) to the point where they had to ride the bus or subway to work—assuming they had a job at all. As a result, many limo drivers quickly found themselves unemployed.

We're describing this in terms of generalities, without having any way of knowing whether it's relevant to *your* business. Our studies indicate that Wall Street firms, banks, insurance companies, and telemarketing-based firms, among others, are highly vulnerable; small businesses, farmers, and proprietors of small neighborhood stores, delis, and pizza parlors may be less vulnerable. It's up to you to examine the company you work for and the environment you work in. If it's a large company with lots of computer systems, track down the appropriate computer experts and managers and ask them. If you get a blank look when you ask the question, our advice is to grab your paycheck, cash in your stock options, and get out as fast as you can.

And, watch out for the computer manager who pats you on the shoulder and says, "Don't you worry your pretty little head about something like that. It's too complicated to explain to you, but we've got the problem under control." Yes, the technical details of fixing the software may be difficult to understand if you're not in the computer field, but the overall "scorecard" is pretty straightforward. How many programmers within the organization are working on the problem? How large is the "portfolio" of computer systems, and how much of it has already been converted to ensure Year-2000 compliance? If there's not enough time and not enough resources to finish the job by December 31, 1999 (which is almost certain to be the case), what kind of triage of computer systems has been carried out? Which computer systems have been judged noncritical (and thus likely to be abandoned), and what impact will the failure of those systems have on the organization? What steps have been taken to ensure that the "end-user" programs—e.g., spreadsheets developed in Lotus or Excel, desktop databases developed with Microsoft Access, Foxpro, and dBase IV—have been identified for Year-2000 compliance? You don't have to be a rocket scientist to ask questions like these, and you don't have to be a rocket scientist to understand the answers. If you can't get straight answers to these questions, or if it appears that the relevant computer managers in your organization haven't begun thinking about them, then— to paraphrase Stephen King—be afraid. Be very afraid.

And this is just the beginning. If you get adequate answers concerning the planning for *direct* Year-2000 failures, then you need to show Figure B.5 (from Appendix B) to your computer managers and ask them whether they've planned for *non*-compliant computer systems feeding input to your company's computers, and accepting output from your company's computers. What if your largest customer begins sending computerized orders to your company that are non-Year-2000-compliant? What if the bank and the IRS reject your loan payments and tax payments after January 1, because your computers are sending Year-2000-compliant transactions, but their computers aren't working correctly? Any computer manager who has thought about this possibility for more than a few minutes realizes that there will be a period of time when your company's computers will have to be capable of coping—somehow—with a mixture of both compliant and non-compliant computer systems in other companies.

Interestingly, that's about as far as the typical computer manager is likely to extend his or her thinking. You'll have to talk to your senior *business* managers about the consequences of outright failure (e.g., bankruptcy) on the part of the suppliers, subcontractors, customers, and other entities illustrated in Figure B.5. What are the chances of survival if your three top customers go bankrupt? How long can the business survive if the company's bank scrambles its computers and refuses to provide any revolving credit or line-of-credit loans for six months? How long would it take to find a replacement if the company's chief supplier of "raw materials" (which could be anything from pizza dough to iron ore) went bankrupt?

The questions go on and on, and our experience is that most senior managers will become increasingly frustrated if you continue asking. If they were honest, most of them would tell you they've made no contingency plans for such disasters. But their official statement is more likely to be, "These scare story scenarios you're inventing are so preposterous that they're not worth talking about in a serious way." And the blunt reality is that if some of these events *did* occur, there would be no practical way to recover. Your company would shut down—period, full stop, end of story. Small startup companies often have to contemplate such possibilities even in normal times, and it's not considered heresy to raise such questions. But, large, established companies, with a noble history of decades or centuries, have a culture that finds it virtually impossible to consider their own demise. If you ask too many blunt questions, you're likely to be branded a heretic and rabble-rouser; so, be discreet and indirect, if necessary. But, don't fall into the same "denial of reality" trap that your company may be suffering—just because your management is behaving in ostrich-like fashion and your company goes bankrupt, it doesn't necessarily mean that you have to behave in the same way.

Keep in mind that even if the Year-2000 problems are severe in your company, it doesn't necessarily mean that things will abruptly shut down on January 2. If the company can't get access to its customers or the funds in its corporate bank account, it may still be able to limp along for a month or two before it closes the doors. If it can't process orders and invoices properly because of Year-2000 problems, it could find itself bleeding to death over a period of six months to a year. And it's quite possible, of course, that through the heroic efforts of both computer people and businesspeople throughout the organization, all of the problems and computer screwups that emerge after January 1, 2000 might be corrected before they become fatal. If you're a loyal employee with a vested interest in keeping the company alive, you may very well want to offer every possible bit of support.

But, be very careful if you find yourself in this position. It's one thing to work 16-hour days for a few months to help put your company's accounting records back together. It's one thing to suffer through a few months of no heat, no air-conditioning, and no phone systems in the office because the company's "process control" computers fell apart. But when the company tells you that it will be a couple of months before anyone can be paid, and that there's some question about the status of your company-funded 401K retirement plan, then you have crossed the line between loyal employee and lender/investor in the company. If you *really* love your company, perhaps you'll be willing to risk a few months of your salary; it's obviously inappropriate for us to tell you where you should draw the line. But, at least we can remind you to think carefully about what you're doing; after the stroke of midnight on December 31, 1999, we'll be entering perilous times, where the usual corporate promises and assurances are likely to be worth very little.

Fallback Advice: The Two-Day Shutdown

Will anyone bother making special plans to cope with a two-day work shutdown caused by a Year-2000 problem? Probably not; for most, it will seem like an unplanned holiday, much the same as the blizzard, tornado, or hurricane that occasionally shuts down the schools and keeps prudent parents and workers at home.

A particularly benevolent employer would treat this as a crisis beyond the control of the employee, and continue to provide a salary for the missed day or two at work. If the potential loss of a couple days' pay concerns you, it would be a good idea to check with your boss, or with the Human Resources Department in your company. As noted above, the Year-2000 policy should be much the same as for other kinds of natural disasters. If yours is the kind of company that does *not* pay for such missed days (which we might expect of the hypothetical Vinnie and his pizza parlor, for example), you should see whether you can use sick days, vacation days, or other mechanisms to avoid a reduction in your paycheck.

Ironically, there are likely to be a few situations where the employee wants to stay home (perhaps because of concern about the safety of transportation, which we'll discuss in Chapter 4), but the employer desperately needs the services of the employee. Doctors and nurses are obvious examples; and there are a variety of other jobs where the employee is supposed to show up, come hell or high water ... or Year-2000 breakdown. If yours is a job that falls into this category, the best thing we can advise is to have a calm, rational discussion with your employer *now*, before any crisis occurs. The most likely date for Year-2000 problems may be January 1, 2, or 3 of the Year-2000—but there will inevitably be problems both before and after these dates. You may need to find alternative ways of getting to and from work; you may also want to think about the circumstances that are *beyond* the reasonable call of duty. You may already have some experience with dealing with the demands of your job when blizzards or hurricanes are involved; but, none of us have yet experienced a Year-2000 shutdown.

Fallback Advice: The One-Month Shutdown

This is where things get serious: for whatever reason, your office, factory, or place of work shuts down for a month ... or maybe two months, or three. The interesting thing here is that your employer may not be able to give you a firm date for resuming normal operations. Again, since nobody has experienced the kind of software problems associated with the Year-2000 bug before, it's very difficult to offer a precise estimate of the time that will be required to get past the crisis stage.

There's one important exception: the situation where an office is shut down because of the "cleanup" effort required *after* a Year-2000 problem. This could happen in almost any kind of company where the day-to-day operations are highly dependent on computer-generated plans, schedules, etc. Let's take a simple, hypothetical case: You work as a teller in a major bank, and your primary job is to stand behind the teller's window and process deposits and withdrawals for those customers who don't use the ubiquitous ATM machine. It's easy to imagine that you might have far more customers to deal with than normal, in the event of a Year-2000-based failure in the ATM machines; but even ignoring this potential problem, you may find that your employer tells you to stay home for a month.

Why? Because a Year-2000 bug causes the kind of problem discussed in more detail in Appendix A. During the normal overnight processing of checks, payments, deposits, etc., an erroneous computer program scrambles *every* customer's database record, thus making it impossible to tell what any customer's true balance is. Let's make the optimistic assumption that the problem occurs on January 1, when everyone is likely to be especially alert for such a problem. And let's assume that the programmers scurry into the office on January 2 (which happens to be a Sunday) to fix the bug. Unfortunately, even though the bug has been fixed (so that any subsequent processing of checks and deposits will be handled correctly), the damage has been done. What now awaits the computer department within the bank is a massive cleanup job: The pre-January customer balances and associated information must be restored, and the erroneous processing must be re-run (correctly, this time). It's like cleaning up after a serious tornado. The tornado itself might only have lasted for a few moments, but the cleanup can easily take weeks.

In any event, if you've been told not to come into the office for a month, chances are that you won't be paid during the idle period (we'll ignore the additional complication that it might not be possible to run the payroll system or deposit your check in the bank anyway, though it's precisely this kind of compounded "ripple effect" that we're most concerned about with regard to the overall Year-2000 situation). The bottom line is: If your company is shut down for a month because of a Year-2000 problem, you're probably going to lose a month's income.

Don't count on your insurance company to make up the difference, either. Again, there is the ripple effect problem to worry about. Your insurance company is likely to be hard-hit with its own Year-2000 problems, and it won't be sending its agents out in Boy Scout fashion, the way it would with a fire or weather-related danger. But aside from that, the simple fact is that you don't have Year-2000 insurance; take a look at your insurance policy to confirm it for yourself. You may be covered for fire, flood, earthquakes, meteor showers, theft, plagues of locusts, and a variety of other familiar problems, but chances are that there's also an explicit clause that absolves the company of any responsibility for damages associated with hang-gliding, parachute-jumping, wars, and a catch-all phrase known as "acts of God." The Year-2000 problem is definitely an act of Man, but under the circumstances, it defies credulity to assume that a typical insurance company would send you a check for a month's lost wages because of a computer programming bug.

What does all of this mean? You'll have to make your own judgment about the likelihood that a Year-2000 bug *could* keep you from earning your normal paycheck for a month. But if you think it's a reasonable possibility, then you have two choices: find a job that's guaranteed *not* to suffer Year-2000 problems, and do so before New Year's Eve, 1999; or, make sure that you've got a month's worth of living expenses available. The first option is a bit extreme, and we'll discuss it in more detail for the more serious possibility of a one-year loss of income. But the second option is perfectly sensible. After all, even without the bizarre phenomenon of a Year-2000-induced loss of income, today's turbulent economy could put any one of us out of work for a month. Even civil servants learned this sobering fact when the political squabble between Republicans and Democrats effectively shut down the federal government for two weeks in early 1996. As noted earlier, the generation that grew up during the Depression era would find it odd that we even bother to talk about this: *"Of course,"* they would say, *"you have to assume that you might have to go a month or two without income because your company has closed its doors for a while."*

The authors of this book represent two generations, one of whom was born at the end of World War II when the common advice was to make sure that one always had 6-12 months living expenses in the bank in case of unforeseen economic difficulties. We heard this from our Depression-age parents, for whom it was very real indeed; but since we Baby Boomers had not experienced the Depression personally, we didn't always follow the advice. Successive generations, including the Generation-X represented by the other author of this book, sometimes watched their Boomer parents suffer from episodes of corporate downsizing and reengineering, but they were even further removed from the experiences of their grandparents in the Depression.

Such experiences are only a part of today's economic situation, but the overall situation is grim indeed if one imagines the consequences of a one-month loss of income occurring both randomly and pervasively across the U.S. landscape. Our strong advice: Take a look at your savings account today. You still have nearly two full years to put yourself in a position where you *could* survive a one-month lapse in income without any serious repercussions. It won't be so easy to do in October 1999.

By the way, beware the usual reaction from today's middle-class consumer: charging things on a credit card and then "catching up" later on may not be an option. This was a common trick of the Wall Street yuppies who were caught unexpectedly by the 1987 stock market crash; one of the authors was applying for a home mortgage during this period, and was astounded by the stories from loan officers of the practice of upper-middle-class New York residents to run up credit limits of $25,000 or more on each of half a dozen credit cards while looking for a new job.

If the banks manage to avoid the Year-2000 problem, and *if* the MasterCards, Visas, and American Expresses of the world are equally successful in avoiding problems in this area, and *if* merchants and suppliers are willing to accept credit card charges as a form of payment, maybe you can get away with charging a month's worth of living expenses while you cope with the loss of income. But it seems to us that this is a greater risk than any prudent person should take. It's far more realistic to assume that you won't be able to live on credit for the first few months (if not longer) of the next decade—at least while the Year-2000 problems are being sorted out.

Indeed, you may not even be able to depend on the normal functioning of the banking system during the early days or weeks of the next decade. One advantage of growing up as a child of Depression-era parents is that one hears, first-hand, of the experience of the "bank holiday" that took place in the U.S. during the early days of the FDR administration. The word "holiday" conjures up an image of a day or two of gaiety and celebration—but it's worth remembering that many of the banks in the U.S. were closed for *ten days* in March 1933. It's even more sobering to realize that more than 4,000 banks failed during this period; whether we'll suffer this level of crisis is something we'll discuss further in Chapter 5.

Thus, if you're feeling somewhat paranoid about all of this, our advice is to have a month's living expenses in cash, *outside* your normal bank. You'll lose a month's interest, but interest rates are so low in 1997-98 that the loss of interest income for most people is literally a couple of dollars.[6] It should be noted that withdrawing a month's income *now*, and hiding it under your mattress (or wherever you hide such valuables), is unlikely to have any effect on the nation's economy, especially as only a tiny percentage of U.S. citizens are likely to worry about such things in early 1998. However, if it suddenly occurs to a substantial percentage of the population to behave in this fashion in late 1999, then we'll have an old-fashioned *run* on the banks. We haven't seen this phenomenon since the days of the Depression; it's unclear whether the population, banking officials, or the government is capable of dealing with such a phenomenon in a rational fashion today. If you're concerned about this sort of thing, we recommend early action for obvious reasons.

Indeed, if you're *really* paranoid, you might wonder whether the dollar bills stuffed under your mattress will be worth anything. In Chapter 5, we'll briefly discuss the impact of Year-2000 bugs on the overall banking system; depending on the details of the situation, we could find the national economy faced with either a sudden, acute deflation or an equally sudden, government-initiated inflation. The primary experience of the Depression era in the U.S. was a substantial *de*flation, including falling prices in almost every sector of the economy. However, the experience in both 1920s-vintage Germany and Austria, as well as 1970s-vintage Brazil and Argentina, has been that of massive hyperinflation. Both scenarios might be a problem for those who wish to store their life's savings under their mattress, as we'll see in Chapter 5.

Fallback Advice: The One-Year Shutdown

Now the situation becomes *much* more serious. Suppose that the Year-2000 problem is sufficiently serious that you're without work for a year? This is a good example of the point that we stressed in the previous chapter: There are *qualitative* differences as one increases the dimension of the Year-2000 problem by an order of magnitude.

If a Year-2000 problem causes your office to shut down for a month, and thereby causes a loss of income for a month, the natural instinct is to respond, "Well, it's a serious, annoying problem, but not one that requires me to change my lifestyle." In the best of cases, you've got a month's income stuffed under the mattress; in a reasonable scenario, you can borrow money from a credit card lender or from sympathetic neighbors, friends, or parents; in the worst case, you simply accept some level of deprivation for a month.

But, when the problem extends to a year, things are different. Parents may be willing to take their children back into the house for a year; after all, that has been a common experience with Generation-X children in recent times. But it's much more difficult to live off the generosity of friends and parents for a year; and, it's extremely difficult to imagine living off a credit card for a year. What would *you* do if you were without income for a year?

Let's put this in the proper context. It's highly unlikely that your boss will come to you on January 3, 2000 and say, "Gee, we have a serious Year-2000 problem and we won't be able to employ you for quite a while—check back with us next year.

We should have everything back to normal by then." It's conceivable, we suppose, that a Year-2000-induced problem could drag on from one month to the next, until a full year had transpired. But the most likely scenario is fairly simple: Your current employer shuts down unexpectedly, and it takes you a year to find a replacement job in the same industry. This could happen not only in the Year-2000-sensitive industries like banking and insurance, but in any industry that suddenly discovers that it is highly dependent on other industries that have been bankrupted by Year-2000 problems.

Such a scenario could result from a *conscious* decision, reached during the "triage" planning described earlier, to shut down a part of the business for which Year-2000 repairs could not be scheduled. This kind of planning is beginning to take place in 1997 and 1998, and could even lead some organizations to shut these non-compliant parts of the company down, in an orderly fashion, a few weeks or months prior to December 31, 1999.

For those lucky enough to earn upper-middle-class salaries in these Year-2000-related (computerized) industries, the prospect of switching fields is probably not attractive; the 32-year-old Wall Street investment banker who enjoys a million-dollar salary probably doesn't want to trade it in for a modest $20,000 income running an antique shop. But, the 45-year-old investment banker who has managed to stash away a large nest egg (the vulnerability of which is a separate topic in Chapter 5), and who has grown weary of the pressure and politics of a high-stress job, might want to take the opportunity to change his or her lifestyle in 1998 or 1999, before things go awry. And the vast numbers of people who hold less-glamorous clerical, administrative, and service-oriented jobs—jobs

that are nevertheless vulnerable to Year-2000 failures—might
have even less hesitation about finding an alternative lifestyle.

Our advice: Take a look at your industry now, and make
appropriate changes before it's too late. Some of the changes
may be industry-related. You might decide that it's not a good
idea to be a bank teller or an insurance agent as the century
comes to an end. But, it's also likely that the problems will be
geographical. The situation could be more serious in banking
communities like New York City. Ironically, Washington may
turn out to be one of the best places to live and work, for even
if all the government computers shut down for a year, the civil
service bureaucrats will still show up and sit at their desks. It
has sometimes been difficult to tell if they were doing anything useful, and one could even make a plausible argument
that they'll cause *less* trouble if they don't have access to their
computers. Washington has another interesting feature: It's the
home of the Treasury Department, where fresh money can be
printed, if necessary. Obviously, the situation is more complex
than just asking the Treasury Department to print some new
dollar bills for all the government workers; but the fact
remains, as we'll discuss in more detail in Chapter 5, that the
federal government *controls* the currency and thus maintains
some benevolent power over its employees (as well as various
other groups toward whom it may feel benevolent).

State governments may not fare so well. A confluence of
Year-2000-related problems (including massive shortfalls in
tax collections, for example) might exhaust the state treasuries
and leave the legislators with no choice but to furlough large
numbers of their employees. So it may well turn out that cities
like Sacramento, Albany, Trenton, and Austin are not the
places to be, from a job-hunting perspective.

There's a further irony to all of this: One job category that probably will remain in high demand for several years after January 1, 2000 is that of computer programming. Whether or not you blame this group for having caused the Year-2000 problem in the first place (most of them would tell you it was their predecessors' fault, or their bosses' fault), the fact remains that many organizations will be critically dependent on programmers, systems analysts, database designers, networking and telecommunication experts, and various other specialties. Not only are these people considered valuable in today's good times (there was an estimated shortage of approximately 300,000 software specialists in the U.S. as this book was being written), but it's quite likely that an even larger number will be required for post-Year-2000 cleanup activities. Thus, if you don't mind walking into the eye of the storm, as it were, this might be a good time to consider getting a two-year degree, or some other credentials, in computer programming.

One last piece of advice: Make sure your resume is updated, and that you've printed or photocopied an adequate number of "hard" copies. It would be an irony of the worst kind if your resume was locked within your company's *non*-Year-2000-compliant computer.

Fallback Advice: The Ten-Year Shutdown

Though the notion of being without work for a decade is incomprehensible for the vast majority of Americans, it bears noting that an unfortunate minority is already grimly familiar with the experience. The welfare class, the terminally unemployable, and the handicapped probably have a lot to tell the rest of us about the ordeal of going year after year without a real paycheck. Yet another irony is that a Year-2000 failure in the unemployment and welfare payment systems (including such things as food stamps) could create a particularly volatile situation for unemployed/welfare people who have no other financial resources at all.

If there should be such a Year-2000 failure in these government-sponsored payment systems, we don't think it will last longer than a month or two; the political pressures for finding some remedy—any remedy—will be too great. Indeed, a minor version of this problem occurred years ago when the computer systems of the U.S. Veterans' Administration collapsed. Because the problem could not be fixed quickly, and because the constituency was politically vocal, matters reached the point where administrators of the government agency began hand-writing checks in whatever amount they thought appropriate. The subsequent cleanup operation to straighten out the accounting records was horrendous indeed.

It's conceivable, of course, that a massive Year-2000 failure might cause one or more social welfare systems to be shut down completely. It's hard to predict in advance what the political mood of the country is going to be in the post-Year-2000 years, but the current political climate in Washington and many state governments is already oriented towards cutbacks in the social services.

In any case, our primary concern here—notwithstanding the desire to provide care for the unemployed and welfare recipients who need it—is with the working-class majority. As we've already suggested in this chapter, most work-related problems are likely to involve minor disruptions of a couple days, or moderate disruptions of a month. A disruption of a year is serious indeed, but most of the victims of this level of Year-2000-induced problem are probably *not* going to change careers, even though we've suggested that it could be a good idea; instead, they'll seek other jobs in the same field. If you've been a bank teller for ten years, there's a good chance that you'll want to continue your career as a bank teller; if your own bank shuts down, then you'll apply for a job at another bank—even if it means moving to a different city.

But what if the entire industry disappears? What if your profession vanishes? We hasten to note that banking is unlikely to disappear, no matter how serious the Year-2000 problem turns out to be. Greenbacks might be printed in a different color; old banks might be replaced by new banks; but, money and banking have survived for thousands of years, and will continue to exist in some form. The day-to-day operational activities of a bank teller might change, but it's reasonable to assume that someone who performs competently today in this profession will be able to adjust to the newly-defined bank teller jobs that might emerge a few years hence.

We can't be so confident about the future prospects of other job categories—e.g., tax attorneys, especially those who specialize in dealing with the IRS. What if a Year-2000 catastrophe brings about the downfall of the IRS and the entire hodgepodge of tax regulations, all of which is replaced with a simple flat tax mechanism that can be calculated by any third-grade school child? The highly paid tax attorney may well find that there is no requirement for his or her expertise at all ... nor will there be for another decade, until the inevitable tendency of bureaucrats to add exceptions and loopholes to the flat tax eventually brings about the need for a new generation of tax attorneys.

In recent years, there has been much political debate about the long-term disappearance of jobs and professions in the U.S. because of political agreements like NAFTA and the gradual globalization of industry. But over the past two hundred years, since the beginning of the Industrial Revolution, a much larger threat to many jobs and professions has been *automation*; and in the past 50 years, much of that automation has involved computers. Indeed, it has been argued that the major reason for the massive layoffs of middle-level managers in the last recession was the realization that desktop computers had eliminated the need for human managers to process and refine raw data from the bottom-level workers and then manually pass that data upward to senior managers.

In any case, it's almost a tautology that the workers in companies most vulnerable to Year-2000 failures are those who are computer-literate, to one degree or another. Why should we expect that any of their jobs might go away as a result of a massive Year-2000 failure? The reason is that many computer-supported activities within organizations exist to provide a service that society has deemed necessary or desirable; if society changes its mind about such matters, the service may no longer be needed, and the organization will cease to provide it.

This is particularly true of services that are imposed by government regulation, and which no organization would *ever* bother carrying out if not forced to. Take a look at the Human Resources Department in your company. The reason it's no longer called the Payroll Department is that it spends much of its time collecting data about the age, gender, nationality, race, and other details of its work force, in order to file appropriate reports with EEOC, OSHA, IRS, SSA, and various other government agencies. As noted earlier, it's hard to predict the political mood of the country if the Year-2000 problem turns out to be as serious as we think it might be; but it's not impossible to imagine one or more government agencies collapsing, especially if they were incompetent, disorganized, or on the verge of collapse *before* the Year-2000 problem came along.

A bizarre example will illustrate this point. One of the authors happened to be in South Africa in the early 1990s, when that country's government was taking its first steps to dismantle apartheid prior to Nelson Mandela's release. One of the government actions was to eliminate the racial classification scheme that had existed for decades, a scheme which defined each citizen as being a member of one of seven racial classifications (the consequences of which, throughout the rest of that citizen's life, were profoundly negative unless the classification was "white"). The decision was given front-page coverage in all the newspapers, as one might imagine, and one of the Johannesburg papers also carried a sarcastic editorial. What should be done, the newspaper asked, with the large group of government bureaucrats who had spent their entire professional lives classifying humans into such categories? What industry could possibly use the skills these individuals had developed? Perhaps, said the editorial writer, the local South African mines could use people who could divide rocks into different colors, so that gold and diamonds might be more easily recognized; but that was ultimately rejected, and the editorial concluded by noting, with grim satisfaction, that these government bureaucrats had no useful role to play in society ever again.

Fortunately, we have no bureaucrats in the U.S. government with such offensive duties; but, we *do* have bureaucrats, and many of them enforce regulations, make policies, and generally fill up their day with activities that might—in the lucid moments following a Year-2000 crisis—be judged no longer necessary or appropriate. The key point to remember here is that it's not just the government bureaucrats who are affected by the dismantling of such activities—it's all the people in private industry who have built careers around such activities.

When Prohibition was ended in the 1930s, for example, how many jobs were lost?

It's also possible that certain careers or professions will vanish because of sharp changes in the fashion, taste, mood, or hobbies of society following a massive Year-2000 failure. Maybe we'll abandon baseball as the national hobby—a change that will not only be catastrophic for today's highly-paid athletes, but also for those who sell peanuts and beer in the baseball stadium. Obviously, things like this are difficult, if not impossible, to predict; we merely wish to point out that such changes *could* occur.

Given that it's possible, what should we do about it? There's not much chance that you'll convince a highly-paid baseball star to abandon his career and take up farming; nor would such advice have any impact on the seller of peanuts and beer. We might advise the baseball star to start socking away most of his money in conservative investments, rather than spending it wildly; but, the peanut-seller is probably operating on such a tight budget that he or she wouldn't listen to such advice. Indeed, it would be hard enough to persuade *anyone* in the middle-class or lower-middle-class to put away a month's expenses in cash and a year's expenses in a savings account; and, suggesting that a ten-year nest egg should be squirreled away would be rejected as sheer lunacy.

Only the very affluent can consider a ten-year nest egg, and these individuals have the ironic problem of wondering where and how they can store their nest egg without running into Year-2000 problems. Those of us who enjoy middle-class incomes may have to worry about the danger of losing a one-year nest egg if the local bank collapses, but that's a more manageable problem. As for the problem of a decade-long collapse in our chosen career or profession, the only intelligent thing we can recommend is *flexibility*. Certain professions may be safe (prostitutes, for example, will continue to flourish!), but given the pervasive impact of computers on society, most of us have no guarantee at all that our current experience or credentials will be worth much at all in the post-Year-2000 years.

It's a sobering thought, but one that is beginning to be discussed independently of the Year-2000 problem. Jim Taylor and Watts Wacker, for example, offer the following advice in their intriguing new book, *The 500 Year Delta:*[7]

> *How do you plan for the inevitability of disaster? By taking the blinders off. By seeing the world as it is. By counting on the certainty of uncertainty, rather than the certainty of certainty. Not by trying to wish the bad away, but by acknowledging that things are going to happen soon to you and your business — things that by all your current reasoning schemes are anything but reasonable. Here's an exercise that we have our clients do: Take out a sheet of paper. Write down the 10 worst things that could happen to your business in the next 500 days, the next 500 weeks, and then start acting as if they will happen, because in a chaos world they or something very similar will.*

Even more sobering is the impact that a pervasive Year-2000 problem is likely to have on different generations. Just as the Great Depression had a different impact upon children, young adults, middle-aged people, and the elderly, we're likely to see a similar range of reactions to the Year-2000 crisis. Freedom, as one of the folk songs of the 1960s lamented, means you've got nothing left to lose, and a younger generation with no savings and no mortgage and no retirement plan may well find a Year-2000 crisis refreshingly liberating. An older generation is likely to have more to lose, and is likely to find it far more difficult to abandon a lifetime career because a Year-2000 bug has rendered it useless. The generational issues are indeed profound; we have neither the space nor the expertise to pursue the topic further in this book, but we strongly encourage you to study an eloquent and thought-provoking discussion in *The Fourth Turning,*[8] by William Strauss and Neil Howe. The Year-2000 crisis, in our opinion, is likely to be the formative event that will unleash what Strauss and Howe call a "fourth turning," the last example of which was the Great Crash of October 1929.

Jobs will certainly be at risk if the Year-2000 bug causes such a "fourth turning," but that will be just the beginning. In the next chapter, we'll look at the impact on utilities, such as what happens if the lights don't work and/or we have no oil or gas.

Endnotes

1. Capers Jones, quoted in "The Day The World Shuts Down," *Newsweek,* June 2, 1997. Also, see Capers Jones, *The Year 2000 Software Problem: Quantifying the Costs, Assessing the Consequences* (Addison-Wesley, 1997).

2. One of the authors visited Brazil annually during the late 1980s and early 1990s. Inflation was so bad that a new currency was introduced on at least two occasions, thereby rendering the leftover currency one had from the previous year's visit entirely useless. The Brazilians joked that you could tell how bad inflation was by watching to see whether people took buses or taxis; in one case, the fare is determined at the beginning of the ride, but in the other case, the fare is determined at the end of the ride—by which time it might have gone up!

3. One of the authors had the opportunity to visit Venezuela in 1994, during a prolonged period of high inflation and widespread distrust of the major banks. It was amazing to see that even the most modest of white-collar workers, including secretaries and clerks, all had U.S. dollar accounts in Miami-based U.S. banks. The standard practice was to immediately convert one's paycheck into dollars and deposit it in a U.S. bank. Small amounts of cash, sufficient to cover a day's normal expenses, would then be withdrawn on a daily basis and converted back into the local currency.

4. For statisticians and economists, we note that the correlation between consumer confidence and the savings rate has been -0.31 since 1978, and -0.45 since 1990.

5. Note that this involves the concept of system dynamics, which we discuss in more detail in Appendix B. The U.S. economic system is indeed a highly dynamic system, and if one wants to manipulate it successfully, it's crucial to

have a sense of the time-delay and feedback loops associated with actions being contemplated.

6. Let's say, for the sake of argument, that your normal monthly living expenses are $3,000. If you kept that amount of money in a savings account for a year, at today's typical savings account interest rate of 3.25%, the interest earnings would be $97.50; that's roughly $8 per month, or a quarter per day.

7. Jim Taylor and Watts Wacker, *The 500 Year Delta: What Happens After What Comes Next?* (HarperCollins Publishers, 1997).

8. William Strauss and Neil Howe, *The Fourth Turning: What the Cycles of History Tell Us About America's Next Rendezvous With History* (Broadway Books/Bantam Doubleday Dell, 1997).

Year-2000 Impact on Utilities

In preparing for battle I have always found that plans are useless, but planning is indispensable.

Dwight D. Eisenhower, quoted by Richard Nixon in Six Crises, "Krushchev" (1962).

Introduction

Most Americans, except those in dire economic straits, take a number of comforts for granted. Among these are the common utilities: electricity, running water, gas for cooking, and either gas, oil, or electricity for heating and cooling. Like so many other comforts, we can do without them for a few days—indeed, we sometimes do so willingly when camping or hiking. But take all this away for a month, and we would be a cold, odiferous, grumpy, miserable lot. Take them away for a year, and American society would be thrown backward a century, to the candle-lit days of the mid-nineteenth century.

It's not a prospect that anyone relishes. Indeed, it's so unthinkable that it's easier not to think about it at all—but that's what we'll do in this chapter. Our primary focus is the possibility of Year-2000-induced failures in the electrical utility industry. A similar investigation could be made of gas, oil, and water—but it would be largely repetitious, so we've skipped it to focus instead on suggesting some measures for coping with such a failure.

How Could Such Failures Happen?

The first thing to realize is that such failures already *have* happened, on numerous occasions—but they weren't caused by Year-2000 bugs, and most of them have been relatively brief. Throughout the U.S., we've all seen temporary failures in the delivery or supply of electricity, gas, oil, and even water. Most of the examples have been weather-related—e.g., a tornado or a blizzard knocks down power lines and cuts off electricity for a period of a couple days up to a week. Floods and problems in a city's sewage system or water supply have occasionally deprived communities of potable water for a few days. Industrial strikes, bad weather, and other problems have sometimes prevented delivery of heating oil. The list goes on…

The second thing to realize is that Year-2000 problems could easily become "systemic" because of the ripple effect phenomenon. If the entire city of New York, Chicago, or Los Angeles suddenly has the lights turned off, it *will* get some attention. And if it spreads beyond that … well, if you're old enough, you may remember the chaos surrounding the 1965 blackout that shut down much of the Northeast; that was followed, a decade later, by the blackout in the summer of 1977. If you're too young to remember those events, think back to July 3, 1996, when a power outage knocked out electricity in parts of eight western states and two Canadian provinces. We'll discuss these events in more detail below.

The third thing to keep in mind, as you begin planning for all of this, is that there are two fundamentally distinct aspects of a Year-2000 problem with utilities: one has to do with the physical delivery of the utility to your home, and the other has to do with the business computer systems, operated by the utility companies, that determine whether the utility service *should* be delivered. We'll comment on both aspects below, but the latter one is fairly obvious: If the electric company (or the gas company, or the oil company, etc.) decides that you owe them $357 million and that you haven't paid your bill for six months, it could decide to shut off your power, even if the generators are working just fine.

The Electrical System

With little doubt, electricity is one of the fundamental linchpins of modern society. If power shuts down, a great deal of the rest of society shuts down with it.[1] And as noted above, the nation's electrical generating system is definitely an area where ripple effect problems could occur. Within the U.S., there are 6,000 electrical generating units, 500,000 miles of bulk transmission lines, 12,000 major substations, and vast numbers of lower-voltage transformers. They're all linked together in a grid—and even with redundancy and fail-safe mechanisms (which were improved after the 1965 and 1977 experiences), it's still possible for a problem in one part of the system to ripple elsewhere.

A good example of this is the outage that occurred on July 3, 1996. We've excerpted and condensed one of the news reports that was filed shortly after the outage; it will give you an idea of how massive the problem of no electricity can be.

> *Across the West, a power outage knocked out electricity and phone service Tuesday to 1.5 million customers on a day of record heat above 100 in some places. The blackout shut down elevators, air conditioners and subway cars, and briefly darkened flashy casinos. The sporadic outages in at least*

*eight states from California to Colorado, and into Canada,
didn't last long—from 1 to 1 1/2 hours. But it was enough
to reveal the vulnerability of the region's linked power grid.*

*Utility officials prepared today to investigate the outages,
which came amid heavy usage in the heat wave. "Having an
interconnected system really makes for more efficient use of
our natural resources and keeps the cost down" said Lynn
Baker, spokeswoman for Bonneville Power Administration,
which oversees the power grid in the Pacific Northwest. "But
it means when something goes wrong, it can cascade through
the system."*

*At the center of the outage were three 500-kilovolt transmis-
sion lines that extend from the hydroelectric dams in the
Northwest down to the Southwest. All three lines, which can
supply up to 2.2 million homes, were knocked out at one
point. Authorities were unsure whether the lines caused the
outages or were affected by a problem elsewhere.*

*Elsewhere in California, hundreds of thousands lost power.
Thrill seekers at the Del Mar Fair outside San Diego were
surprised when the rides suddenly shut down. Subway cars in
San Francisco's Bay Area Rapid Transit system stopped in
their tracks. Los Angeles briefly shut down seven of its giant
water pumps.*

*Some stores, banks and restaurants closed; others operated
without cash registers, computers, lights and refrigeration. In
northern Nevada, police in Reno and Sparks reported so
many traffic lights out of service that they ran out of temporary stop signs. Casinos in Reno briefly lost power. Las Vegas
was unaffected.*

*Most hospitals and emergency services were able to switch to
auxiliary power. Federal Aviation Administration officials
in Seattle said air traffic controllers were able to use backup
power generators. Elevators were knocked out for about two
hours at the 19-story Ambassador East condominiums in
Denver.*

*The outage touched parts of Oregon, California, Idaho,
Utah, Wyoming, Colorado, Arizona and Nevada as well as
the Canadian provinces of Alberta and British Columbia.
At least 700,000 people lost power in northern Nevada, east-*

ern Oregon and southern Idaho, and at least 500,000 customers were blacked out in California, utility officials said. In Boise, Idaho, most offices and state agencies sent workers home and banks locked their doors during a two-hour outage.

All of this from a power outage that lasted only between one and two hours; think what the consequences would be if the outage lasted for the time periods we've focused on in this book: a few days, a month, a year, or a decade. It's quite unreasonable to assume that electricity would disappear from our lives for a decade; in the worst of all cases, the nation would rebuild its electrical infrastructure from scratch, if it had to. The most likely scenario, in our opinion, is the blackout that lasts for a couple days; a less likely scenario, but one we feel should not be ignored, is the one-month blackout. Why? Because it could take that long to fix whatever Year-2000 problems are discovered in the hours after midnight on December 31, 1999, and it could take that long to restart the system. While most of us would agree that a 2–3 day blackout could be tolerated with only moderate discomfort, the prospect of a one-month failure obviously needs to be taken more seriously.

Having said this, we should emphasize that there are knowledgeable professionals in the field who strongly disagree with us on this point. For example, Dick Mills, a senior consultant in the power and electrical industry, reviewed an early draft of our book and commented to us:

> *There has never been a widespread month long blackout in more than 100 years of experience. I think the statement also implies that the less than perfect history, makes Y2K extrapolations more plausible. Actually, just the opposite is true. It would serve the public better to point out that it is the system which has never failed and thus which remains largely un-*

tested that is most vulnerable to complete collapse. The more frequently a system fails the more real life experience we have about how they fail and the consequences of failure.

The non-technical reader reading the non-technical descriptions of the ripple effect and descriptions of the power system might reasonably come away with the impression that the systems are fragile. In other words, they might believe that nearly everything has to work right, or else it blacks out. The reality is just the opposite. Steam power generating plants are enormously complex, the power system itself is enormously complex, and dependent on all these power plants. The power system has operated for more than 100 years, and all during that time there has never been an instant when there were not thousands of malfunctioning, or aberrant devices participating. It's also probably true, that there has never been an instant when some isolated customer wasn't inadvertently without power. There has never been a case, hurricanes and tornadoes notwithstanding, of a national blackout, or a regional blackout lasting much more than 24 hours. That knowledge puts quite a different light on things.[2]

Notwithstanding this reassurance, we still argue that there *could* be Year-2000 bugs in the computer software associated with the electrical power grid. Each of the 6,000 generating units throughout the U.S. has its own computer systems to regulate the amount of electricity that is generated by hydroelectric dams, oil-burning generators, or nuclear generators. The entire network, or grid, is controlled regionally by more than 100 separate control centers that coordinate responsibilities jointly for the impact upon real-time network operations throughout the country. The control centers have computer systems too, of course, and these too can fail.

Generally speaking, the computer software for electrical generating utilities has been written more carefully, and tested more thoroughly, than the business software in most companies. But these systems do have date calculations embedded within them; as such, they are vulnerable to Year-2000 failures. Dick Mills, whose comments we noted earlier, pointed out to us in the following that while the actual generation of electricity is not based on date-sensitive calculations of 'anticipated' demands for power; the date calculations are elsewhere:

> *The generation of electricity is regulated according to actual demand. There is no practical way to store massive amounts of electric energy, so it must be generated at the instant of demand. When you flip on the light switch in your bedroom, you actually cause the nation's electric system to increase the generation just enough to power the lights. The details are too technical to discuss here, but if you think about it, if the electricity can't be made in advance and stored, there's simply no other way.*

> *The point is, the calculations for regulating power generators and power systems are in-general not date sensitive. Indeed, the regulating computer programs don't even need access to the date for any purpose. Hourly, daily or seasonal variations in demand have nothing to do with it. That's terribly important.*

> *What is date sensitive, are the forecasts of what might happen tomorrow, or next week or in six months. We use this information to plan. On days of low forecast demand, the workers at some plants might be told to stay home. During weeks of high demand, we make sure that no schedulable maintenance is scheduled. These plans are certainly date sensitive, but at the same time they are much more subject to human reasonableness checks than are automatic controls. If, for example, a Y2K bug causes an outlandish forecast that says in the next year New York City will use no electricity while Sandusky, Ohio will use seven zillion times its previous use, what will the effect be. Do we expect humans to actually act on such forecasts uncritically? Of course not. The safest of all automated systems are those which retain a human in-the-loop as the final filter. I encourage anyone who doubts the truth of this, to book his flights on airlines that no longer put pilots on board their airplanes.*

One of the things we must continue reminding ourselves about in discussions of this kind is the ripple effect phenomenon: Even if a utility company's Year-2000 computers are *all* Year-2000-compliant, is this enough? Well, consider the dilemma faced by utilities that depend on coal, oil, or natural gas for the generation of their power. What happens if the raw materials are not available? Martyn Emery, a UK-based Year-2000 expert, provided the following note as a sobering reminder of how interconnected everything seems to be:

> *In the UK, 8 miles from my home is a chemical/petroleum plant that processes UK oil requirements, it requires a crude oil tanker delivery every day, and within 2 days this has been refined and delivered to petrol stations. They really have no more than 4–5 days buffer. Directly next to the refinery is a power station that produces electricity for the region using the refined oil. Water companies can not operate without power.*
>
> *At a recent presentation by a petroleum company they estimated that 17% of all computer systems on a tanker were Non-y2k compliant, and they have a fleet of over 100 tankers. Changing and testing all the system is impossible in the next 18 months, they simply do not have the dry dock facilities or labor resource. So they will not be able to get the approval from the Marine Safety Agency to issue sea-worthy licenses and hence they will not be able to insurance from 1.1.1999. The business impact is very significant.*

In the case of coal-, gas-, and/or oil-powered generators, perhaps all of this still will fall into the "nuisance" category. An expensive, serious, annoying nuisance to be sure, but probably not life-threatening. But, there's another source of electrical power—one we've learned to treat carefully after the famous incident at Three Mile Island in 1979—*nuclear* power generation. Interestingly, there's an entire government bureaucracy devoted to this area, the Nuclear Regulatory Commission. Fortunately, this agency is aware of the Year-2000 problem, but whether they have taken adequate steps to prevent serious problems (e.g., radiation leakage a la Chernobyl) is debatable. We'll let you make your own decision by taking a look at NRC Notice 96-70,[3] issued on December 24, 1996:

UNITED STATES
NUCLEAR REGULATORY COMMISSION
OFFICE OF NUCLEAR MATERIAL SAFETY AND SAFEGUARDS
OFFICE OF NUCLEAR REACTOR REGULATION
WASHINGTON, D.C. 20555

December 24, 1996

NRC INFORMATION NOTICE 96-70: YEAR 2000 EFFECT ON COM-
PUTER SYSTEM SOFTWARE

Addressees

All U.S. Nuclear Regulatory Commission licensees, cer-
tificate holders, and registrants (hereafter referred
to as licensees).

Purpose

The U.S. Nuclear Regulatory Commission (NRC) is issuing this information notice to alert addressees to the
potential problems their computer systems and software
may encounter as a result of the change to the new
century. It is expected that recipients will review
the information for applicability to their facilities
and consider actions, as appropriate, to avoid potential problems. However, suggestions contained in this
information notice are not NRC requirements; therefore, no specific action nor written response is
required.

Description of Circumstances

Earlier this year, the U.S. House of Representatives
held hearings on an issue known as the "Year 2000"
software problem. These hearings identified that some
of the most important computer software used by the
Federal government may not work correctly starting in
the year 2000, because the software can only use single years or decades in performing calculations; it
will not be able to recognize a change to the new century. Many computer systems will potentially fail to

recognize this change to a new century and will mis-
read "00" or the year 2000, as 1900, and thus may
cause the system to fail or generate faulty data. The
NRC, along with several other Federal agencies, is
currently examining computer software used to support
Agency functions that may be affected. Specific problems have already been identified and will be corrected. In some instances where future dates are used
to schedule actions, problems have already occurred—
well before the end of the century.

Discussion

The Year 2000 issue affects everyone. It will have an
impact on State and local governments, NRC licensees,
and businesses. The magnitude of the Year 2000 issue
poses a challenge to all those potentially affected.
Dates are involved in many facets of computer systems
and software. Neither industry nor the Federal government has yet identified the scope of the situation.

This issue may affect NRC licensees in many different
ways. For example, computer software used to calculate
dose or to account for radioactive decay may not recognize the turn of the century, which could lead to
incorrectly calculated doses or exposure times for
treatment planning. Other examples of software that
may be affected include security control, radiation
monitoring, technical specification surveillance
testing, and accumulated burn-up programs. Also,
equipment that licensees have purchased may contain
computer software susceptible to the Year 2000 problem. The problem could occur not only in computer
software or data that have been acquired from external
sources, but also in programs developed by licensees
or consultants. For many licensees, this issue may not
prove to be a significant health and safety concern.
However, to prevent any other potential problems this
issue may precipitate, licensees are encouraged to
examine their uses of computer systems and software
well before the turn of the century. In assessing computer software, licensees may want to consider review-

ing those programs that are used to meet licensing requirements or those that have safety significance. To facilitate the exchange of information among licensees, NRC, and the public, information related to the Year 2000 problem is posted on NRC's World Wide Web server (www.nrc.gov.) under the "News and Information" option. An example of information that has already been posted is contract language developed by the Federal government for acquisition of new information technology to avoid the Year 2000 problem. In addition to the information presented on NRC's homepage, an Internet list server has been established to encourage discussion of Year 2000 issues. To subscribe to this list, Internet e-mail may be sent to listproc@nrc.gov with the message: subscribe year-2000 username, where the username is the first and last name of the individual making the request (e.g., John Doe).

Licensees may wish to consider what actions may be appropriate to examine and evaluate their software systems, and whether to designate an individual to monitor the continuing activities in government and industry to determine the extent of potential problems and proposed solutions. Any additional contact regarding the Year 2000 problem between NRC and licensees will be made through the addressee of this information notice, unless a separate point of contact is designated by the licensee. Licensees who wish to designate a separate point of contact should provide the contact name and address, including telephone and fax number and email address if available, to the appropriate technical contact of this information notice. Holders of Title 10 of the Code of Federal Regulations (CFR) Part 50 licenses are requested to provide this information to the appropriate Office of Nuclear Reactor Regulation (NRR) project manager (courtesy copy to the *NRR technical contact listed below).*

This information notice requires no specific action nor written response. If you have any questions about the information in this notice, please contact the

technical contacts listed below or the appropriate
regional office.

signed by   signed by
Donald A. Cool, Director   Thomas T. Martin, Director
Division of Industrial   Division of Reactor Program
and Medical Nuclear   Management Office of
Safety Office of Nuclear   Nuclear Reactor Regulation
Material Safety and Safe-
guards

Technical contacts: Mark A. Sitek, NMSS, (301) 415-
6155, E-mail: mas6@nrc.gov

Michael Kaltman, NRR, (301) 415-2905, E-mail:
mxk2@nrc.gov

We find the last paragraph of this notice particularly trou-
blesome: NRC licensees are advised that the notice "requires
no specific action nor written response." We're delighted that
the NRC took the trouble to advise its licensees of the problem, and we're confident that all the licensees are responsible,
intelligent people who will work hard to avoid a Year-2000
problem, but we're still concerned about the ripple effect. As
the NRC points out in its notice, "The problem could occur
not only in computer software or data that have been acquired
from external sources, but also in programs developed by licensees or consultants." And we're further concerned by the
assessment of Year-2000 expert Capers Jones that only 3% of
the public utilities are ahead of schedule on their Year-2000
conversion efforts, while 50% are on schedule, and 47% are
behind schedule.[4]

By the way, disruptions in the electrical system are typically
exacerbated by extreme weather conditions; the July 3, 1996
failure described above was partially caused by a massive 100-

degree heat wave that blanketed much of the western U.S. The Year-2000 problem begins, of course, on January 1; if it happens to be a cold winter, much of the middle and northern U.S. could be drawing large loads of electricity for heating purposes. And as if that wasn't enough, it turns out that the year 2000 will also be a period of intense solar flares, which have caused severe electrical disruptions in the past. The subject of solar flares, as you might imagine, is far beyond the expertise of the authors of this book; however, if you have access to the Internet, we invite you to browse http://www.sel.noaa.gov/info/Cycle23.html to see the U.S. government's summary of flare activity in 2000-2005. You should also browse http://www.pathfinder.com/@@yQsh2AUABc4 RMSCY/time/magazine/domestic/1996/960909/space.html to see an article in the September 9, 1996 issue of *Time* that warns about the impact of flare activity on the nation's electrical system.[5]

Additional Year-2000 Problems for Utility Companies

Everything we've discussed so far is concerned with the actual creation and distribution of electrical power. But as noted above, problems could also occur even if this part of the utility industry completely avoids Year-2000 software bugs. Electricity—and in a similar fashion, oil and gas and water—are delivered to customers for a price; we all get a monthly bill, and the utility company expects us to pay that bill in a timely fashion. We may be given various payment options (e.g., spreading payments over a period of months to reduce the impact of high usage during summer months), and we may have occasional interactions with the utility when we move into a new home or switch from oil heat to gas heat. All of this, of course, involves interactions with the business computer systems within the utility company; and, these computers are obviously vulnerable to the kind of software problems discussed in Appendix A.

One of our concerns involves billing. A faulty utility computer might send you a multi-million dollar bill, or it might come to the conclusion that you're a deadbeat who never pays his or her bills. But, any number of other problems could occur. An aberrant computer could accidentally delete your database record so that the utility company doesn't even know that you exist, or it could come to the mistaken conclusion that you asked to have your service terminated.

If problems of this kind occur, the important question is. Will the decision to shut off your service be made by a human or a computer? In the case of a large utility company—e.g., the gas/electric utility for a metropolitan area—it's easy to imagine that all of this has been automated, because the numbers are too large for humans in the utility's Customer Service department to deal with. Thus, we might expect a wave of automated service shut-offs in the event of a Year-2000 problem; but, the hue and outcry associated with such an action would probably be large enough that most utilities would be forced to quickly program an "override" into their system to disregard any such actions. (However, even this could take a few days or weeks to program, test, and install within the computer system.)

In today's normal operating conditions, we don't know whether the decision to shut off electric, gas, or water service is made automatically or manually in our own city, let alone yours. You might want to call your Customer Service department to find out; we attempted to do so in New York City, but (as is common with calls to the Customer Service department of banks, automobile companies, and many other large firms these days), our call was answered by a puzzled representative who had never heard of the Year-2000 problem, and who forwarded us on to another representative who was equally puzzled, who forwarded us to another department, where an automated voice-mail system recorded our question and never got back to us. C'est la vie.

Our real concern is the small utility services in suburban and rural areas. Even in these cases, the electric and gas utilities are somewhat centralized; but other utilities—especially the delivery of heating oil, for example—are likely to be in the hands of small companies who service a limited number of customers. These companies are likely to have far less sophisticated computer systems, and are likely to encounter far more serious Year-2000 problems—indeed, it's far more likely that in mid-1997, as this book is being written, they're completely unaware of the problem. The local heating oil distributor is more likely to have a human involved in any decision to shut off your deliveries, and one might expect more humane decisions to be made in the event of a Year-2000-induced billing mistake. On the other hand, the delivery schedules in such companies are also computerized; a Year-2000 bug could easily cause your house, and a hundred others, to be left off the list for regularly scheduled deliveries of winter heating oil.

By the way, while you're worrying about electrical utilities from *your* perspective, some of the utilities apparently haven't begun to worry about the problem at all. Rick Cowles, who has organized an excellent Year-2000/utility Web site at http://www.accsyst.com/writers/ele2000a.htm notes that two separate surveys conducted in early 1997 indicated that 32-36% of the nation's utility companies had not begun any formal Year-2000 planning efforts. Cowles summarizes the Year-2000-

related business issues facing the utility companies in the following way:[6]

> Here's a short list of business areas every utility should be thinking about and the systems that should be considered as 'mission critical:"
>
> **Human Resources**: The obvious—payroll. But how about mundane systems such as Resumix? How about your benefits systems, pensions systems, job posting systems, etc. People are supposed to be your number-one priority, so make your HR systems one of your first priorities in conversions and compliance.
>
> **Financial Control**: The biggie. The SEC, Moody's, Barron's, and a host of other financial risk organizations are going to be looking to see if your FI systems are Y2K compliant. Your company's bond rating depends on an aggressive Y2K compliance effort (and not just the fact that you're "implementing SAP"). Can you pay your bills? Can you process your receivables? Can you do such routine things such as track the market and park your free cash wherever it's going to make the most ROI? Can you budget? How about FERC accounting—will your FERC module crash because you can't close the 1999 books post-01/01/2000? How about closing the 2000 books post-2001? And the cost of money? (That's discussed under INVENTORY.) Most importantly—have you tested? (Particularly your ACH software, which your utility probably doesn't own, and attendant financial networks....)
>
> **Plant Maintenance**: Can your maintenance control and administrative systems, both at the plant level and corporate level, cut simple workorders to repair your in-house equipment? Can the systems track and schedule, into the future, preventive maintenance and surveillance testing? Will maintenance demand and timetables for spare parts appropriately drive MRP in your purchasing systems? Will your workorder system and HR systems work in tandem to schedule resources for maintenance? (Remember, it's the interdependencies in Y2K that are going to be the killer.)

Purchasing: Can you interact with your suppliers? This means, simply, cutting purchase orders, tracking and expediting orders, and paying the bills. EDI. Petty cash purchases. Procurement cards (will your cards work with local vendor POS systems?). MRP driven orders. ¡Ay, caramba! There's a lot of systems and inter-relationships to check here. Also, have you included Y2K compliance clauses in all of your current day purchasing documents?

Inventory Control and Warehousing: Here's something to consider, and it relates back to the earlier Financial Control discussions. Many companies are not only reviewing in-house computer systems, applications, and hardware, but are also considering contingencies should a supplier not weather Y2K too well, and not be able to supply needed material or services because THEIR systems crashed. One of the Y2K contingencies that most 'material intensive' organizations are considering is to increase stocking levels of consumable and safety stock commodities prior to 01/01/2000. How is this going to impact your bottom line? If you increase safety stock on $100 million inventory (typical for a major U.S. utility) just 20 percent, well, you do the math. That's $20 million of extra inventory sitting on the shelf and not working for your organization or generating revenue in some other manner. Just in case, not "just in time."

Fallback Advice: The Two-Day Failure

Two or three days with no heat or electricity is manageable, right? Indeed, if you knew exactly when the problem would occur, you could plan ahead for it: empty out the freezer, stock up on candles and batteries, make plans to eat out, etc. Unfortunately, if a minor Year-2000-related utility problem does occur, there's no guarantee that it will happen at the stroke of midnight on New Year's Eve, 1999. Depending on the nature of the problem, it could occur at almost any point during the year; for example, a shutdown caused by a Year-2000-related billing problem might occur on January 31 or February 29; a problem with delivery of your heating oil could occur in the middle of January or in the middle of February.

Nevertheless, the basic precautions mentioned above do make sense. Suburban and rural residents are already aware of the desirability of having candles and batteries, as well as some extra wood for the fireplace in the event of a short-term utility outage. It's the city-dwellers who are likely to be the least prepared; after all, the lights *never* go out in New York City ... except in 1965, 1977, and perhaps in 2000.

A small point to keep in mind: If problems with the electrical industry should continue on through the summer, you should be prepared for brownouts and "spikes" in the power supply. A colleague of ours lives in northern Nevada and works as an independent computer consultant. When the July 3, 1996 power outage occurred, it zapped three of his desktop and laptop computers, despite the surge suppressor in the "power strip" he had purchased in the local hardware store.

Along those same lines, we got an e-mail note from Rob Jones [jonesr@med.ge.com], who reviewed the first draft of this book and commented:

> ...surge protectors/transient suppressors (the kind the hardware store typically sell) should be replaced about once a year. Many people are surprised when suddenly their equipment is damaged. But often these devises have been taking a beating and saving the equipment far more often than they might realize. These are not like fuses (in serial with the equipment) but are a bypass for spikes (in parallel)... So when they wear out, instead of preventing the equipment from running (like a fuze or circuit breaker) they simple cease to provide a bypass for future spikes. They silently stop working. I think a lot of people are putting more faith in old surge suppressors than they should. It doesn't take Y2K outages to destroy your electronics, a good thunderstorm will do.

Fallback Advice: The One-Month Failure

If the lights go out or the gas gets shut off for a month, it's more likely to be the result of a major disagreement with the billing department of your utility than a Chernobyl-style meltdown. This distinction may sound academic, however, because a month without utilities would be unpleasant, regardless of the reason why it happens.

If the problem is that a faulty computer thinks you owe seven zillion dollars for last month's electric power, it's possible you can rectify the problem by dealing with a human being. If you're concerned about the possibility of this kind of Year-2000-induced failure, one of the most important things you can do is ensure that you have not only the current utility bill and a canceled check to confirm that it was paid, but also the appropriate bills and payment records for the last several months. You may need to show all of this to an intelligent, sympathetic clerk at the gas company or electric company to confirm that you're an honest bill-paying citizen and to get your utilities restored. There's nothing complicated about this, of course, but it's amazing how many people throw away the bills once they're paid, and manage to lose all of their canceled checks. Forewarned is forearmed.

The notion of actually speaking to a utility company clerk face-to-face may not seem strange to suburbanites or residents of small towns, but it's unlikely that any city-dweller has ever done such a thing. For most of us, a call to a utility company, the bank, the phone company, or any other large institution means that we interact with a confusing series of voice-response messages ("If you're calling about a problem with your bill, press 1; if you want to discontinue your service, press 2") before ever talking to a human. And if we do speak with a human, we never learn his or her name—and it's never the same person we spoke to the last time we called. In some cases, large organizations deliberately design their customer service systems this way: If you ask a customer service representative's name, he or she will tell you that giving you that information is not allowed. Even if you do find that you're discussing your billing problem with Joe Shmoe, you'll discover that it's impossible to call the Customer Service department and ask to speak specifically with Joe. You'll be told—typically by another automated voice-response system—that you can only speak with "the next available representative," whoever that turns out to be.

If that's the way things work in your utility company, we offer our sympathy—it works that way in New York City where we live too. But, it's worth testing the system to see how it works, and to determine whether the automated anonymity can be circumvented; the point of all this discussion is that it may turn out to be *very* valuable to have a direct, human contact within these vast organizations, should there be a Year-2000-related problem that causes your utility service to be disrupted. There may not be much point in attempting this in 1998, for people move around and change jobs rather frequently; but sometime in the middle of 1999, we suggest that you nurture a personal relationship with someone at your electric company, gas company, and heating oil company. Call someone to get an explanation of your bill in mid-1999 (even if you understand your bill completely), and then send a thank-you note to the customer service representative to show how much you appreciate the assistance. Send a note to his or her supervisor, send a birthday card, send a box of candy, send ... well, you get the idea.

All of this may or may not help in the event of a month-long shutdown of utility services. Other strategies, such as stockpiling may or may not be relevant, depending on your situation. You can't stockpile electricity or gas, but you may be able to stockpile oil to some minor extent. Make sure the tank is completely full toward the end of December 31, 1999, and then try to get it topped off every time it falls to the halfway mark.[7] Batteries and candles may be worth stockpiling too, though it's doubtful that many of us will be willing to put up with reading by candlelight for more than a month.

Indeed, this is the real question: When do we reach the point where we decide that we can't stand it anymore—and what options do we have at that point? As you can imagine, it's extremely unlikely that anyone is going to make a proactive decision to move to a different location in mid-1999 because of the possibility of a utility company failure in the post-2000 era. After all, who's to say whether such failures are more likely in a big city like New York or a small city like Boise? Who can really say whether the suburban residents of Long Island, New York are more vulnerable than the ranchers in Montana? Wherever we happen to live, we're likely to stay put—as long as utility company failures are the only form of Year-2000 disasters we're concerned about.

It's also unclear whether we'll be able to tell that we're entering a month-long failure at the outset. If there's a physical failure in an electrical generating facility (e.g., a generator burns out because of an errant computer or, God forbid, a radiation leak occurs in a nuclear power facility), perhaps you'll see an official announcement that power won't be restored for a certain number of weeks or months. But if the disruption is caused by a billing system that erroneously decided to terminate your service because of non-payment, you could be faced with a day-to-day battle with customer service representatives to get things restored. Keep in mind that you won't be the only one dealing with such a problem; everyone else in your neighborhood or city may be complaining about it too, which may keep the Customer Service department from fixing *your* problem for quite a while.

Bottom line: If a problem of this magnitude occurs, you're not going to be able to do much about it. Depending on where you live, what the weather is like, and how much you're able to stockpile, you may be able to survive a few weeks of utility service disruption. We figure that a month is about the most that anyone can be expected to put up with before some drastic action needs to be taken; it could happen even sooner if an entire city is without heat or electricity. But, there is the possibility that banks and businesses and government agencies will be able to maintain operations, while a miserable 10% of the population carries on a battle with the utility company to restore their service.

In any case, if it comes to this, you should be prepared to leave town until the situation is resolved. Make sure that your network of relatives, college roommates, and other friends is intact; you may need to move in with them for a few weeks. Make sure that you've got enough money—in cash, or in whatever bank is functioning in the post-2000 era—so that you can afford to leave town without hitch-hiking.

Fallback Advice: The One-Year Failure

A one-year failure, in our opinion, is *not* likely to be the result of the billing mix-up we described earlier. If a situation like this persisted for more than a month or two—especially if it's fairly pervasive so that large segments of the population are affected—it is likely to result in drastic action by the utility companies themselves, or by government regulation. One can almost imagine Congress passing the Electrical Relief Act of

2001, decreeing that all citizens are entitled to electric power regardless of the status of their bills.

So a problem of this magnitude—which we think is unlikely, but nevertheless minimally possible—would almost certainly be associated with a physical/mechanical shutdown of the utility provider in the affected area. If there are massive power failures throughout the entire national grid, for example, then it's conceivable that the repair effort could be so expensive and time-consuming that certain rural areas would be put at the bottom of the priority list. If the distribution network itself is damaged or rendered inoperable, then it may be impossible to switch electrical power from a region that has escaped Year-2000 problems to one whose local generation capability has collapsed because of a Year-2000 failure.

In the unlikely event that something like this occurs, the "escape" option mentioned earlier will be even more necessary. Indeed, the real question is whether things will still be intact when you return. Think for a moment about the plans you make when leaving your house behind for a one-month vacation versus the plans you would have to make if you were leaving the country for a year. And, think about how much more difficult such planning would be if you had to assume the absence of heat, light, water, or gas during that absence. Now factor in the likelihood that your neighbors will be gone too; at some point, for example, you might have to worry about the possibility of looting or break-ins.

One thing is for certain: People who rent are going to be in much better shape than people who own in a scenario like this. Those who rent have the option—in the worst case—of piling themselves and their family and their most precious possessions into the car and driving away; if they default on their rent and lose the rest of their household possessions, it

won't be a severe disaster. Those who own their homes can also
drive away in the family car, but they leave behind the largest
part of their financial equity. If they return a year later and
find that the house has been ransacked, trashed, or burned to
the ground, it will be that much more difficult to recover.

Is anything like this even remotely possible? That depends on
your opinion about two things: first, the likelihood of a Year-
2000 breakdown; and second, your opinion about the possibility of a social breakdown following a Year-2000 breakdown. As
we've said, we think it's highly unlikely that we'll see a one-year
disruption of utility services. We think it's particularly unlikely
in the urban areas, if for no other reason than the political pressure that will be imposed to restore such services. On the other
hand, if Year-2000-induced utility breakdowns are compounded by breakdowns in banking, communications, and
other areas discussed in this book, then the social reaction—
especially in the urban areas!—could deteriorate rather quickly.
A month without power in the middle of winter is not something that the residents of New York City, Boston, Chicago, or
any of the other northern cities of the U.S. are likely to accept
with good humor and civic spirit. The residents of these cities
are already understandably grumpy about the circumstances in
which they live; a three-month, six-month, or nine-month utility disruption could easily lead to rioting in the streets.

Endnotes

1. Several people who reviewed an early draft of this book argued that water is even
   more fundamental.
2. These comments were sent to the authors during the summer of 1997 and are
   posted on Mr. Mills' Web site at http://www.albany.net/~dmills/fallback/
   chapt5.htm
3. You can find this information on the Internet at http://ftp.fedworld.gov/pub/
   nrc-gc/in96070.txt and, as you'll see in the NRC document, you can visit their
   Web site and subscribe to an Internet mailing list for updates.

4. Capers Jones, *The Year 2000 Software Problem: Quantifying the Costs and Assessing the Consequences*, page 82.

5. See also "Geomagnetic Storms Can Threaten Electric Power Grid," by John G. Kappenman, Minnesota Power, Duluth, Minn.; Lawrence J. Zanetti, Johns Hopkins University, Applied Physics Laboratory, Laurel, Md.; and William A. Radasky, Metatech, Goleta, Calif. Earth in Space, Vol. 9, No. 7, March 1997, pp. 9-11. You can find this on the Internet at http://www.agu.org/sci_soc/eiskappenman.html

6. See http://www.accsyst.com/writers/business.htm for the full text of Mr. Cowles' comments on the business ramifications of Year-2000 problems for utility companies.

7. But keep in mind that the pilot light on your oil furnace is probably powered by electricity—so that if the electricity fails, you may also be without heat.

Year-2000 Impact on Transportation

As machines become more and more efficient and perfect, so it will become clear that imperfection is the greatness of man.

Ernst Fischer, The Necessity of Art, *Chapter 5 (1959).*

Introduction

In the hilarious movie, *Planes, Trains, and Automobiles,* actors Steve Martin and the late John Candy demonstrated that when things go wrong, it requires almost superhuman effort to travel from New York to Chicago in time to be home for the holidays. While the movie-based predicament has nothing to do with Year-2000 problems, it does provide a rough idea of how difficult things could be if the Millennium Bug disrupts the transportation system.

While perhaps somewhat less important than electric power and the telephone, the transportation system is obviously crucial to the nation's economy—not to mention our own individual lives. Many of us think nothing of hopping in our car each morning for a 50-mile ride to the office, completely forgetting that fifty miles was often a day's journey in the mid-nineteenth century. Others ride to work each day on a complex network of trains, buses, subways, ferries, and other carefully synchronized devices. Even more amazing is the practice of business executives, some of whom fly from the East Coast to the West Coast for a one-hour meeting, then zoom cross-country at 35,000 feet back to the East Coast in time for David Letterman or Jay Leno on late-night TV.

Of course, it doesn't always work perfectly. Everyone has experienced automobile breakdowns, delays in the train schedules, or canceled airline flights. Indeed, that was the whole point of *Planes, Trains, and Automobiles*: What should have been a straightforward two-hour flight to Chicago, at the end of a business meeting in New York City, turned out to be a marathon experience of one disaster after another.

While it sometimes seems that these travel-related problems are occurring more frequently than they were in the "good old days" (whenever that might have been), a realistic appraisal would have to conclude that overall, transportation works pretty well. But a similar appraisal would conclude that the Year-2000 bug could wreak havoc upon all of this. We're not suggesting that American society will retreat back to the horse-and-buggy days, but for reasons that should be familiar to you by this stage in the book, we *do* believe that there will be a significant number of minor transportation problems that will persist for two or three days. There will be some that last a month, with moderately serious consequences; and yes, there could be one or two problems that create transportation hardships that take a year or more to undo.

Automobiles

We begin our discussion with automobiles, which have two salient characteristics: first, there are a lot of them; and second, they operate under the personal control of the owner. As this book was being written, there were nearly 100 million automobiles on the highways and byways of the U.S., many of which were manufactured during the current decade.

The last statistic is relevant, because it has only been the past five years or so that we've begun to see a significant increase in the number of microprocessors embedded within the typical consumer automobile. The numbers vary from model to model, and from manufacturer to manufacturer, but the typical car has about 50 microprocessors—i.e., tiny embedded computers. Some of these computers are relatively passive; for example, they provide readout displays of the current temperature (in both Centigrade and Fahrenheit, just to show how clever they are) or the average mileage since the car was last powered on. But, some of the computers provide *control* functions: they regulate the mixture of air and fuel in the carburetor, they provide "intelligent" braking and suspension capabilities, and so forth. Under the appropriate circumstances, they can signal alarms or flashing lights on the driver's dashboard—or they can initiate more serious actions, such as inflating the air-bags in the event of a crash.

What happens if one or more of these computer systems fail? In some cases, the results are merely annoying. Perhaps you won't see a display of the outside air temperature or a display telling you your average mileage and speed on this trip. Lack of information could be more serious, though, if there's a failure in the microcomputer that controls the digital display on the entire dashboard in front of the driver. And there is, of course, the possibility of more serious trouble, such as faulty braking, faulty suspension, faulty fuel mixture, etc.

Obviously, the relevant question is: How dependent are these systems on Year-2000-related date logic? At first glance, one would think the answer is "not at all." We can't recall ever having seen a calendar in any car we've ever driven, so why worry about a "rollover" program on New Year's Eve in 1999? The problem has to do with the nature of "embedded systems" in general. In general, the problem is that the computerized chips which form the core of the embedded systems are now generic commodities, and they often contain functions that the end-user (in this case, the manufacturer of the automobile) has no interest in. By analogy, take a look at the digital wristwatch you're wearing. How many of its embedded functions are you using? Almost all watches have a stopwatch, a timer, and other simple functions; and, many of them can record a hundred telephone numbers, and even carry out mathematical functions. Since you paid only $19.95 for the watch, it doesn't bother you that there's a lot of unused functionality buried within the watch—all you want is the basic task of keeping the time of day.

That's not a fully satisfactory answer for our automobile situation; after all, why would an auto manufacturer buy a generic chip with date calculation capabilities to display the car's temperature and gas mileage? The answer is simple: Even though a car may not need to know the calendar date, it *does* have to know about the passage of time intervals. The microcomputer that controls your carburetor has to recalculate the fuel mixture several times a second; the microcomputer that displays your average gas mileage on a trip probably recalculates its figures once a second. Calculating a time interval is indeed a "generic" piece of computerized functionality; the fact that the chip manufacturer (e.g., Intel, Texas Instruments, Motorola, AMD, or a dozen others) enlarged upon that functionality to keep track of the day-of-year is probably not something the auto manufacturer stopped to think about.[1]

A more likely example of a date-related problem is the embedded computer system that keeps track of the elapsed time and/or mileage since the car was last serviced. These computers are normally reset by a technician each time a car is brought in for servicing, so that it can begin 'counting down' again. When the counter reaches zero, an audible alarm is sounded, or a red light is flashed on the dashboard. While this is obviously not a fatal problem, it could take a driver by surprise if it occurs at the stroke of midnight on December 31, 1999; it could also lead to a number of unnecessary visits to the auto service center to fix the problem.

Note that such a mechanism could be implemented in a very simple fashion that does not appear to involve any awareness of specific dates. If the computer has a counter that can be set to an integer value—e.g., 100—then with each passing day, the computer can decrement the counter until it reaches zero. However, even this simple approach requires that the computer be able to keep track of the passage of a day, which may rely upon some hardware logic that *is* date-sensitive, and therefore Year-2000-sensitive. On the other hand, if the counter is tracking the car's mileage, then no dates are involved at all. Every time the odometer clicks up a mile, the time-for-service counter clicks down a mile. The simplest solution to this problem is to ask your service technician if any of his or her diagnostic tools allow a date to be set *anywhere* within the car; if so, ask him or her to certify (in writing) that the relevant computer systems are Year-2000-compliant. Chances are that he or she won't be willing or able to do so; in that case, ask to have the date set back several years.

We'll discuss the issue of embedded systems in more detail in Chapter 11; as you can appreciate, such a problem could also occur in household appliances, factory devices, and an enormous variety of other man-made gadgets that now have computer chips embedded in them. For now, we'll simply summarize. Some percentage of on-board automobile micro-computers are probably date-sensitive, and some percentage of these "sensitive" computers are carrying out "mission-critical" functions (e.g., fuel mixture) for which a sudden failure could have life-threatening consequences. We don't know which cars might be subject to such a problem; for what it's worth, none of the major automobile companies anywhere in the world have yet published any guarantee, or even informal assurances, that their automobiles *are* Year-2000 compliant.[2]

The good news, if one can call it that, is that the vast major-ity of Year-2000 problems in these embedded automobile sys-tems will occur right at the stroke of midnight on December 31, 1999. After all, there are no business-oriented billing sys-tems in an automobile, and no databases to corrupt. If some-thing goes wrong, it's likely to go wrong right away. Regardless of whatever assurances or warranties the automobile manufac-turers may eventually publish, we think that simple prudence dictates that you stay off the highway at midnight on that fate-ful New Year's Eve. In the best of cases, your car will work, and so will all the other automobiles on the road. In the more plausible situation, one or two of the cars on the highway (and hopefully not yours!) will experience some kind of malfunc-tion, which could cause them to behave erratically. And in the worst of cases, it could be *your* car that suddenly shuts down while you're hurtling down the highway at 60 mph.

The bad news about a Year-2000 automobile problem is that it could lead to an automobile "recall" situation unlike anything the auto industry has ever seen. The auto manufac-turers will almost certainly be facing their own problems, deal-ing with the logistics of continuing to manufacture new cars in the face of Year-2000 problems. If they also have to repair mil-lions upon millions of faulty cars that are already on the high-

,way, it will compound their problem enormously. And as a practical matter, the chances of getting your car fixed quickly are relatively small. There may be only one or two chips that need to be replaced, but the waiting list for such repairs will be horrendous.

Let's assume for the moment that we've gotten past this category of "immediate" problem with Year-2000-sensitive automobile systems. What else do we need to worry about? The details will vary from person to person, but the two obvious categories are:

- *Gas, oil, and other supplies* —You can't get very far in your car if you can't refill the gas tank. Sooner or later, you'll need to change the oil, replace the spark plugs, and repair anything else that breaks down. Putting gas in your car requires that: (a) the distributors have managed to deliver adequate supplies to your gas station; (b) the gas station has electrical power; (c) panic hoarding of the kind we saw during the oil crisis of the late 1970s hasn't occurred; and (d) your credit card works, or you have adequate cash, to pay for the gas.

- *Bridges, tunnels, and other parts of the highway system*—Bridges and tunnels are likely to be controlled, to some extent, by computers; it's another variation on the embedded system problem. Not only that, many parts of the country charge tolls for access to the bridges and tunnels. That means the toll collectors have to be in place, and all of their computerized support systems have to be somewhat operational. The latter problem could be ignored in an emergency, of course; an appropriate government decree could allow free access. But if bridges can't be raised or lowered, and if tunnels can't have carbon monoxide exhaust fumes pumped away, then we've got a problem.

Public Transportation: Trains and Buses

From a Year-2000 perspective, trains and buses are significantly different than automobiles. There are fewer of them, they carry more passengers, and their operations are *scheduled*. Because of their size and complexity, they're likely to have more micro-computers than a standard automobile, and those computers may, of course, have the same possibility of Year-2000 problems. We've found no written indications yet that such computers have been tested for Year-2000 compliance, nor have we found any formal assurances from public transportation companies that they'll indeed carry out such testing before December 31, 1999. Common sense says that such testing *will* be done, but as the American humorist Will Rogers once remarked, "Common sense isn't common." It's up to you to decide whether you want to be riding a bus or train at the stroke of midnight on New Year's Eve, 1999.

Assuming that such testing is done and that any Year-2000 problems associated with the embedded systems have been fixed, there's a separate issue that must be dealt with: scheduling. Whether it's a city bus, a Trailways/Greyhound bus, or an Amtrak Metroliner between New York and Washington, it's virtually certain that a computerized scheduling system is used to determine departure times, scheduled arrival times, frequency of service, etc. Those systems are typical of the business-oriented computer systems we discussed earlier in the book; there are numerous opportunities for Year-2000-related bugs in such systems. In the case of a bus, it may mean that the standard 7 AM bus that you ride to work on Monday morning, January 3, doesn't arrive. Or, perhaps two buses will arrive; or, some other bizarre scheduling mishap could occur.

In the case of buses, none of this is likely to have life-threatening consequences; in the case of trains, there's a more serious problem to worry about—two trains could be scheduled to operate on the same section of track at the same time. Assuming that the conductors are alert, and assuming that mechanical fail-safe mechanisms operate correctly, such a double-scheduling snafu should be detected and dealt with before the trains crash into each other. On the other hand, more and more of the information used by conductors and dispatchers throughout the rail system is computerized; and, more and more of the fail-safe mechanisms themselves are computerized. Train collisions occur a few times a year throughout the U.S., even when things are supposedly operating in a normal fashion; the risk of such a failure is arguably higher given the possibility of Year-2000 computer glitches.

Planes

Commercial airplanes are similar to trains and buses in the sense that: (a) there are far fewer of them than automobiles; (b) they carry many more passengers than automobiles; and (c) they operate on a scheduled basis. But unlike buses or trains, Year-2000 problems in mid-air run a more serious risk of fatal injuries. On the other hand, it's also fair to say that the airlines are operated by more highly skilled and trained personnel (i.e., pilots, navigators, etc.) than is the case with buses.[3]

Commercial airplanes are also, to put it mildly, *much* more complex pieces of equipment than cars, buses, or trains. Not only does a Boeing 767 or a McDonnell-Douglas MD-11 represent $100+ million worth of engines, wings, and chassis, but it's also much more heavily computerized. One of the authors had the experience last year of listening to an airline pilot brag to all the passengers on his flight that the airplane they were riding on contained some 500 computers. Some of these, as with the automobile, are performing functions whose failure would be nothing more than annoying—perhaps the onboard movie wouldn't work, or perhaps the airline meals would be even more badly cooked than normal. Obviously, what we're concerned about is the "control" systems that produce all the displays (most of which are now digital) on the cockpit instrument panel, as well as those that assist the pilot and copilot with takeoff, landing, collision detection, navigation, communication with air traffic controllers, and numerous other functions. Are all of those systems Year-2000-compliant? So far, we've not seen or heard any reassuring statements from Boeing, McDonnell-Douglas, British Aerospace, Airbus Industrie, or any of the other major aircraft manufacturers (nor, for that matter, from any of the commercial airlines!).

Then there is the Federal Aviation Administration (FAA), the central government authority that defines, develops, and coordinates the air traffic controls systems throughout the U.S. The FAA air traffic control system is one of the nation's largest and most complex computer systems; it's also one of the oldest, and has been the subject of a major redesign and redevelopment for the past several years. In a nutshell: The current FAA software was *not* Year-2000-compliant as of the date this book was drafted, but the FAA is very, *very* aware of the effort required to fix the problem. If you have access to the Internet, it's worth taking a look at the massive, detailed document describing the agency's Year-2000 plan; it's located at http://www.faa.gov/ait/year2000/2000home.htm and it begins with the following summary:

> *Aging information technology (IT) application systems across Government and industry will face a critical juncture as they begin to be used in the Year 2000. Often referred to as the "Millennium Time Bomb," date dependent calculations can cause inaccurate results or total application collapse. When will the problem surface? Some systems may have already failed—some of these have been noticed and fixed; some may be producing erroneous results that have not been noticed. Between now and Jan. 1, 2000 systems that use dates in the future may begin to fail (forecasting, long term expirations, archival and backup). There are systems that may fail during the transition period—for instance global networks due to the rollover to 1/1/2000 in different time zones. And the remainder of the systems may fail as of 1/1/2000.*
>
> *The Year 2000 effort is decentralized within the FAA. The Integrated Product Team for Information Technology Acquisition (AIT-400) has been designated as the focal point for Year 2000 within the FAA. This role includes disseminating information to the FAA Lines of Business (LOB), participating on the Interagency Year 2000 Committee, chairing the FAA Year 2000 Steering Committee, and gathering status information for FAA management, the Department of Transportation, and to respond to Congressional inquiries.*

To its enormous credit, the FAA appears to be maintaining a policy of "high visibility" and openness about its plans; thus, it should be possible to monitor its progress during the final two years of the decade. It goes without saying that all but the most rabid terrorists desperately hope that the FAA will succeed in its Year-2000 efforts, providing a positive example for other government agencies. At the same time, it must be noted that there is no guarantee that the efforts will succeed, or that they'll be finished on time.

Let's move beyond the embedded systems within airplanes and the FAA's air traffic control systems (as well as the various information systems and business systems that the FAA needs to operate properly). What else is required to avoid a significant Year-2000 impact upon airline transportation? Here are the issues that appear most significant to us:

- *Aircraft maintenance and repair*—The FAA establishes the regulations for scheduled maintenance and repairs, and carries out appropriate investigations to ensure that it's done properly; in addition, aircraft manufacturers establish guidelines and recommendations for maintenance and replacement of engines, tires, and other parts of the plane. But, it's the *airlines* that carry out the maintenance. From an operational perspective, if you're a passenger on XYZ Airlines, you're more concerned that XYZ's maintenance scheduling computer systems are working in the days and weeks after January 1, 2000 than you are about the well-established guidelines and policies of the aircraft manufacturers and the FAA.

- *Scheduling of pilots, crew, and flight attendants*— This is fairly obvious: No crew means no flight. If you've done any amount of flying on commercial airlines, you're probably already aware that this is a fairly complex business; it's not uncommon to see flights delayed because the flight crew was stuck in another city because of bad weather. The bad news, of course, is that Year-2000 problems could thoroughly scramble these elaborate, computer-generated schedules; the good news is that there are very strict regulations that prevent the airlines from responding to such problems in a fashion that might otherwise occur—i.e., politely, but firmly, asking the crew to work additional hours to compensate for scheduling mistakes. Again, if you're a veteran flyer, you've probably seen this already. After a certain number of hours of continuous service, the crews walk off the plane to avoid operating a flight when they're too tired to perform properly.

- *Airline reservation systems*—Arguably, this is not a life-and-death issue, but the absence of today's highly sophisticated, worldwide reservation systems would throw the airline industry into a state of utter chaos until things were resolved. "Shuttle" flights, like the ones between New York and Washington, would be fine; but, anyone who needed a confirmed reservation for a cross-country flight or an intercontinental flight would be out of luck. Obviously, if such a situation persisted for any length of time, the airlines could fall back to the kind of manual systems that existed prior to the 1960s; but, it would be *extremely* costly, chaotic, and painful. (Note, by the way, that this problem essentially doesn't exist with trains and buses. You show up at the terminal and get on.)

- *Airport infrastructure systems*—The airports at most major cities across the country (and around the world) are small cities unto themselves; they

have upwards of 10,000 employees, and they
have a transient population that sometimes
numbers in the hundreds of thousands. There
are dozens, if not hundreds, of shops and restaurants; acres upon acres of parking lots; intricate
schedules of shuttle buses; and a complex traffic
control network to ensure that the ebb and flow
of passengers doesn't screech to a halt. Again,
computers are heavily involved in all of this; and
on top of all of that, we've got the electrical, oil,
gas, and telephone services discussed in other
chapters of this book. A reasonable subset of this
vast infrastructure must work for the airport to
stay open. (A similar statement could be made
about bus and train stations, but it's on a much
smaller scale; indeed, many such facilities are so
antiquated that it appears nothing has changed
since the 1940s, prior to the appearance of the
modern computer!)

Another Transportation Problem: GPS Rollover Failures in 1999

While most of the problems discussed in this chapter are
directly attributable to the Year-2000 rollover problem, there's
another rollover problem that will occur approximately six
months earlier—specifically, on August 22, 1999. The problem involves the Global Positioning System, a set of satellites
installed by the U.S. Navy to provide navigational data for
ships, planes, and missiles. The system is not only used by the
Defense Department, but by an estimated *ten million* commercial planes and ships.

The problem with the GPS system should sound familiar to anyone who has become involved in the Year-2000 crisis. The GPS satellites record the time-of-day with remarkably accurate atomic clocks. The time is recorded in terms of seconds, minutes, hours, days, and *weeks* since the inception of the system on January 5, 1980; unfortunately, the computer memory assigned to keep track of the "week number" is only 12 "bits" long, which means that it will roll over after 1,024 consecutive weeks of operation. As luck would have it, that will occur on August 22, 1999. Lest you think we're making this up, here's the official announcement from the U.S. Navy:[4]

The GPS Week Number count began at approximately midnight on the evening of 05 January 1980 / morning of 06 January 1980. Since that time, the count has been incremented by 1 each week, and broadcast as part of the GPS message. The GPS Week Number field is modulo 1024. This means that at the completion of week 1023, the GPS week number will rollover to 0 on midnight of the evening of 21 August 1999 / morning of 22 August 1999.

Week beginning at 0000 GPS Time on	GPS Week Number broadcast by satellites
08 Aug 1999	1022
15 Aug 1999	1023
22 Aug 1999	0
29 Aug 1999	1

Once the rollover has occurred, it is the responsibility of the user (i.e., user equipment or software) to account for the previous 1024 weeks.

Depending upon the manufacturer of your GPS receiver, you may or may not be affected by the GPS Week Number Rollover on 22 August 1999. Some receivers may display inaccurate date information, some may also calculate incorrect navigation solutions.

Contact the manufacturer of your GPS receiver to determine if you will be affected by the GPS week number rollover.

The problem is a serious one indeed, especially since it affects guided missiles, bombers, and commercial airlines, as well as the weekend hobbyist who has just installed a fancy new navigation system in his boat. We're not sure whether it's a good thing or bad thing that the GPS problem will occur approximately four months before the Year-2000 problem; it would be ironic indeed if the Year-2000 problem became irrelevant because all of our GPS-sensitive transportation vehicles were grounded several months before New Year's Eve, 1999.

One last irony: The GPS system is widely used not only to help vehicles determine where they are at any given time, but it's also used by many *non*-transportation systems (including many of the major banks in the U.S.) as a standard mechanism for recording the time-of-day. Because the accuracy of the GPS atomic clocks is among the highest in the world, and because it can be accessed by anyone with a GPS receiver, thousands of financial systems use the GPS for their time calculations; they need the accuracy of the GPS because interest calculations on multi-billion dollar loans is sometimes calculated to the nearest millisecond. Thus, in addition to all of the other banking problems that we'll be discussing in Chapter 5, there is the additional problem that some banks may lose track of which week it is, beginning in late August 1999.

Fallback Advice: Two-Day Problems

Like most of the other areas discussed in this book, a two-day loss of transportation services is something that you can probably tolerate with only minor inconvenience. Note that we're probably dealing with failures in the public-sector forms of travel here—i.e., bus, train, or air travel. If something goes wrong with your car, it's more likely that: (a) it will be a minor problem (e.g., an incorrect readout of the outside air temperature) that you can ignore; or (b) a problem that requires sending your car to the repair shop, where you're likely to wait for a month or two before the replacement "chip" arrives.

If a problem does occur with any form of transportation, it's likely to occur at the stroke of midnight on December 31, when the Year-2000-sensitive embedded systems fail. Thus, if you're concerned about this level of failure, the obvious precaution is not to count heavily on public-sector travel during the first few days of January. January 1 and 2 are, respectively, a holiday and a Sunday; most people will be home relaxing, celebrating, or recuperating anyway. By January 3, it will be widely known whether planes are flying and whether the public transportation system is operating on schedule—i.e., you'll know whether it's safe. But if you're scheduling a business trip for January 2000, and if you have any flexibility at all, schedule it for the middle of the month.

There's a corollary to this advice: Don't travel in, or on, anything more sophisticated than a bicycle or horse-and-buggy at midnight on December 31, 1999—unless you're the type who enjoys Russian Roulette as a pastime. As noted already, none of the companies who manufacture transportation devices (cars, planes, trains, and buses) are in a position in mid-1997, when this book was being written, to unconditionally guarantee that their products are Year-2000-compliant. It's quite possible that one or more of these companies *will* make such a claim in 1998 or 1999, which you may or may not find credible.[5] But even if you're confident that your car is Year-2000-compliant, it doesn't necessarily mean that all other cars on the highway are Year-2000-compliant. All it takes is one malfunctioning car, perhaps compounded by one inebriated driver, to cause a major traffic accident.

Fallback Advice: One-Month Problems

One-month problems could occur for a number of reasons. For example, your car malfunctions, and it takes a month to get a replacement chip for the carburetor, the braking system, or some other critical component. The bus company finds that its database of drivers has been destroyed, and it has no idea which drivers should be assigned to which routes; union-management disagreements compound the problem, and nobody shows up to drive the buses for a month. The commuter train company finds that its database of train schedules has been clobbered, and it can't figure out which trains should occupy which tracks at which time. The airline that you depend on for your business flights has discovered that its maintenance/repair systems are misbehaving, and the FAA discovers that airplanes are disappearing off the radar scopes at the air-traffic control centers.

Aside from the automobile recall problem, most of the other scenarios described here could occur at random times during the first few months of 2000; just because we reach January 5 without problems doesn't necessarily mean that we can rule out the possibility of Year-2000 bugs. The transportation companies could run into problems as a result of computer processing that they carry out on January 31, or February 29 (which the computers might not recognize as a legitimate leap-year), etc.

In any case, what will you do if this level of disruption occurs in the transportation systems you depend on? Since everyone uses different forms of transportation and has different needs, we can't offer any simple, universal guidelines; but, here are some possibilities:

- Avoid scheduling any personal or business trips requiring air transport for the month of January. January is a slow month for many businesses anyway, as people recover from the holidays and winter vacations. Such a scheduling delay will obviously create hardships for some; consider video conferencing as an alternative; or try to schedule your trips for December instead of January.

- Plan ahead for backup travel arrangements. If the trains aren't working, perhaps you can take the bus—or vice versa. If your car doesn't work, perhaps your neighbor's does; since your neighbor is faced with the same potential Year-2000 problem, perhaps you can make advance arrangements to carpool to your respective offices in the event that either of your cars malfunctions.

- Investigate "personal" transportation mechanisms—e.g., walking or bicycling to the office. If the problems actually begin in January 2000, then this won't be a pleasant option for those living in the northern half of the country; but, it might be an acceptable option for those living in Florida, Arizona, and most of California.

Fallback Advice: One-Year Problems

Like most of the other topics discussed in this book, the prospect of a one-year disruption in service is difficult to imagine. However, even though we might judge such a scenario as highly unlikely, it *is* possible. Worse-than-expected problems in the FAA air traffic control system could conceivably ground the nation's airlines for a year; larger-than-expected automobile recalls might mean a one-year delay in getting your car repaired; etc.

In the case of individual transportation systems—e.g., cars —the straightforward advice is: Make sure you have sufficient funds to get a replacement, Year-2000-compliant transportation system. It's an expensive, unpleasant option, and it presumes that not all automobiles will be subject to fatal Year-2000 problems. But for those who depend heavily on their car, there may not be a viable alternative.

As for the public transportation systems, there's not much we can suggest besides looking for backup alternatives. If the airlines are grounded for a year, we'll become a nation of train-riders once again, which might even have a positive impact on the aging, decrepit, poorly-serviced train infrastructure. If the trains break down for a year, we'll eventually get used to riding Greyhound and Trailways.

For the few who are inclined towards proactive planning, here's a thought: This might be a good time to move to an area where you're not so dependent on public transportation systems or even an automobile. Many of us today live in congested urban centers where the transportation infrastructure barely works even without a Year-2000 problem. Indeed, some of us have already begun asking ourselves why we put up with a daily commute of two or three hours, and whether it really makes sense to live in an area where highway congestion, or weather-related breakdowns in the trains and bus system, sometimes extend that commute time to four or five hours. Changing one's job or residence is not a casual decision, but even today there are some who make such a decision based on the inconvenience and unpredictability of transportation. If such thoughts have occurred to you, you should re-examine the situation in 1998 or early 1999, before Year-2000-related travel difficulties occur.

Fallback Advice: Ten-Year Problems

The only aspect of transportation where we can imagine the possibility of a severe Year-2000-related software crisis extending beyond a year is the FAA air traffic control system. As noted earlier, the FAA is well aware of the problem, has set up an organizational structure to deal with it, and has already begun committing resources to fix its software. Unfortunately, the existing hardware/software complex is so aged and overloaded that it has been on the verge of collapse for several years. And, the project to replace the existing system with a new generation system has been mired in such political controversy and technological confusion that it's years behind schedule. Thus, while we would like to believe that the FAA will have all its Year-2000 problems fixed before December 31, 1999, the age and intrinsic complexity of its systems, coupled with a less than stellar track record in the past few years, makes us somewhat more pessimistic.

The worst-case situation for the FAA is likely to be *much* worse than would be the case for Amtrak or Greyhound Bus Lines. If the entire FAA computer infrastructure collapses and has to be replaced from scratch, it will be a massive undertaking. Rome wasn't built in a day, and the existing FAA system certainly wasn't built in a year; building a completely new FAA system could easily take 3–5 years, and with the political bureaucracy that seems to surround most FAA activity, it wouldn't be surprising to see such a project drag on for 5–7 years. Whether there would still be an airline industry at the end of such a long period is an interesting question to contemplate.

In the meantime, society would muddle along somehow. We don't expect 250 million Americans to commit mass suicide simply because United Airlines is unable to fly the friendly skies between Chicago and New York. But while most of us *would* muddle along in some fashion, such a long-term disruption in air travel could indeed turn out to have permanent, tragic consequences for anyone whose business or profession depends critically on being able to travel between New York and Chicago (or any other such pairs of cities) on a daily basis. We can't predict the likelihood of such a situation, though we do believe it to be quite small; as with the other aspects of society we explore in this book, the possibility of a ten-year disruption essentially changes life as we now know it.

Endnotes

1. There is enormous debate about this point, and we received e-mail messages from several software engineers who responded to the first draft of this book with emphatic statements that embedded computer systems are not date-sensitive. They may be right, but unless your auto company is willing and able to guarantee it in writing, you're putting yourself at risk. Some embedded computers, for example, are designed so that when they're first activated, they set the year to an "epoch date" (which, in one case, turns out to be the birth-year of the founder of the engineering company that builds the chip). Thus, if the "epoch date" is 1980, the chip will experience a "rollover," with possibly unpredictable behavior, after 20 years of operation; if you bought your car in 1985, you won't have a problem until 2005.

2. Why not? Because they don't know! According to an article in the May 1, 1997 *Detroit News* ("Fix millennium glitch, group tells auto suppliers," by Joel J. Smith), the Big Three auto manufacturers (Ford, GM, and Chrysler) have devoted substantial funds to their own Year-2000 cleanup efforts, but there's less confidence that all 1,300 companies that form the automobile parts industry will be compliant. The vast majority of these parts have no embedded computer chips, but if the suppliers can't produce the parts, the auto companies can't build the cars.

3. We haven't focused on charter airlines or the small airplanes piloted by individual "amateurs." The equipment involved here is obviously smaller and simpler, but still capable of experiencing severe Year-2000 problems. The risk of massive

fatalities is presumably smaller, though the training and supervision of the pilots is generally less strenuous.

4. "GPS Week Number Rollover Approaches," located on the Internet at http:// tycho.usno.navy.mil/gps_week.html.

5. We'll discuss the credibility of such claims of Year-2000 compliance in more detail in Chapter 11, when we examine the broader issue of embedded systems.

Year-2000 Impact on Banking/Finance

Money is a singular thing. It ranks with love as man's greatest source of joy. And with death as his greatest source of anxiety. Over all history it has oppressed nearly all people in one of two ways: either it has been abundant and very unreliable, or reliable and very scarce.

John Kenneth Galbraith, The Age of Uncertainty, *Chapter 6.*

Introduction

By now, it should be no surprise when we suggest that your bank account, your credit cards, and your stocks and bonds might be vulnerable to Year-2000-induced computer failures. Indeed, the only reason you might be surprised at all is that American society has been so trusting of its financial institutions for the past several decades. Notwithstanding the occasional stock market slump, the savings and loan "crisis" of the 1980s (a phenomenon the average citizen would be hard-pressed to explain in any detail), or the occasional story of credit card fraud, the prevailing opinion in this country is that the dollar is stable and the institutions in which we store our dollars are equally stable.

Yet the elder generation—those who were young children or young adults on October 29, 1929—still recall an era in which thousands of banks failed. And any study of economic history[1] over the past three hundred years will illustrate numerous panics, depressions, bank runs, and crises in which people discovered that the money they had deposited in their local bank was gone, or that their money had become worthless, or both. The proximate causes of these crises have varied from war to speculation (as in the case of 1929) to corruption and malfeasance on the part of bankers and government officials. While none of these unpleasant forces have vanished from the earth, they are not the focus of this chapter. Instead, we'll worry about the impact of a unique technological failure upon our financial institutions.

Ironically, it's conceivable that speculation, malfeasance, and corruption could further aggravate a Year-2000-induced financial crisis. While some investors seek profits from rising stock prices, others sell short if they anticipate a decline; there are already investors and analysts on Wall Street who are looking for ways to profit from the Year-2000 difficulties, and some would argue that the stock price of Year-2000-related computer vendors borders on speculative fantasy. And just as unscrupulous businesspeople and charlatans prey on the hopes of AIDS victims by promising a miracle cure, we should not be surprised to see wild schemes emerging in 1998 and 1999 whose purpose is to relieve nervous citizens of their life savings in return for a phony scheme to protect those savings.

In this chapter, we'll discuss three primary financial institutions with which most of us have some day-to-day contact: the banks that provide checking and savings accounts, the credit card companies that fill our wallets with plastic, and the stock market industry that provides innumerable ways in which to invest our funds. As usual, we'll then conclude with some advice for coping with minor, moderate, serious, and cata-strophic failures in these institutions.

Year 2000 and the Banking System

Appendix A of this book provides the technical details of a simple example of a Year-2000-related banking problem: Erro-neous date arithmetic could cause a bank's computer system to go awry, or to generate hysterically incorrect results, when computing the interest on your car loan or your home mort-gage. The fundamental problem is that nearly every computer system within a bank is concerned with "transactions," and those transactions have dates attached to them. Whether it's a deposit transaction, a withdrawal transaction, or a transaction describing the transfer of funds from your checking account to your savings account, they're all vulnerable.

Lest you think this discussion of banking problems is aca-demic, take a look at the news report summarized below, which appeared in the on-line version of *USA Today* as we were preparing this chapter in the fall of 1997:

> *07/10/97—04:43 PM ET*
>
> *Experts: Banks not ready for year 2000 computer glitches*
>
> *WASHINGTON—Lost transaction records, funds sudden-ly made inaccessible, miscalculated interest and even failures of some banks.*
>
> *The financial industry is especially vulnerable to year 2000 computer problems, yet only about 10% of banks and other companies have completed programs to handle them, an ex-pert said Thursday.*
>
> *The potential computer crisis starting Jan. 1, 2000, could cause consumers to lose faith in the security of their banks and the financial markets, several experts told a hearing of the Senate Banking subcommittee on financial services and technology.*

Sen. Christopher Dodd, D-Conn., said there likely would be "a deluge of litigation" against banks and financial companies by consumers who lose money.

The warnings came as the White House released a report concluding the federal government could face a partial computer crash in 2000 because it is moving too slowly to fix the millennium problem. Of the nearly 4,500 critical computer systems the government must repair, including those for national defense, air traffic control and income taxes, only 6% have been fixed, according to the report by the Office of Management and Budget.

When the forerunners of today's massive computer programs were first designed, storage space was at a premium. To save memory space on the old-fashioned mainframes, code writers simply omitted the first two numbers of a date. That means 1998, for example, would read as 98, 1999 as 99, and so on. The year 2000 would be read as 00. Since the systems are coded to assume that all years begin with 19, computers will interpret 00 to mean 1900, if changes are not made.

The financial industry, too, is running out of time to repair the problem, the experts told the Senate panel. Companies need to have a solution in place by the end of next year in order to allow a year for testing in 1999, said Larry Martin, president of Data Dimensions Inc., a consulting firm based in Bellevue, Wash.

"We have figured out a way," Martin said. "But is there time for everyone to get the job done? Not unless they start immediately." Otherwise, he warned, "there will be failures" of some financial institutions.

Martin estimated that only around 10% of the banking and financial industry is ready for 2000. "The lack of concern and action on the part of the international banking community is particularly distressing," he testified. "The ability of international banks to operate effectively after the year 2000 is, in our estimate, seriously in question."

If there are bank failures resulting from the year 2000 problem, taxpayers would ultimately foot the bill for any government bailout, noted Jeff Jinnett, president of LeBoeuf Computing Technologies.

One large U.S. bank, BankBoston NA, expects to spend some $50 million over four years to cope with its 2000 problems, said David Iacino, senior manager of the bank's Millennium Project. Even if a bank is prepared, it could be adversely affected by its close links to other financial institutions that are not, Iacino said.

The parent of the Nasdaq Stock Market, the nation's second-largest, started its 2000 program in June 1996 at a cost of around $20 million, Nasdaq President Alfred R. Berkeley III told the subcommittee.

Even if nearly all the nation's banks and financial institutions become prepared for 2000, a highly publicized computer system failure of one of them could have a negative impact on stocks of other financial companies, some experts believe.

A second fundamental problem is that banking (along with insurance companies and government agencies) was one of the first industries to begin automating its operations in the 1950s. Thus, unlike many small companies that only began computerizing when the price of desktop computers fell below $2,000, banks have accumulated 30-40 years of old "legacy" computer programs. Obviously, some of the old programs have been replaced by newer programs; the newer programs (e.g., those that are only, say, ten years old) may also have Year-2000 software problems, but they're likely to be written in more familiar programming languages, with some vestiges of useful documentation with which the programmers can figure out where the corrections need to be made.

Along with the ancient age of these legacy programs, there's also the problem of magnitude. Banks have vast amounts of software that has to be fixed. Citibank and Chase, two of the country's largest and most visible banks, are widely reported to have roughly 400 million and 200 million program instructions, respectively, in their "portfolio" of computer applications; one can expect similar numbers at Bank of America, Wells Fargo, First Bank of Chicago, and the rest of the top 50-

100 banks.[2] Indeed, it would be rare to find a bank of any significant size—i.e., a bank with branches in more than one locality—that has a portfolio of less than a hundred million program instructions.

These numbers are more mind-boggling than you might realize. Despite the fact that we might only have a few hundred dollars in our personal bank account, we tend to be blasé about the notion that banks wheel and deal with hundreds of millions, if not billions, of dollars. We're also blasé about the numbers associated with computer hardware. A desktop computer can carry out a million calculations a second, it can store a billion characters of data on its hard disk, and so forth. But, the program instructions that comprise the bank's software were written by hand, one instruction at a time; the typical productivity of programmers creating such software is about 20-30 tested, debugged program instructions per day. The process of examining all those instructions, repairing the ones that have faulty Year-2000 date arithmetic, and testing the modified programs, can be greatly assisted by computerized tools (which explains the sudden prominence of software vendors who provide such tools)—but there is still an enormous amount of manual labor involved. A bank with 100 million program instructions can expect to devote approximately 8-12 *thousand* person-months of effort, and approximately $100-150 million to fix the problem.[3]

If it were merely a question of time and money, society would shrug its collective shoulders—few of us, if any, would lose any sleep worrying about the big banks spending some of their accumulated profits. On the other hand, it's quite possible that such expenses could be the straw the breaks the camel's bank for the marginal banks. And, it could easily turn out that the diversion of resources (i.e., the assignment of programmers to Year-2000 projects who would otherwise be working on "new" development projects) will further erode the competitiveness of those marginal banks. And there's a further point to keep in mind, something we learned when we saw how the banks responded to their problematic real estate and Third World loans in the 1980s: To recoup their Year-2000 expenses, the banks will raise the fees and interest charges they levy upon individuals and small companies.

Still, this is not what really troubles us. Our concern is that computer software is notoriously complex in even the best of cases, and computer development projects are notorious for being substantially behind schedule (as well as being over budget, which merely aggravates the problem described above). *The typical large business-oriented software project is 100% over budget and one year late.*[4] There were over 9,500 main offices of separate, discrete, FDIC-insured commercial banking institutions in the U.S. at the end of 1996; every one of them will be—indeed, already *are*—working on the problem. Thus, in terms of typical software industry statistics, about 25% of them will be late finishing the job, and an embarrassingly large minority will be substantially late (and this ignores the normal industry behavior of canceling 24% of all development projects before they finish!).

There are more than 55,000 branch offices of these commercial banks, and of course, the computer systems of each individual branch must be Year-2000-compliant. These commercial banks have over $4 trillion in assets. There are also over 600 savings banks which are insured by various other agencies that are regulated by the FDIC, and these banks have almost $300 billion in deposits. There are also a few thousand thrifts, credit unions, and other savings institutions. For reasons discussed below, most banks are trying to finish their

Year-2000 conversion projects by December 31, 1998; thus, if they're only a year late, they may wrap things up just before the New Year's Eve party at the end of the decade. But, some banks will not finish the task in time for the inexorable deadline; the only question is whether it will be your bank, or our bank, or some other hapless soul's bank.

As mentioned above, computer software is notoriously complex; that is, programmers have a very difficult time ascertaining whether their programs will behave correctly under all the possible conditions and scenarios to which they might be subjected. For a tiny computer program of, say, 100 instructions, it's possible to construct a mathematical proof of correctness; by the time one reaches the size of 1,000 instructions, such an effort is sufficient to gain a Ph.D. degree in our best universities. As one might imagine, such an effort is far beyond the ability of the most brilliant programmer—or team of programmers—when dealing with computer programs of 100,000 instructions or more. Obviously, most computer programmers are intelligent people and they don't make a lot of mistakes; but, the chances for error are much greater when: (a) working under extreme pressure; (b) modifying a computer program written by someone else; (c) working in a programming language with which one is not particularly familiar or experienced; and (d) working on a program for which there is no current documentation. These four conditions are exactly what most Year-2000 projects face.

The remedy, such as it is, consists of *testing*—massive testing to ensure correct behavior of the computer programs under every condition that the programmers can imagine. That's why the banks want to finish the main part of their work by December 31, 1998. They need to test "normal" conditions, end-of-month conditions, leap-year conditions, and as many other scenarios as possible during the full year of 1999. Indeed, the Federal Reserve system, as we'll see below, has strongly recommended a more aggressive stance. The Fed suggested that banks should finish their planning efforts by September 1997 so that they can spend 1998 converting and testing their own (internal) systems, and 1999 testing *interbank* scenarios.

We assume that all of this will be done by intelligent, dedicated, energetic people; indeed, it's fortunate that the software industry is populated by people who are relatively young and energetic, and who are already accustomed to working massive amounts of overtime. But no matter how intelligent, and no matter how industrious they may be, the reality is that they will make mistakes. Not many, but more than you might suppose. One of the most depressing statistics about the computer software industry is that its professional practitioners deliver allegedly well-tested software to their customers with an average of approximately one defect (often referred to as a "bug") for every *hundred* program instructions. With good discipline, sophisticated tools, and sufficient resources, the average IS/IT organization within the typical American company can reduce the defect levels by approximately two orders of magnitude— i.e., to the level of one bug for every 10,000 program instructions. The "best of the best" organizations—e.g., organizations like Lucent (formerly Bell Laboratories), Motorola, and the NASA Space Shuttle software group—can improve upon this by another two orders of magnitude, thus achieving a minuscule one bug for every million program instructions.

The layman may well find these figures so appalling as to be unbelievable; indeed, it raises the obvious question: How on earth have we ever managed to get today's computer systems to work at all? The answer is: with great difficulty, at great cost, and with frequent embarrassment along the way, over a period of 30-40 years. The defects mentioned above are the ones that are discovered in operation, e.g., when the computer abruptly halts, or when it produces incorrect output. The problem is then repaired, the programmers congratulate themselves on having found what they assume is the "last" bug, and the computer system is put back into operation again. Thus, what's really significant about the legacy banking systems is that the banks have had 30-40 years to shake almost all of the defects out of their computer systems. Even today, under normal circumstances, there will be the occasional hiccup; interest payments will sometimes be incorrect, deposits or withdrawals will be double-booked, etc.

Consequently, the real problem with the Year-2000 projects in the nation's banks (and, in a similar vein, other banks around the world) is that all of the software will be investigated, corrected to eliminate Year-2000 problems, and tested as thoroughly as possible until time runs out on New Year's Eve, 1999—*but there will still be residual errors that will gradually become evident during the first few years of the new decade.* A bank whose portfolio of computer applications contains 100 million program instructions, and whose programmers are geniuses on par with the very best in the world, may wrap up their work at the very end of the decade with only a hundred residual bugs. But the typical bank will have 10,000 such bugs, and the worst will have as many as a million defects.

Let's assume that your bank is one of the average ones, and that it marches bravely into the new millennium with hastily-modified software containing some 10,000 bugs.[5] The majority of these bugs will be nothing more than minor annoyances—e.g., an expanded date field on your monthly banking statement will chop off the first two characters of your name.

But a few of the bugs are likely to have more serious consequences, such as:

- Incorrect statements, with erroneous information about deposits, withdrawals, transfers, and balances.

- An inability to withdraw money or to credit deposits and payments properly.

- An inability to provide loans, mortgages, letters of credit, and other financial instruments.

- An inability to support normal banking operations via ATM machines, thereby requiring a retreat back to a practice long abandoned by many individuals—waiting in line to deal with a human bank teller.

These, and many other similar problems, are all internal and localized—that is, they involve the internal consequences of the bank's Year-2000 computer problems. But a potentially larger problem exists when banks communicate with one another—e.g., when your employer gives you a paycheck drawn on ABC bank, and you deposit it in your account at XYZ bank, the two banks have to communicate to accomplish the shift of funds from ABC to XYZ. Even if all of the computer software in ABC is Year-2000-compliant, problems could occur if XYZ's software is *not* Year-2000 compliant. And since we're dealing with two different organizations, finger-pointing and accusations will be the typical response when a Year-2000 problem emerges. The bugs that remain in the software of both banks after January 1, 2000 will most likely be the subtle, obscure bugs (the obvious ones will have been found and removed by then), so it may not be at all evident which of the banks is responsible for the Year-2000 problem if your paycheck mysteriously disappears in transit between ABC and XYZ.

In some cases, the communications (or the "system interfaces," as computer people like to call them) exist in a more-or-less straightforward fashion between two banks, as implied above. But the country's banks have become remarkably sophisticated and complex during the past hundred years, and even something as simple as the clearing of a check written on ABC and deposited into XYZ is likely to involve several other financial institutions that operate in a manner invisible to the average citizen, but nevertheless highly dependent on computers.

The country's check-clearing system actually operates in a couple of different ways. To illustrate the most common approach, imagine that Joe Consumer writes a check from his checking account at Bank A to Joe Merchant, who sells him some merchandise. The merchant physically brings the check to his bank (Bank B) and deposits it—but because the consumer's check is not drawn on an account at the same bank, Bank B must collect from another institution. Bank B begins the funds collection process by physically presenting the check to the bank on which it was written. Before these funds are collected, the merchant can't access them, and the bank puts them in a separate account, usually labeled Cash Items in the Process of Circulation (CIPC). When the funds become available, the CIPC account is reduced by the amount of the check, and the bank's reserves are increased. The funds, of course, are now available to the merchant. It doesn't seem like there will be many unique Year-2000 problems here because this mechanism involves physical, tangible paper (i.e., the checks themselves) being transferred between banks. The most likely Year-2000 problems that would arise in this kind of processing mechanism would be in the banks' own internal systems—and presumably these will also arise along with other functions the bank performs. Smaller banks would be more likely to use this traditional approach to check-clearing than the largest banks in the country. The Federal Reserve also operates an air courier service to transfer checks between member banks across the country, which could conceivably suffer its own Year-2000 problems if there are transportation problems of the nature discussed in Chapter 4.

In addition to this traditional check-clearing mechanism, there are public and private electronic payments systems, the former being the Federal Reserve and the latter being bank clearinghouses and the CHIPS international payment system. In the example above, if an electronic payments system is used, Bank B will deposit the check from the customer into its own account at its regional Federal Reserve Bank branch. The Fed will then transfer funds electronically from Bank A's reserve account to that of Bank B. The Fed then sends the check to Bank A and it is subtracted from the customer's account. This assumes that there are sufficient funds in the account to cover the check. Indeed, most checks do have sufficient funds, so the Federal Reserve performs this funds transferring service for checks drawn on banks in other Federal Reserve districts. The Fed's bank wire transfer system is used by over 11,000 institutions. This same function is performed by clearinghouses.

The problems here, of course, are compounded by the sheer volume of transactions, and the magnitude of money involved. Bank B communicates not only with Bank A and the Fed, but (directly or indirectly) with thousands of other banks; it processes not just your paycheck and the others within your company, but millions of deposits and withdrawals made by its various account-holders. The *daily* volume of "clearing" activity, including public and private payments systems, is more than $2 trillion in payments and electronic securities transactions.

This electronic payments system is where we believe most check-clearing-related Year-2000 problems could occur. The payments system can be endangered by an institution defaulting on payments to other institutions, or if liquidity decreases sharply. These problems arise if an institution has no more assets it can transfer to others for cash. For example, a liquidity crisis occurred in 1985 when the Bank of New York encountered a computer malfunction which enabled it to continue buying government securities, but prevented it from selling those securities. The Bank kept buying government securities, and was quickly running out of cash. This did not result in a crisis because the Bank was able to borrow from the Federal Reserve—and it did so to the tune of more than $20 billion on an overnight basis. The Bank was therefore able to meet its outgoing payment commitments until the computers were fixed. This was by far the largest one-day borrowing from the Federal Reserve's discount window (the facility by which credit is extended to eligible institutions).

Private clearinghouses sometimes argue that they can clear checks more efficiently (on a cost and time basis) than the Federal Reserve. The Federal Reserve is, however, the only institution that can *guarantee* payments and cause money to be created. Thus, the Fed is able to safeguard the payments system, but in doing so, also assumes payment systems risk. To reduce that risk, the Fed has instituted certain rules which include a limit on how much banks can overdraw on their reserves account during the day. (Banks are required by the

Fed to keep a certain percentage of their customer deposits on reserve with the central bank. These reserves can be in the form of cash held in the banks' vaults or in accounts held at the Federal Reserve.) This rule was implemented because the Fed wanted to ensure that the bank would be able to replenish its reserves account by the end of the day. When a bank is overdrawn, it must either stop payments temporarily until it has received more deposits, or it must borrow additional reserves from other banks (in the Fed Funds market).

Thus, a Year-2000 problem could hamper the check-clearing system, and could indeed start a severe liquidity crisis. Computer glitches can also hamper all of the steps outlined in the above paragraph—borrowing reserves from the Fed Funds market and monitoring reserves accounts are all done electronically. Unlike in the Bank of New York example above, though, Year-2000 computer problems would be very unlikely to be fixed in a day or two. Imagine, for example, how serious the problem would be if Citibank, BankAmerica, or Chase found itself in a position where it could pay out funds, but not receive any, because of computer glitches.

It's important to keep in mind that the Fed can create money, and is the protector of the payments systems. Thus, we would expect the Fed to provide unlimited liquidity if needed, much like in October 1987, when the stock market crashed. Indeed, official statements from the Federal Reserve show it is well aware of all the potential risks, and is letting us know that it intends to act as the lender of last resort. This was indicated in testimony made by Federal Reserve Governor Edward W. Kelley, Jr. to the U.S. Senate on July 30, 1997, which we've excerpted below:

> *We already have arrangements in place to assist financial institutions in the event they are unable to access their own systems. For example, we are able to provide financial insti-*

*tutions with access to Federal Reserve computer terminals on
a limited basis for the processing of critical funds transfers.
This contingency arrangement has proven highly effective
when used from time to time by depository institutions experiencing major hardware/software outages or that have had
their operations disrupted due to natural disasters such as the
Los Angeles earthquake, hurricane Hugo in the Carolinas,
and hurricane Andrew in south Florida. In these cases we
worked closely with financial institutions to ensure that adequate supplies of cash were available to the community and
also arranged for our operations to function virtually without interruptions for 24 hours a day during the crisis period.
We feel the experience gained from such crises will prove very
helpful in the event of similar problems triggered by century
date change. We are also beginning to formulate responses for
augmenting certain functions, such as computer help desk
services and off-line fund transfers, to respond to short-term
needs for these services...*

*We recognize, nonetheless, that despite their best efforts, some
depository institutions may experience operating difficulties,
either as a result of their own computer problems or those of
their customers, counterparties, or others. These problems
could be manifested in a number of ways and would not necessarily involve funding shortfalls. Nevertheless, the Federal
Reserve is always prepared to provide information to depository institutions on the balances in their accounts with us
throughout the day, so that they can identify shortfalls and
seek funding in the market. The Federal Reserve will be prepared to lend in appropriate circumstances and with adequate collateral to depository institutions when market
sources of funding are not reasonably available. The terms
and conditions of such lending may depend upon the circumstances giving rise to the liquidity shortfall.*

Unfortunately, Year 2000 differs from the natural disasters
outlined above. Year 2000 will not occur in one geographic
area....it will occur at the same time, everywhere, to everyone,
in every country around the world that has a banking system.
We believe that there will likely be delays in the clearing of

some checks, and this, we think, will be the main ramification of Year-2000 problems in the check-clearing system.

More Serious Banking Problems

That Year-2000 software bugs could cause problems in the nation's banking system is hardly in doubt; the real question is how many such problems will occur, and how serious will they be? If the problems were confined to one bank, and if they were resolved within a matter of days, it would be annoying for those involved, but not a matter of serious national concern. Similarly, if your paycheck is the only item lost among the millions of transfers between banks ABC and XYZ, it won't make you feel any better, but the programming staff at both banks will feel they've done a pretty good job. Sooner or later, your paycheck will be found (or the check will be canceled, and a new one issued) and life will go on.

A study of economic history reminds us, unfortunately, that things can occasionally be much worse: at intervals of approximately 20-30 years prior to the legislation associated with the New Deal era, there have been waves of bank runs, bank failures, and currency collapse. As noted earlier, many of these acute problems have been caused by war, massive speculation, or corruption; and while today's banking laws may be adequate for dealing with those issues, they may not be sufficient to cope with a "systemic" Year-2000-induced banking crisis.

One of the classic problems is that of a "run" on the bank, caused by a real or imaginary fear on the part of depositors that their funds have vanished, or that the bank is in imminent danger of being shut down. There is an interesting paradox here, one that exists not only in the modern American banking system, but one which has been true since banks were first created. In recounting the history of banking in Amsterdam, for example, Galbraith notes that:

> In 1672, when the armies of Louis XIV approached Amsterdam, there was grave alarm. Merchants besieged the Bank, some in the suspicion that their wealth might not be there. All who sought their money were paid, and when they found this to be so, they did not want payment. As was often to be observed in the future, however desperately people want their money from a bank, when they are assured they can get it, they no longer want it[6]

Unfortunately, the converse is also true: When depositors are no longer confident, their natural instinct is to withdraw their money as quickly as possible. Given the nature of banking, this almost always causes problems even when the bank is fundamentally sound and operating in a conservative fashion—because only a fraction of the aggregate funds of depositors is actually lodged within the bank. The rest has been loaned out to individuals, corporations, other banks, and even governments. Federally-chartered banks (i.e., those that belong to the Federal Reserve banking system) are required to maintain 10% of their demand deposits (checking and others from which transfers can be made to third parties) "in reserve," but are not required to maintain any reserve for time deposits. This "fractional reserve" system is designed to ensure that if you want your money, it will be there. While carrying out the research for this book, we found a Dallas-based software company, Carreker Antinori (http://www.carreker.com), whose software product makes it possible for banks to "sweep" funds from accounts with reserve requirements, to those without reserve requirements. This software, and similar software developed internally at banks, uses "artificial intelligence" to determine what the optimal amount of funds is to leave in the account from which funds are being swept. In other words, banks are sweeping money out of accounts from which checks are paid and funds are withdrawn, to accounts which cannot readily have funds withdrawn, and which are not subject to reserve requirements. This practice is permitted by the Federal Reserve as long as the number of transfers per month is limited. It thus permits banks, as a practical matter, to carry fewer reserves than the 10% required by law. This practice is used more than we thought. Our source at Carreker Antinori informed us that most of the top 200 banks use this process, and that approximately $80 billion has been "restructured" using this process. We find this alarming, given the potential problems banks face entering the new millennium.

Unfortunately, even a conservative reserve policy may be insufficient to stop a true panic. If a substantial majority of the bank's depositors demand to liquidate their account and withdraw their cash, it's virtually certain that the bank will be unable to honor the demands—unless, of course, it can borrow funds from other banks or from the "lender of last resort," the Federal Reserve. It was the lack of such a backup system that was largely responsible for the bank failures at the beginning of the Great Depression. For those of the current generation who may have slept through their high school civics class when this topic was being discussed, a brief summary of the statistics may be useful:

> In 1929, 659 banks failed, a fair number after the crash. In 1930, 1352 went under and in 1931, 2294. Failures were still the most numerous among the small non-member banks of the old compromise. But now, when the rumours spread and the lines formed, no bank was safe... By the end of 1933, nearly half of all the nation's banks had disappeared.

> ... The [Reconstruction Finance Corporation] notwithstanding, the runs continued. And by late 1932 and early 1933, they had ceased to involve individual banks and small banks and now spread over whole communities and even states. They also extended into the principal financial centres

> *and to the big banks. The remedy that now occurred to the*
> *authorities, as the runs became pandemic, was to close up all*
> *the banks in the community before their depositors closed*
> *them up anyway. At the end of October 1932, all the Neva-*
> *da banks were thus placed on vacation...when Roosevelt was*
> *inaugurated, only the banks in the Northeast were still doing*
> *business. On 6 March 1933, by Executive Order deriving its*
> *authority from the Trading with the Enemy Act of the First*
> *World War, the holiday was made nationwide.*[7]

Sobering though these statistics might be, the common reaction from both layman and expert in today's society is, "Such a thing could never happen again." And perhaps the strongest reason for this faith in today's banking system comes from one of the final legacies of the banking debacle in 1933: the creation of the Federal Deposit Insurance Corporation, known to most citizens simply as the FDIC. As Galbraith puts it:

> *In the banking legislation passed in 1933, there was one pro-*
> *vision that was opposed by conservatives and the new Ad-*
> *ministration alike. This was written by Representative*
> *Henry B. Steagall of Alabama, who had a reputation for ec-*
> *centricity, even crankiness, where money was concerned, and*
> *by Senator Arthur Vandenberg of Michigan; it provided for*
> *the insurance of bank deposits. A special corporation, the*
> *Federal Deposit Insurance Corporation, would be chartered*
> *and capitalized by the Treasury and the Federal Reserve*
> *Banks. Insurance would be available to the depositors of all*
> *banks—state or national, members or nonmembers of the*
> *Federal Reserve—which chose to join...*
>
> *In all American monetary history no legislative action*
> *brought such a change as this. Not since, to this writing, have*
> *the lines formed outside one bank and then spread ineluctab-*
> *bly to the others in the town. Almost never have the lines*
> *formed at all. Nor was there reason why they should. A gov-*
> *ernment insurance fund was now back of the deposits; no*
> *matter what happened to the bank, the depositors would get*
> *theirs.*[8]

There is only one problem with this noble scheme: The FDIC is based on the same "fractional" reserve system as the banks themselves. Its officers and supporters would doubtless prefer to describe the situation in some other terms, but as noted by Professor Galbraith in the comments above, the FDIC is first and foremost an *insurance* entity; thus, its existence is predicated on the statistical probability that only a small number of its member banks (and their respective depositors) will need assistance at any given time. The FDIC can bail out a single bank, or even a handful, but it lacks the reserves to bail them all out at once, nor can it realistically handle a large wave of simultaneous bank failures. This sobering reality came to light during the 1980s, when the failure of several smaller banks in the so-called "savings and loans" scandals sorely tested the financial resources of the FDIC. As a result, we think it's useful to look at why and how the FDIC was created, and the history of bank failures and why they arose—for it may give us a better understanding of the possible impact of a systemic Year-2000-induced jolt to the system.

After the Crash of 1929 and the failure of many banks and corporations, the Banking Act of 1933 established the Federal Deposit Insurance Corporation (FDIC), and some faith returned to the banking system. The FDIC was created as an independent federal agency responsible for the regulation of federally-insured savings banks, the Bank Insurance Fund, and the Savings Association Insurance Fund (SAIF). The FDIC works much like a medical insurance company in that it charges premiums to its members based on the probabilities of bank failures and depositors it might have to pay off. Unlike a medical insurance company, however, the FDIC has actually returned premiums when it has had surpluses at the end of the year.

Obviously, anyone but the most fanatical extremist devoutly hopes that the FDIC will never be called upon to handle more than a few Year-2000-induced bank collapses.

The authors of this book have modest savings accounts too, and those accounts are just as vulnerable as the accounts of the readers of this book. But wishful thinking and collective optimism may not be enough to prevent a serious problem. If indeed there does turn out to be a banking crisis on the scale of the Great Depression, we believe that it's almost inevitable that government legislation and regulation will be created to cope with it. It's impossible to tell, at this point, precisely what kind of action will be taken; the only certainty is that it will be surrounded by massive partisan, political debate and that it will be enacted months or years after the crisis begins. Though history rarely, if ever, repeats itself with precision, we can't help wondering how many parallels there may be between the Great Depression of the 1930s and the potential crisis caused by Year-2000-induced banking failures. It's worth noting, in this context, that three years, four months, and seven days elapsed between the Crash of October 29, 1929 and Franklin Delano Roosevelt's declaration of a national banking holiday on March 6, 1933.

One of the shortcomings of the creation of the FDIC was that it created a "moral hazard" problem. People just assumed that if their bank offered federally-sponsored insurance, then it was a safe bank. In fact, federally-insured banks are subject to frequent examinations, including the CAMEL (Capital adequacy, Asset quality, Management competence and control, Earnings, and Liquidity) exam. If problems are found to be serious after a few examinations, a bank receives a "cease and desist" order that forces it to make the necessary changes.

The renewed faith brought about by the creation of a federal agency charged with insuring bank deposits resulted in a dramatic drop in the number of bank failures during the Depression. Between 1930 and 1933, before the FDIC was created, an average of more than 2200 banks were failing every year. Between 1934 and 1942, however, an average of only 54 banks failed every year. The annual number of failures continued to be minimal until the 1980s, when deregulation, higher interest rates, regionally weak economies, and bad loans to less developed countries put pressure on many banks, and especially S&Ls. Between 1983 and 1987, an average of 119 banks failed ever year, while in 1988, 228 banks went out of business.

Federal deposit insurance covers deposits up to $100,000. It must be obtained by all federally-chartered commercial banks, savings banks, savings and loans, and credit unions from one of the federal insurance funds. Federal insurance is also provided to credit unions' depositors shares through the National Credit Union Share Insurance Fund (NCUSIF). The NCUSIF was established in 1970, and gives insurance of up to $100,000 for participating credit union members' shares. By contrast, state-sponsored insurance funds have fallen out of favor, since so many failed in the 1980s. They are generally considered less secure than federal funds because state governments don't have the ability to print money, like federal governments do. In addition, state governments are usually very reluctant to raise state taxes to bail out banks if the state funds run out of money. Many state insurance funds encourage state-chartered banks to get state insurance wherever possible, but state-chartered institutions can also get federal insurance as long as they meet the standards set by the particular fund they are trying to get insurance from.

It's instructive to review the policies adopted by federal agencies to deal with bank failures during the 1980s, because it seems likely that any bank failures resulting from Year-2000 problems would be resolved in a manner more similar to that of the 1980s than of the 1930s. Two policies were imple-

mented in the 1980s by the federal insurance funds mentioned above. The first was called a "purchase and assumption"
policy, under which the fund had two procedures it could follow when a bank was in danger of failing. The first procedure
was simple and straightforward: If a bank failed, the depositors
would first be paid for their deposits up to $100,000. After the
$100,000 ceiling was hit, depositors would either receive par-
tial or zero settlement when the assets of the bank were sold.[9]
The second procedure consisted of allowing another bank to
purchase an endangered institution and assume its liabilities,
rather than letting it fail. The rationale for the second procedure is that if all the liabilities of the endangered bank are
assumed, no depositor loses any money; however, it's interesting to note that in some cases, the FDIC may decide to assist
the acquiring bank in its purchase.

The second policy adopted by the insurance funds is known
as a "too big to fail" (TBTF) policy. It had always been
assumed that the FDIC was hesitant to close down large
banks, and that the agency would try and organize purchases
of ailing institutions. In 1984, the FDIC actually announced
that one ailing bank in Ohio, the Continental Illinois
National Bank, was too big to fail. In addition, the FDIC said,
the eleven biggest banks in the country were also too big to
fail. This policy was implemented in the case of the Ohio bank
in 1984, and then again in 1988 for two large banks in Texas.
In both cases, and for the "too big to fail" policy in general,
federal regulators announced that 100% of deposits would be
paid, regardless of the size of the deposits.

Historically, bank failures have usually occurred either
because of a lack of liquidity, or from risky business and lending practices. In the 1980s, both problems occurred—especially in the case of S&Ls, which concentrate on acquiring

funds from issuing checking accounts and different time deposits, as well as purchasing long-term mortgages. By contrast, commercial banks use the funds acquired from various forms of savings accounts, time deposits, and checking accounts to create a diversity of loans to businesses, individuals and state and local governments, as well as underwriting certain forms of securities. Throughout the 1970s, S&Ls did very poorly when interest rates were rising, because government-imposed interest rate ceilings at the time prohibited them from paying competitive rates. Because of the ceilings, funds would flow out of S&Ls, as market interest rates rose, to institutions and accounts which would pay a higher interest rate. S&Ls were also prohibited from conducting any business besides accounts and deposits, and guaranteeing home mortgage loans.

Deregulation legislation passed in the late 1960s and the 1970s, which helped the S&Ls' profitability, but ultimately led to the demise of many. And in the early 1980s, more regulatory changes were made to help S&Ls increase profits (as opposed to the original focus of the S&Ls to promote housing and home ownership). In 1980, the Depository Institutions Deregulation and Monetary Control Act (DIDCMA) removed the ceiling on interest rates that had to be paid, and also increased the federal deposit insurance limit. These acts were relatively benign, but in the early 1980s, less benign legislation followed that allowed some dubious accounting standards, and which allowed serious dilution of the ownership of institutions. For example, in December 1982, the Nolan Bill was passed, which allowed California-chartered S&Ls to invest 100% of deposits in any kind of venture. Similar bills were passed in Texas and Florida.

Texas became one of the first regions where the consequences began to be visible because of excessively speedy
deregulation, fraud, unsound methods of operation, and the
plunge in the price of oil. Consequently, several Texas banks
collapsed. Many in Texas had become quite rich in the 1970s
and 1980s, when the price of oil skyrocketed; but when oil
prices fell by over 65% in the mid-1980s, many institutions
failed. In 1982 and 1983, for example, Amarillo National
Bank and First of Midland collapsed because they had
expanded so rapidly that management control and oversight
began to fail. It was later discovered that workers in both
banks were getting kickbacks. Similarly, Texas Commerce was
acquired by Chemical Bank when it ran into trouble from bad
loans to individuals in the oil and real estate businesses. Then,
the troubled Interfirst Bank merged with Republic Bank. The
new bank, First Republic Bank, also failed when the real estate
market took a plunge. With help from the FDIC, First Republic was sold to another bank and all depositors were repaid in
full, in line with the "too big to fail" policy.

One of the banks that almost certainly would have failed in
1984 without help from a federal agency was the Continental
Illinois National Bank. At the time, it was the seventh largest
bank in the country, and it was in trouble because of bad loans
it had made in the energy and agricultural sectors, which
started performing very badly. In addition, a senior loan
officer at the bank bought some bad loans from another bank
after being approved on a large personal loan. As reports and
rumors about the possible demise of the bank began to circle,
the bank quickly began losing deposits. Within three days, the
bank lost almost *$4 billion* in deposits. Government action
started almost immediately. The Fed provided loans at the discount window (where banks can borrow reserves from the

Fed). Also, the FDIC proceeded to guarantee the full deposits of all the bank's depositors up to any amount, not just up to $100,000. This last action was undertaken because of the "too big to fail" approach outlined earlier. In this case, too, the "almost" bank failure came about because of both unsound practices and liquidity problems.

While failures of this nature may or may not occur at the turn of the millennium, it's interesting to see how relatively recent events in the 1980s have been influenced by the appearance or disappearance of government regulations. A more severe form of regulation, which many people assume has vanished since the 1930s, is the *bank holiday*, i.e., where the bank is closed for some period of time by order of the government. The obvious explanation for such an event in early 2000 would be that the programmers need more time to fix their Year-2000 software problems, rather than the concomitant problem that the banks have no cash in their vaults. In any case, it's important to realize that bank holidays are *not* a forgotten relic of the Great Depression; in March of 1985, a bank holiday was called because of the anticipated failure of the Home State Savings Bank of Cincinnati, and the possible depletion of the state insurance fund. All Ohio S&Ls were required to close, but eventually—after nearly a year—all those that could qualify for state insurance were allowed to reopen. In May of 1985, S&L failures caused a loss to state deposit insurance funds and Maryland taxpayers of $185 million. As a result of problems like these, there was only $4.6 billion left in the FSLIC insurance fund by August of 1985.

Aside from bank holidays, additional governmental regulations could involve currency regulations (e.g., prohibitions against importing or exporting foreign currencies), daily limits on cash withdrawals from banks, or restrictions on ownership of gold.[10] Unfortunately, the government doesn't always respond to bank failures in the most efficient manner. When the government takes steps to correct any problem, blame must inevitably be assigned to someone, and no one in government wants to be the scapegoat. If the government must take action to help banks suffering from Year-2000 problems, the American people will undoubtedly ask, "Why weren't banks more prepared? Why wasn't more attention paid to the warnings from those members of Congress who were aware of Year 2000?"

To illustrate the politics that we might look forward to in the event of Year-2000-induced banking problems: Even into the late 1980s, S&L losses were allowed to grow because political pressure was put on the FSLIC to keep some unhealthy banks open. No member of Congress wanted S&Ls in *their* district to be declared insolvent. Not only did Congress put pressure on the FSLIC, but they wouldn't give the FSLIC sufficient funds to cover the losses it would incur by shutting down the insolvent savings and loan associations. Needless to say, Congress never admitted that it had contributed to and, yes, aggravated, the problem.

Finally, in January of 1987, the General Accounting Office (GAO) declared the FSLIC insolvent by almost $4 billion; as of December 1987, it had a negative net worth of almost $13 billion. It continued to operate because people continued to take FSLIC promissory notes and guarantees; FSLIC, in turn, continued to hope that Congress would make good on its pledge to make future payments. In 1989, under the Financial Institutions Reform Recovery and Enforcement Act (FIRREA), the FSLIC was abolished, and S&L regulation was shifted to the newly created Office of Thrift Supervision; meanwhile, the deposit insurance function was shifted to the

FDIC. Also under this act, $50 billion in government-backed bonds were sold and transferred to the newly-created Resolution Trust Corporation, which took responsibility for all institutions that were shut down, merged, or aided by the FSLIC.

When the government sells bonds, it is borrowing money and increasing its debt. The revenues the government earns are principally from taxes, and principally from personal income taxes. Thus, when the government issues (sells) bonds to pay for bank failures, it is revenue from future income taxes that will be used to pay off the debt. *In other words, it is really the U.S. taxpayers who paid for the mismanagement of S&Ls and the poor handling of the situation by the U.S. Congress.* This was obviously not popular with taxpayers, and has been a general embarrassment to the Congress. Perhaps to pacify the U.S. taxpayers (but probably to reduce current and future embarrassment to themselves!), Congress made penalties stricter on fraudulent directors of institutions, and strengthened laws and regulations of federally-chartered and federally-insured financial institutions.

Economic pessimists can look beyond the possibility of bank closings to the possibility of a long-term deflation caused by the reduction of money in circulation—i.e., monies that vanish because of bank failures. Conversely, we may find ourselves faced with massive inflation. A plausible political response to massive runs on the major national banks could be an equally massive printing of new dollar bills, with massive loans from the Federal Reserve Banks to its member banks. The real question here is what the citizenry of the U.S. would do if it managed to successfully withdraw the funds currently sequestered in banks; a fearful population that observes its phones, its cars, its jobs, its banks, and its government reeling under the attack of Year-2000 bugs might well decide to use its cash to purchase tangible goods such as food and clothing. The phenomenon of large quantities of cash chasing after a fixed amount of goods (indeed, potentially a shrinking supply of goods, since the nation's manufacturing facilities may also be affected by Year-2000 bugs) could cause massive inflation.

By the way, there's one last irony to mention: In the past, whenever a country has faced a banking or currency crisis, those who are wealthy and/or nervous about their money have traditionally moved it to a safe haven in another country. The U.S. has traditionally benefited from this tendency, particularly within the past 200+ years of warfare in Europe and political instability in other parts of the world. Conversely, some Americans have found it prudent to store a portion of their wealth in Switzerland and other so-called tax havens. Thus, the potential banking problems discussed in this chapter might prompt the suggestion to remove one's money from Citibank, or Chase, or BankAmerica and move it ... where?

And therein lies the irony. The problems faced by American banks are the same as those faced by British, Japanese, and yes, even the fabled Swiss banks. Indeed, U.S. banks may be better off than many of their international counterparts, simply because the awareness of Year-2000 problems is higher, and the U.S. banks have gotten an earlier start. The problem is now getting global, coordinated attention. In a press release by the Governors of the G-10 central banks, it was said:

> At their meeting in Basle on 8th September 1997, the central bank Governors of the Group of 10 reviewed the need for financial institutions to check all their computer applications in advance of the new millennium. Not only will a large number of applications have to be converted or replaced, but extensive testing will be necessary to ensure that all operations run smoothly after conversion. While the major financial market participants are well aware of the problem and are taking steps to address it within their own

institutions, time is running out for those institutions that have not yet addressed the problem. Further delay may prove costly not only for these institutions but also for their counterparties.

In spite of the above statement, much of the attention, as well as the scarce programming resources, of the European banks is being concentrated on the creation of a unified European currency called the "Euro." It is hard to imagine how there will be ample resources to do the computer work necessary for both the Euro and the new millennium, a fact we fear has not been sufficiently considered by the financial markets. As *Computerworld's* Allan E. Alter puts it:[11]

> *The last thing IS executives need is another big conversion project. But it's looming, right on the heels of the year 2000 problem: the arrival of the European Union's new currency, the Euro.*
>
> *Already, information systems managers in the European Union (EU) are preparing for European Monetary Union (EMU) and the Euro, which is expected to gradually replace the national currencies of EU members between 1999 and 2002.*
>
> *Banks will feel the impact first: In 1999, they will have the option of conducting electronic funds transfers in Euros. For other businesses, the crunch comes in 2002, when the Euro begins circulating and national currencies are phased out.*
>
> *For now, many U.S. firms doing business in Europe are putting the Euro on the back burner. "I think the year 2000 is still the highest [priority]," says Lauris Nance, vice president and year 2000 project executive at Equifax, Inc., an Atlanta business information services firm. "People keep hoping [the Euro] will be delayed." Others question whether the adoption of the Euro will stick to its timetable or whether all EU countries will adopt the currency...*
>
> *But European banks are planning for the Euro's impact on information technology. The initial goal for bankers is "multicurrency capability" adjusting applications so they can handle multiple currencies. The Federal Association of Ger-*

man Banks says automated teller machines, statement print-
ers and system connections to customers and other banks will
be affected.

By 2002, retailers will need point-of-sale systems and cash
registers capable of handling two currencies as well as the
century change. Companies will have to adjust their finance,
accounting, payment and billing systems.

All told, converting to the Euro should cost about $100 bil-
lion worldwide, according to Bruce Hall, former research di-
rector at Gartner Group, Inc. in Stamford, Conn. That
compares with $300 billion to $600 billion worldwide for
the year 2000 problem.

What's the Fed Doing About All of This?

One thing that politicians and government regulators cannot control with laws, acts, restrictions, levies, or taxes is the
inexorable advancement of the calendar. Not since the days of
Pope Gregory XIII (in the late sixteenth century) has someone
tried to change the calendar, so it's unlikely that even the most
ambitious President or proactive Congress could manage to
pass legislation that would prevent the arrival of January 1,
2000 at the pre-ordained hour, minute, and second.

On the other hand, the potential for serious chaos within
the financial community is beginning to provoke some action
within the Federal Financial Institutions Examination Council
(FFIEC), an agency within the Federal Reserve system that
appears to be in charge of imposing Year-2000 policies and
guidelines upon member banks.

In a May 5, 1997 press release,[12] the FFIEC congratulated
itself for having first alerted the banking industry to the Year-
2000 problem in June 1996, and for having recommended
that institutions perform risk assessment and plan a strategy
for repairing their Year-2000-vulnerable systems. Since this
vintage-1996 advice apparently had negligible impact upon

the banking industry, the May 5, 1997 statement put things in somewhat stronger language:

> *Today's Statement outlines a project management process that strongly encourages federally insured depository institutions to complete an inventory of core computer functions and set priorities for Year 2000 goals by September 30, 1997. Banks are expected to largely complete programming changes, and have testing well underway for mission critical systems by December 31, 1998.*
>
> *In an appendix to the Statement, the Task Force included an examiner questionnaire to help regulatory agencies conduct assessments of financial institution planning efforts, which are expected to be completed shortly. Based on the results of these assessments, regulators will prioritize supervisory reviews, using examination procedures contained in a second appendix to the Statement. The regulators expect to complete examinations of conversion efforts by mid-1998.*
>
> *Federal financial regulators are concerned that systemic disruptions and potential failures could result if computers used by financial institutions cannot properly read date-sensitive information when the calendar year changes to 2000. For this reason, an institution's reprogramming planning should include consideration of the vendors whose products and services a financial institution uses; the other banks, clearing houses and customers with whom it exchanges data electronically; and, corporate borrowers, whose creditworthiness might be diminished by significant service disruptions.*

Our interpretation of this language is as follows: The FFIEC will begin auditing its member banks, beginning in mid-1998, to determine whether they are Year-2000-compliant. Considering that: (a) there are more than 9,000 FDIC-insured commercial banks in the U.S.; (b) each of those banks has a software portfolio averaging 100+ million program instructions; (c) both technical/IT and business managers within the bank may suffer the usual human tendency to minimize or even hide the extent of their problems; and (d) the regulators are unlikely to be computer experts, we find it quite difficult to believe that this nationwide audit will be complete, comprehensive, and accurate. Nevertheless, the FFIEC auditors may be able to obtain a statistically-credible estimate of the "degree" of Year-2000-readiness for the nation's banking system as a whole; and that will leave 1999 for the inevitable political battles. Meanwhile, the clock will continue to tick.

Credit Cards

One of the authors is a computer consultant who makes regular business trips of one or two weeks' duration, not only across the U.S., but to clients and computer conferences in Europe, Asia, Africa, and South America. It's relatively easy to make such a trip, for which the overall travel expenses can amount to several thousand dollars, with no more than ten or twenty dollars in cash for the occasional tip to hotel porters, or for a magazine in the airport. The rest, including taxi fares, can be paid by credit card. Without the wallet full of plastic cards that most of us carry today, business trips and many of the other details of day-to-day life would be considerably more tedious.

We won't re-hash the basics of date-arithmetic problems here; suffice it to say that credit card transactions are essentially the same as banking transactions. Whether it's a purchase, payment, or any other activity on your credit card, it's virtually certain to have a date attached to it. And as with our discussion about banking above, it's important to keep in mind that a typical credit card transaction involves several parties: the customer, the merchant, the credit card company itself (e.g., MasterCard, Visa, American Express), and a member bank with which the card is associated. In many cases, there are other organizations involved. It's common, for example, to have a credit card linked to one's airline frequent-flyer account, so that each dollar of purchases produces a credit of one frequent-flyer mile.

There's at least one other item that distinguishes credit cards from bank accounts: Credit cards traditionally have expiration dates, while the typical bank account has no termination date. Since most credit cards have an expiration date two, three, or four years after the date of issue, it means that most credit card companies are already experiencing Year-2000 problems. At the time this book was written, all of the major credit card companies in the U.S. were restricting the expiration date of new cards to 1999 (or before), because of potential problems with merchants rejecting cards with an expiration date of "00".[13]

The other aspect of credit cards that differs substantially from one's checking or savings account involves the concept of liabilities versus assets. Our savings account is an asset. It's our money, and it belongs to us, and we have merely placed it in the bank's vault for temporary safekeeping. As noted above, if we suddenly get the impression that the bank has lost the money, or has closed its doors, it creates an emotional reaction of outrage; accusations of theft and embezzlement are hard to resist.

A credit card, on the other hand, involves a liability—i.e., a mechanism for incurring a debt. This is not true of the newer "debit cards," but these are not yet widespread in the U.S. Most of us use the familiar MasterCard or Visa plastic that allows us to accumulate a month-to-month debt. American Express expects us to pay off that debt, in full, when each monthly statement is rendered; MasterCard and Visa are content to accept a minimal payment, in return for the privilege of levying interest charges that, in more conservative times, would have been labeled usurious.

The reason for reminding you of this difference is to suggest that the public reaction to a Year-2000-induced failure of credit cards might be considerably different than a Year-2000-induced failure of the banks themselves. If we can't withdraw the funds from our savings account, the reaction is immediate and visceral; lines will form at the bank's front door. But if the merchants and MasterCard and the associated bank somehow fail to send us our monthly credit card statement, very few of us will rush to the bank in an effort to pay off the bill. Indeed, the Year-2000 problem will only cause a visceral reaction for those who depend on credit cards for a ready supply of easy credit, and for those of us who prefer to travel, dine, and shop with a minimum of cash in our pockets. The latter group can learn to adjust; the former group may find it more difficult to do so.[14]

The Stock Market

Like banking and the credit card industry, Wall Street and the entire securities industry depends heavily on computers. Just before the Great Crash of 1929, Wall Street labored enormously to handle then-record volumes of five million shares per day; ticker tapes regularly ran an hour behind actual trading, and exhausted clerks worked nights and weekends to reconcile all of the paperwork. Today, stock market volumes frequently exceed 500 million shares per day, and the massive bookkeeping activities are all handled by computers. No computers means no trading. (The "no trading" phenomenon could also result from having no phones, and no banking system, but that has to do with the "ripple effect" phenomenon discussed in Appendix B.)

Again, the fundamental problem is that all stock market transactions involve dates, which means that almost all computer systems within a securities firm are Year-2000-vulnerable. And, like the banks, the problem is compounded by massive volumes of transactions, massive amounts of software to be converted, and a combination of scarce programming resources and limited time. Australia's *Financial Review* estimates the total Year-2000 price-tag for the securities industry at $5 billion, and the expenses of Merrill Lynch alone as $200 million.[15] Merrill Lynch, by the way, has expressed confidence that it will be finished with its Year-2000 conversions by the end of 1998;[16] if you ask most other Wall Street firms about their plans, chances are that you'll hear the same year-end 1998 date, but without much detail to back it up.

One of the most sobering analyses of the state of Year-2000 activity in both the securities industry and the rest of U.S. industry comes from the respected Wall Street firm of J.P. Morgan. In a May 15, 1997 report, Morgan's analysts summarize the state of Year-2000 preparations in the U.S. private sector as "serious," with the following commentary:[17]

> *Project status varies quite a bit from industry to industry and company to company, although awareness is generally very high (even at senior management levels) and funding for projects is mostly under way. Overall, the insurance industry is a little ahead, while the financial services industry is coming on strong but has a long way to go.(5) Telecommunications, caught in the cross-currents of deregulation and increased competition, also has a lot of work to catch up on. Although these three groups have often been cited as having difficult compliance issues, other industries, such as manufacturing and utilities, may also have big headaches in the form of embedded silicon chips, which may require complete hardware replacement.*

Assuming that Wall Street itself continues to function, there's a related question: What will investors think about the value of their stock holdings in companies whose earnings are already being affected by Year-2000 expenses? What will they think when they begin to contemplate the possibility of massive post-Year-2000 lawsuits against the companies they've invested in—lawsuits that could dwarf the tobacco, asbestos, and silicone-implant lawsuits of recent years?

The impact on corporate earnings was just beginning to emerge in 1997, when this book was written. As *Information Week* magazine points out,[18]

> *Year 2000 expenditures are reaching the bottom line. Several companies say they will cut corporate earnings to account for the cost of the millennium fix as they find they can't fund their entire year 2000 projects from existing IS budgets. Two research reports indicate that many more companies will have to go the same route.*
>
> *In its annual report, Equifax Inc., a $1.9 billion financial services company in Atlanta, deducted 1 cent per share from earnings to account for its 1996 year 2000 spending—and stated that additional year 2000 spending in 1997 and 1998 would trim four to five cents per share. Year 2000 costs ate up $1 million in the first quarter this year alone.*
>
> *Southern New England Telecommunication Corp. expects to spend $15 million to $20 million this year on its year 2000 fix, which means cutting its earnings for the year from $3.20 to as low as $2.90, estimates Scott Wright, a telecom analyst at Argus Research Corp. in New York. "That's not chicken feed," says Wright.*

Cynics might argue that vintage-1997 stock market prices are so far removed from traditional price-to-earnings ratios that a company's earnings hardly matter anymore; what seems to matter more is the investors' assessment of the company's future prospects. Thus, since *every* company is going to be hit with Year-2000 costs, perhaps Wall Street will simply discount the entire Year-2000 phenomenon as a one-time event, and maintain the current level of prices. On the other hand, the savvy investor will realize that some companies, within any given industry, will end up spending substantially more than others, because of a late start, incompetent managers, excessively complex software, etc. More importantly, some companies may come through the Year-2000 crisis in a substantially weakened state, with future prospects dimmed by expensive lawsuits and continuing Year-2000 malfunctions within their mission-critical computer systems. That kind of assessment would almost certainly drive down the price of a stock; and if such an assessment were made, collectively, about a majority of the companies comprising the Dow Jones index, it would not be surprising to see a Year-2000-induced slump that finally brings an end to the long bull market of the 1990s.

Recap: Could Things Really Be This Bad?

Both authors, in their day-to-day lives, are cheerful optimists. We expect the sun to come up every day, and it never crosses our mind that the sky will fall, or that the earth will come to an end. But after reading the words we've written in this chapter, we worry that we might be labeled hysterical, gloom-and-doom pessimists. Hence, a brief recap to put all of this in perspective.

First, it should be emphasized again that we desperately hope that the Year-2000 problems can be overcome by dint of hard work throughout the financial community in the remaining years of the decade. As noted above, we too have savings accounts, credit cards, and even a few stocks and bonds. It is no more in our interests than anyone else's (except, perhaps, a few aging hard-line Communists watching all of this from a remote corner of Russia) to see the American banking system collapse.

And we certainly don't expect a full-scale collapse. From the various commentaries cited above, it's obvious that the financial community *is* aware of the problem, and that substantial financial and human resources are now being committed to fix the problem. If the testimony at Senator Dodd's recent Senate hearing is to be believed, 10% of the banks are already Year-2000-compliant, as of mid-1997. The question is: What will the percentage be at the close of business on Friday, December 31, 1999? Surely it will be higher than 10%, and as optimists ourselves, we would like to believe that it will be 80%, or 90%, or even 95%. But given the late start, the massive size of the Year-2000 problem, and the intrinsic complexity of modifying all of that computer software, we simply cannot believe that the figure will approach 100%.

The consequences of Year-2000 failures in the remaining 5%, 10%, or 20% of the banks is unknown as we write this book, and will probably remain unknown until the new millennium begins. However, if we could be absolutely certain that the Year-2000 problem could be contained entirely *within* the offending banks, then perhaps it would be possible to take proactive measures. As noted above, the FFIEC has implied, with its statement in mid-May 1997, that it will begin auditing banks for Year-2000 compliance in mid-1998. If this is true, and if the FFIEC has the authority to shut down noncompliant banks, then we might have adequate time during 1999 to effect an orderly transfer of funds and accounts to banks that have been certified as Year-2000-compliant.

But this presumes that Year-2000 compliance is a black-and-white, all-or-nothing proposition; it also presumes that the FFIEC auditors have a sufficient supply of time, resources, and competence to accurately determine a bank's compliance. As we noted above, even the most brilliant of computer programmers, equipped with the very best technology and procedures, have not been able to improve upon the record of one defect per million program instructions for large, complex computer systems. Alas, the software professionals working in the nation's banks and financial institutions cannot walk on water; the best that can be said is that they swim through water competently, and we regret to report that there are some who can barely pass water.

This point must be stressed: *Every piece of evidence that we have from 40 years of experience in the software industry tells us that an estimate of one defect per 10,000 instructions is the best we can hope for in a typical organization.* And it must also be stressed: *These are defects that* remain *in the computer programs* after *they have been officially tested and placed into an operational status.* Bottom line: Neither the bank's programmers, nor the FFIEC auditors, can be certain of finding all of the bugs in the Year-2000-sensitive software they examine.

Thus, no matter how intelligent, resourceful, dedicated, earnest, and optimistic the banking community might be, the reality is that we will have an unknown number of defects in an unknown number of programs in an unknown number of banks. The situation in some banks and brokerage firms will be demonstrably better than others; but even in the best of the banks, there may be Year-2000 bugs lurking in the programs, waiting to pop out at an inopportune moment.

If there is any certainty at all in this situation, it is that we will hear an optimistic assessment from business leaders, regulators, and most politicians. As John Kenneth Galbraith observed in the closing words of his history of the Great Crash of 1929:

> But now, as throughout history, financial capacity and po-
> litical perspicacity are inversely correlated. Long-run salva-
> tion by men of business has never been highly regarded if it
> means disturbance of orderly life and convenience in the
> present. So inaction will be advocated in the present even
> though it means deep trouble in the future. Here, at least

*equally with communism, lies the threat to capitalism. It is
what causes men who know that things are going quite
wrong to say that things are fundamentally sound.*[19]

Fallback Advice: The Two-Day Failure

Perhaps there are some who can read this assessment of the
Year-2000 threat to banking and then continue on, without
making any changes to their plans. If Galbraith's gloomy
assessment is correct, that may be exactly what happens at the
level of governmental leadership. But here's a metaphor to
consider: If you were an average citizen in 1928, and if you
had received a divine revelation that told you *precisely* when
the Great Crash was going to occur, and if you thought that
such a stock market crash might well lead to the collapse and
closure of half the nation's banks,[20] wouldn't you do something about it *before* the lines began forming in front of your
bank?

Let's say you invested money in the stock market in January
of 1928. (We think this is a good reference point, since it was
almost two years before the famous Stock Market Crash of
1929, and now we are approximately two years before potential stock market problems that will arise due to Year-2000
problems). The S&P 500 (a broader measure than the more-
publicized Dow Jones Industrial Average) peaked in August
1929, and then fell 79% to its trough in June of 1932. An
investor would actually have lost a bit less money, because the
above figures do not reflect the reinvestment of dividends,
which most people elect to do in their mutual funds and stock
holdings. But in any case, it took *another five years* for the S&P
500 to reach the levels it was at in January 1928.

So here we are, 70 years later. You may be reading this book
in the summer of 1998, or even the summer of 1999. You may
be hearing encouraging words from the public relations

departments of Wall Street brokerage firms and the banking community. You may be hearing optimistic assessments from Senators and Congressmen, and even from the President.[21] Meanwhile, the clock is ticking, and you've seen no definitive proof that all the nation's banking computers have been fixed.

Why worry about stock market corrections, when everyone knows they peak and trough, and when everyone knows you will make your money back eventually? If you are saving for the very distant future, and if your tax-deferred savings are not too substantial, then you must cope with the reality that there will be blips, bleeps, and hiccups along the way in the stock market, no matter what. Hopefully, neither a Year-2000 problem, a Great Depression, or a crash of 1987 will have too material an impact on your retirement finances 30 years from now. But it's very important for you to remember that the stock market returns of the past few years *are not* representative of the last seventy years, of history in general, or of common sense. As a young investor, you should not be fooled into thinking that 30%+ annual stock market returns will continue. Since 1928, the average twelve-month return in the S&P 500 is roughly 7% (without dividends reinvested); since 1940 that return is a little over 8%, since 1950 roughly 9%, and since 1960 and 1970 a bit more than 8%. Since 1980 and 1990, the S&P 500 has risen an average of 12% every twelve months. Since 1995, however, the S&P 500 has averaged over a 20% return for twelve-month periods. This is a boom period, and boom periods do not last forever.

One proactive thing you can do with your 401K or IRA/Keogh nest egg is to make sure that the firm managing your retirement funds is Year 2000-compliant, or is definitely going to be so soon. No one can guarantee the survival of your small retirement nest egg if the portfolio management firm goes out of business—and since those funds are not federally insured, you can't be assured of getting your money back if the companies do indeed fail.

If you're extremely optimistic, perhaps your personal assessment will be something like this: "Well, things might be a little screwed up for the first couple days of the New Year. Maybe the ATM machine won't work right away; maybe there will be a few problems with my credit card; maybe there will be long lines at the bank when it opens on Monday, January 3." The simple solution is to ensure that you have a few days of spare cash in your wallet. That's not difficult, and it won't pose any problem for the banks. It's common for people to withdraw enough cash to last for a few days during the week, or for a weekend away from home.

This level of risk management is, as we've repeatedly stressed through the book, the absolute minimum. Waking up on Saturday morning, January 1, 2000, with only a five-dollar bill in your wallet is the height of idiocy, unless you're one of the unfortunate members of American society who has only five dollars left to his or her name.

Fallback Advice: The One-Month Failure

This, in our opinion, is a more realistic level of risk management, given the variety of problems that could occur. Perhaps your bank won't shut its doors for a full month (though it must be remembered that the bank holiday imposed by FDR in March 1933 lasted for ten days); indeed, perhaps your bank will be capable of serving the rest of its customers with great success. It may turn out that only *your* account is the one that's frozen, because a Year-2000 error deleted your database record, and no one can figure out how much money you have.

If you believe this is a scenario that has some likelihood of occurring, as we do, then there are two things we strongly suggest. The first is the most obvious, but also the most difficult and expensive: Accumulate a month's living expenses in cash, and sequester it away in a safe place *outside* your bank. As noted earlier, we see no benefit in opening a bank account in Switzerland or some other part of the world. *All* of the world's banks will face the same problem at the same time, and the U.S. banks appear to be in better shape than other international banks. We would also be *extremely* wary of a bank that begins aggressively advertising for new customers in 1999 on the basis that it is "certified" as being Year-2000-compliant. Even if the bank is managed by honest men and women, the "ripple effect" phenomenon could create difficulties when the Year-2000-compliant bank attempts to interact with the rest of the banking system.

Putting a pile of dollars under a mattress is not something that the last two or three generations of Americans are familiar with; perhaps more significantly, it can be quite difficult for the families that live from paycheck to paycheck, with only a few spare dollars in the bank. But if you begin preparing for this strategy in early 1998, it should not be an extreme hardship—especially if you focus on the expenses that absolutely *must* be paid in a timely fashion. If you're a month late paying the rent, and you've got the wonderful excuse that your bank is closed, it's unlikely you'll be evicted. It's equally unlikely that your phone will be disconnected and your lights turned off—unless, of course, you have a bad credit record and/or the phone and utility companies are plagued by severe Year-2000 problems of the sort discussed in Chapter 3. But, you will need cash for food, transportation, and other services and products whose providers demand instant compensation.

The second thing you must do to prepare for this scenario is ensure that you have a hard-copy record of your current bank statement, as well as financial statements from your credit card company, stock brokerage firm, and other similar financial institutions (including, perhaps, your insurance company and the firm that provides your home mortgage). If you've got $10,000 in your savings account, and your bank ruefully admits that a Year-2000 bug has accidentally deleted the database record that describes your current balance, you need to have a piece of paper that can document your claim to your money. Indeed, this is a reasonable precaution even for the minor 2-3 day disruption discussed above.

One of the obvious problems banks could begin having in 1999, and after the Year 2000, is a bank run. Much like in the Continental Illinois National bank example we described above, even rumors of bank trouble can cause a *huge* drain on deposits. One big difference between the 1980s and the coming years is that the Year-2000 problem will become more and more public. As Year 2000 evolves from being a "techie" issue, to a Wall Street issue, and then finally becomes a Main Street issue, we believe the problems will begin with a "flow of funds" to banks which can prove (in writing, by an outside examiner, etc.) that they are (as far as they know) Year-2000-compliant from those banks which cannot provide such make a statement. Indeed, we would recommend a similar course of action if you plan to leave some money in the bank. Demand some proof from your bank that they are Year-2000-compliant (of course, we think no one will be error-free, but getting an assurance from a bank means that *at least* they have performed some tests). After all, banks make handsome profits on your money...they don't deserve to have it if they are not acting prudently!!!

We believe this "flow of funds" we outlined above will generally be from small to large banks, with mid-size banks probably being a wash. There is already the most pressure, protection, help, and focus from the Fed on large banks (which, of course, have the monstrous resources to do their best to fix the problem). And as we described earlier, the Fed considers the largest banks in the country "too big to fail." Along these lines, we also expect that the largest banks have some of the more modern computer programs. All of the largest banks are FDIC-insured. Since almost 99% of bank deposits are FDIC-insured, we don't expect there to be too much of an economic effect of people transferring money from insured banks to uninsured banks.

Of course, even if the large banks are what they consider to be Year-2000-compliant, some of them are likely to experience problems lasting for some period of time. Because these banks will have had the most pressure on them, we think many of the most serious problems will have been worked out. When (not if) large banks do experience computer problems, we fully expect the Federal Reserve to publicly announce (as it already has said it will do) that it will provide the necessary liquidity (i.e., that it will loan money) to the banks until their problems are resolved. Nevertheless, we expect large banks to also experience a drain on deposits, though less than smaller banks, and to experience shutdowns or holidays of the duration we have explored throughout the book. We generally expect no outright failures in the large bank sector—if banks are in trouble, we expect them to be forced to merge with other banks. Outright failures of any of the largest banks in the country would have *severe* implications for the domestic economy—including a stock market *crash* (not a correction and not a dip), as well as a recession (if not depression), widespread consumer panic, and general gloom. In addition, the international financial market and economic ramifications are unthinkable. This does not mean there won't be problems—indeed, we think the contrary holds true—but we do not think the Fed will allow even one of the largest banks to fail outright, so long as it has the power to provide liquidity. With the large banks sector, we expect most of the problems to be of the 2-3 day variety, with some of the one-month variety.

In terms of the stock market, it is difficult for us to differentiate here between a one-month and one-year failure. The ramifications of a one-month shutdown in the stock market could be so severe that the effects are felt for over a year. Therefore, we lump the two together, and we recommend a few different courses of action depending on what stage of life you are in, and what your financial responsibilities are. If you are like one of the authors—i.e., in your mid- to late 20s, with some savings, the small beginnings of a retirement nest egg, few financial commitments, most of your savings in a money market deposit account (MMDA) of a *large* FDIC member bank (which has stated it will be Year-2000-compliant)—then your money will be subject to the same risks as a checking or savings account. This money probably represents most of your liquid assets, and the funds you would need for a rainy day or for a few emergency months—and the Year-2000 problem just may be that rainy day. The emergency that young people usually save for is unemployment, and that could be the result of a Year-2000 problem, as well as a sudden downturn in the economy and stock market. Putting your money in a large, federally-insured bank account, which pays some minimal interest rate, is probably the most cautious step you can take (in addition to our earlier recommendation of having *at least* one month's worth of expenses in hard currency in your home).

The small remainder that you leave in mutual funds (or whatever other investment you have) can be treated as a high-risk diversification to your portfolio.

If you have already started contributing to a 401K/IRA retirement plan, you probably have several choices as to how you can allocate your money. If you are young, you probably have the bulk (60-75%) of your small retirement nest egg in equity funds, and you may be worried about these specific funds in case of a downturn in the stock market. We think you should remember that this is *retirement* money, and that you should be treating it as such, without any intention of touching it for at least 30-35 years. Considering the penalties and taxes imposed on premature withdrawals, it is probably more financially advantageous to take out a loan from a bank than to withdraw your 401K/IRA money. If you follow that advice, we think you should leave your allocation alone. Yes, there might be a stock market correction, or maybe even a crash. Your retirement savings is meant for your retirement, and history teaches that during all market downturns, long-term investments will be successful.

On the other hand, what if your situation is more like the other author of this book: a generation older, with retirement looming only 10 years away, and with a substantial amount of savings accumulated over the years? In this case, you probably have a smaller proportion of your investments in equities, though probably a larger absolute dollar amount. We suggest that this group of investors add an extra risk premium to all asset classes. We recommend significantly increasing the percentage of your assets which are in FDIC-insured money market deposit accounts, and decreasing the percentage allocation to any of the riskier classes of assets. In this scenario, the results of past stock market corrections—especially the 1929 crash—suggest that you could lose half of your stock market investment from a serious Year-2000 crisis, and might not be able to recoup the loss in time for a normal retirement.

One of the authors works in the alternative investment industry, which serves avid investors who want to make higher returns than what the money market account of a bank will offer. "Alternative investment" funds and investments are those which target acceptable financial returns in *all* market environments. These funds invest in many different securities; they sometimes employ leverage, go both long and short simultaneously, buy and sell emerging markets' equity, debt, and real estate, specialize in convertible arbitrage, risk arbitrage, commodities, and currencies... and the list goes on and on. These investments are constructed to perform regardless of the state of the U.S. stock market (though we must stress that if investment managers can't buy and sell securities because of Year-2000 problems at the brokerage house they conduct business with, there will be a problem!). Another specialty in the alternative investment world is that of the short seller. If you think there will be a correction, crash, hiccup, downtrend, or other blip in what seems like the eternal rise in the Dow Jones Industrial Average, investigate some of the short-only funds. Finally, many investors believe that traditional hedges like gold and silver are appropriate investments for the post-2000 era. Almost anyone can open a futures account with a broker, and invest in gold and silver through futures contracts. Alternatively, gold and silver can be purchased for physical delivery, along with the emergency cash that you put under your mattress. Some of these alternative investments have high minimums, and others have stringent criteria for investor suitability, but there are some which are more small investor oriented. These alternative investments are subject to all of the same Year-2000 risks as other investments, except that they are designed to be "uncorrelated" with the stock market.

With any investment choice you make, and with any bank you put money in, a high degree of "due diligence" is crucial during the next two years. If a financial institution cannot prove to you in writing that it will be Year-2000-compliant, think twice.[22] Also, it must be emphasized that neither of the authors are certified financial advisers or planners, and you should seek appropriate professional advice to understand the risks you take before investing in any new funds, or shifting the allocation of your own investments.

Fallback Advice: The One-Year Failure

A one-year disruption in access to your funds is clearly a serious crisis. How could such a crisis be allowed to occur? Again, we remind the reader that in the aftermath of the Great Crash of 1929, it took the federal government over three years to create the mechanisms that restored faith to the banking system; in the meantime, over 4,000 banks went under, taking the deposits and savings of millions of citizens with them.

Today, as we've noted, the FDIC exists as a form of insurance against such bank losses; and if it should fail (because of Year-2000 problems, or because of the "fractional reserve" system upon which it too is based), one assumes that the Federal Reserve system and printing presses of the U.S. Treasury could be called in as a lender of last resort, in the event of a severe emergency. Thus, if you're an optimist and a firm believer in the competence and benevolence of government, you may wish to take the position that your funds are ultimately safe. *Even if my bank closes*, you might be thinking, *I'll get my money back, sooner or later.*

There are two problems with this line of thinking. First, it's likely to be "later" rather than "sooner" before your money is restored. If the Year-2000 problem is serious enough to close one bank, it will probably be serious enough to close several banks. Your refund application to the FDIC (for which you might want to get the appropriate paperwork and forms now, rather than later!) will be joined with several hundred thousand, if not millions, of others. Assuming that the FDIC doesn't have its own Year-2000 problems to deal with, it's still likely to take 6-12 months before your funds reappear.

The second problem is that the *value* of those funds could deteriorate significantly in the interim. In the case of bank deposits, this would only be relevant in a period of severe inflation; as we noted above, hyperinflation is theoretically possible as a consequence of severe Year-2000-induced banking/currency problems, though we have no way of evaluating the likelihood of such an event. However, most adults today can recall the early 1980s, when inflation reached nearly 20%. Whatever combination of economic, fiscal, and monetary events caused that unhappy outcome, it was arguably far less severe and traumatic than the impending Year-2000 situation. In any case, there is the risk that the $10,000 that's "frozen" in your defunct bank account might only be worth $8,000, in terms of present purchasing power, when you get it back from the FDIC. In the worst of all cases, if true hyperinflation sets in, it could be worth far, far less.

Indeed, that's what we're concerned about with investments in the stock market. If your stock broker's computer system collapses because of a Year-2000 problem, you can't buy any new stocks from that broker, or—more importantly—sell the stocks held in "street name" by that broker on your behalf. Assuming that you can get through on the phone, you might ask for physical stock certificates; but if the broker's computers have crashed, it may be impossible for them to produce the certificates for several weeks or months.

In the worst case, the brokerage company collapses. Happily, as you may be aware, your account is protected by an FDIC-like agency, up to a level of $500,000. But the question is: If you apply for a refund, will you get cash or stock certificates? If it takes 6-12 months to recoup your stock certificates, the price of the stock may have collapsed. The trivial, brute-force solution to this problem is to insist that your broker deliver old-fashioned, physical, paper stock certificates to you *now*, rather than in the post-2000 aftermath. Chances are that your broker will resist, delay, complain, and argue about how foolish you are—but you have a legal right to obtain those certificates, as long as you own them free and clear (i.e., they haven't been purchased on a margin account).

The more extreme solution is to liquidate your stocks and bonds before January 1, 2000 (or perhaps even before January 1, 1999, if you're really worried!), and keep the proceeds in a money market account, in which case they'll be subject to approximately the same risks as if they were in a savings account at your local bank. This means, of course, that you'll forego whatever profit-making opportunities might exist from further increases in the stock market averages and indices in the remaining months and years of the decade. That's a risk you'll have to evaluate on your own, and on which we deliberately avoid offering recommendations.

As for your bank account, if you are concerned about the possibility of a one-year shutdown of your bank, it's possible to withdraw all of your funds, and put *all* of it under your mattress. Or, slightly less drastic, perhaps you could withdraw sufficient cash to survive for a year without access to your bank account. Measures like these will almost certainly be seen as extreme and excessive, and we don't expect many will take them seriously. And indeed, it may not be necessary, if you can make the following four assumptions: (a) you've got enough cash to survive for a month, or at least until your next paycheck arrives from your employer; (b) your employer has not gone bankrupt, and your job is safe; (c) your regular salary is sufficient for your month-to-month living needs, without access to your savings; and (d) when you finally do recoup your money from the bank or from the FDIC, it hasn't been substantially devalued by hyperinflation. Of these four, assumption (b) is the most crucial; this involves the issues we discussed in Chapter 2.

Unfortunately, the existence of Year-2000 bugs in banks—of all sizes—could cause directors and bank officers to engage in unsound business practices. We do not direct this comment at anyone in particular; however, we worry that, out of fear, some banking executives will say the banks they run are Year-2000-compliant when they are not. Or, out of fear, they will try to rush their process of fixing the Year-2000 problem, and make fatal errors and mistakes. Unsound business practices could also arise out of greed—banks who are Year-2000-compliant could attempt to profit from that through speculation, risky lending practices, etc. Fear and greed can also give way to fraud, which took place in the last major banking crisis in the 1980s. We cannot assign any probabilities to what individuals will do because of fear and greed, nor can we say what kind of fraud will be committed. It is important to remember here that while the actual problem is technical, the manner in which it will be dealt with is determined by human beings. Human beings make decisions based on emotion, and despite all the economic theory, sometimes just do not act rationally.

Because the future of this problem is based on humans, our book is *not* a science, and we cannot give expectations based on any kind of mathematical formula.

Fallback Advice: The Ten-Year Failure

An advanced nation of 260 million men and women would not tolerate the complete absence of a banking system for more than a few months, let alone a decade. We certainly don't foresee any possibility of a Year-2000 crisis taking us back to the days when we relied upon gold coins, bushels of wheat, or other forms of barter to conduct our economic affairs. Even if a nationwide wave of bank runs and a total loss of investor confidence effectively destroyed our existing banks and financial institutions and our currency, something new would emerge as a replacement within a few years. On the other hand, it could be argued that the nation's faith in its financial institutions was severely shaken, if not destroyed, during the decade between 1929 and 1939; if it happened once (and this was by no means the only such event in our history!), then arguably it could happen again.

If a Year-2000 banking crisis turns out to be so severe that it requires a decade to restore faith and confidence in its stability, then it won't be something we can plan for on an individual basis. If all of the familiar banks collapse and are replaced by a new collection; if the Federal Reserve System collapses and is replaced by a new politically-created structure; if MasterCard, Visa, and American Express vanish and are replaced eventually by some new form of electronic credit; if our familiar greenback dollar bills are recalled by the government and then replaced by a new kind of paper known as the Clinton; if all of these things, and possibly more, should happen, how on earth will we be able to protect whatever modest savings we've managed to accumulate in the years leading up to 2000? A few clever souls—those who are the most nimble, flexible, shrewd, and opportunistic—will find a way to profit from all of this; we see ample illustrations of this in modern-day, post-Communist Russia.

Most of us, though, are likely to suffer a fate similar to that of the average Russian. Our savings might well be wiped out; our corporate and Social Security pensions could prove to be worthless; and more fundamentally, the basic guidelines and rationale that we've traditionally used for making economic decisions could be destroyed and replaced by something new. Those without any savings, without any pensions, and without any conscious economic strategy—which means, for the most part, the young adults entering the work force, and the poor—may find that they're no worse off than before, and that new opportunities are opening up. The middle-class, the middle-aged, pensioners, and numerous other members of society who have spent a lifetime "playing by the rules" are likely to find it *extremely* difficult to adjust to the utter elimination of those rules, followed by the creation of an entirely new set of rules. This is an extremely sobering scenario; again, look to post-Communist Russia to see vivid examples of how difficult it can be to adjust to a new economic order.

We repeat, once again, our fervent hope that things will not end up this way; it would be as painful for us, on an individual basis, as it would for any reader of this book. But painful or not, it's a possibility that we feel ought to be considered—even if only briefly, and even if the possibility is rejected after some thought. If you believe that a ten-year financial crisis is more than just a figment of our imagination, then our advice is: Simplify your life, pare down your debt and financial obligations, re-evaluate the real importance of the material possessions in your life in comparison to family relationships and other fundamental values, and organize your affairs so that you can be as flexible and self-sufficient as possible, no matter what may come in the post-2000 years. There are some who will argue that this would not be such a bad piece of advice even without a Year-2000 crisis!

Endnotes

1. One of our favorites is John Kenneth Galbraith's, *Money: Whence It Came, Where It Went*, revised edition (Houghton Mifflin, 1995).
2. See *Investor's Business Daily*, Feb. 12, 1997, for a description of Citibank's efforts, and the March 1997 on-line version of Software magazine (located at http://www.sentrytech.com/sm037f1a.htm) for a discussion of Chase Manhattan's Year-2000 efforts. In a routine filing, Chase Manhattan estimated that it would spend $250 million in Year-2000 costs over the 1997-99 period.
3. To express this in a different way: It's a staff of approximately 300-500 computer professionals, working full-time over a period of two years. Most organizations have no excess software personnel sitting around in the back office, because they were eliminated during the downsizing, rightsizing, outsourcing, and reengineering period of the early 1990s. For the software industry as a whole, there is a nationwide shortage estimated at 200,000 professionals as of mid-1997, and the figure is likely to get worse in the next few years.
4. This is not a casual bit of hyperbole; there have been numerous studies and analyses of software projects over the past 20 years that confirm this unpleasant aspect of computer software. See, for example, Capers Jones' *Patterns of Software Systems Failure and Success* (International Thomson Computer Press, 1997), which also points out that approximately 14% of all projects are late and 24% are canceled before completion. The really bad news, which won't come as a surprise, is that the percentage of projects late or canceled is substantially higher for the very large computer projects.
5. Banks, being somber and conservative, are likely to do their best to provide a positive "spin" on the Year-2000 PR notices they publish during 1998 and 1999; they would probably take issue with our description of "hastily-modified" software. But overall, the effort of the banking industry *is* hasty; as noted in the Associated Press report at the beginning of this chapter, only 10% of the banks had finished their Year-2000 conversion effort at the time this book was written, even though articles in the computer trade press have been warning of Year-2000 problems since as early as 1993 and the Federal Reserve system published its first advisory warning about Year 2000 in June 1996. The fact that the

end of the decade is approaching is hardly a secret, and nobody forced the senior management of the banks (or any other company, for that matter) to dawdle and delay until panic set in during 1997.

6. John Kenneth Galbraith, *Money: When It Came, Where It Went,* op cit., p. 15.

7. John Kenneth Galbraith, *op cit.,* p. 194 ff.

8. John Kenneth Galbraith, *op cit.,* pp. 200-201.

9. Meanwhile, an account with a savings & loan institution is insured up to $100,000 by the Savings Association Insurance Fund (SAIF), which replaced the Federal Savings and Loan Insurance Corporation (FSLIC) in 1989, and which is under the jurisdiction of the FDIC.

10. The U.S. has long since abandoned the gold standard, the last vestige of which was terminated by Richard Nixon in 1971. Thus, whatever else might happen, the government won't have to worry about demands from its citizens to replace paper money with gold.

11. Allan E. Alter, "Your other millennium problem," *Computerworld,* May 26, 1997.

12. "Federal Bank Regulators Outline Year 2000 Project Management Goals" is available in full on the Internet at http://www.ffiec.gov/y2k/y2kpress.htm). The full text of the FFIEC Year-2000 Task Force Statement is available on the Internet at http://www.FFIEC.gov/Y2000/, and can also be obtained by toll-free telephone FAX BACK at 888-882-0982.

13. Of course, it's not the merchants themselves—these folks are inclined to accept any credit card, under even the most dubious of circumstances. But most merchants use a variety of credit authorization terminals, which in turn are connected to banks or other facilities. Depending on the way these authorization systems are programmed, the consumer's card may be rejected despite the most strenuous efforts on the part of the merchant. See "Credit cards offer a visible sign of the Year 2000 Problem," by Lon Wagner, *The Virginia-Pilot,* May 1, 1997 for more details.

14. This is the perspective of the individual citizen; the impact on mail-order businesses is far more severe. If we can't order an item by phone with a credit card, then we're forced to shop by mail (with a check), or in person in the local neighborhood.

15. "Merrill Lynch's $268m plan to kill 2000 bug," *Financial Review,* June 26, 1997. Note that the reference to $268 million, in the title of this article, refers to Australian dollars. The text of the article quotes Merrill Lynch's Year-2000 costs, as well as those of the overall securities industry, in U.S. dollars.

16. Howard Sorgen, "Merrill Lynch prepares for year 2000 conversion," *Computer Reseller News,* May 19, 1997. Note that Mr. Sorgen is a senior vice president and chief technology officer of Merrill Lynch.

17. William D. Rabin and Terrence P. Tierney, "The Year 2000 Problem: it's worse than we thought," accessible on the Internet at http://www.jpmorgan.com/ MarketDataInd/Research/Y2Kupdate/Y2K.HTM. The Morgan analysts describe the state of Year-2000 preparations in local, state, and federal government agencies as "critical," and the European situation as largely unknown but "probably worse than critical."

18. Bruce Caldwell, "Year 2000 Hits The Bottom Line—Companies find they can't fund all projects from their existing IS budgets," *Information Week*, May 26, 1997.

19. John Kenneth Galbraith, *The Great Crash 1929*, revised edition (Houghton-Mifflin, 1997), p. 194.

20. We hasten to add that historians and economists are still arguing about the degree to which the banking crisis of the Great Depression can be blamed directly on the Stock Market Crash of October 29, 1929. But hardly anyone denies that there was some relationship between the two phenomena, and that it was probably a very strong relationship.

21. You can find some encouraging words from President Clinton in the beginning of Chapter 10, where we discuss the potentially serious Year-2000 impact upon the government.

22. To emphasize the seriousness of this advice, we are not aware of any major bank or financial institution that could say it was fully Year-2000-compliant when this book went to press. Indeed, it would have been virtually impossible to make such a statement, since the hardware, operating systems, and database management packages that the banks rely on are not likely to be Year-2000-compliant until sometime in 1998 or 1999. *Caveat emptor!*

Year-2000 Impact on Food

Food probably has a very great influence on the condition of men. Wine exercises a more visible influence, food does it more slowly but perhaps just as surely. Who knows if a well-prepared soup was not responsible for the pneumatic pump or a poor one for a war?

G. C. Lichtenberg, Aphorisms, *"Notebook A," aphorism 14 (written 1765–99; translated by R. J. Hollingdale, 1990).*

If you're going to America, bring your own food.

Fran Lebowitz, Social Studies, *"Fran Lebowitz's Travel Hints" (1981).*

Introduction

We did not originally plan to devote a chapter to the subject of food, but then we were reminded of Samuel Johnson's astute comment that "he who does not mind his belly will hardly mind anything else."[1] Indeed, without a regular supply of food, we would hardly be in a position to worry at length about the state of our banks, our transportation systems, and the various other topics discussed in this book.

The vast majority of people in this country are in the happy position of having an ample supply of food, whenever and wherever they want it. Relatively few of us grow any of our own food these days, unless gardening is a hobby and we have a plot of land in the backyard. Even those who nurture a few tomatoes in the backyard, or who catch a few fish during their weekend visit to the lake, are likely to visit the local grocery store on a weekly basis to stock up on a dazzling array of meat, fish, fruits, vegetables, dairy products, pasta, bread and bakery items, desserts, beer, wine, and so forth.

Even more interesting is the fact that many of us have largely abandoned cooking during the past twenty years. In both the urban and suburban environments, breakfast often consists of a donut or bagel, or perhaps a bowl of cereal and a cup of coffee; lunch is a Whopper at Burger King or a slice of pizza at Pizza Hut; and dinner consists of whatever we can find at Kentucky Fried Chicken or Taco Bell, because it's too much trouble to throw a pre-packaged meal into the microwave oven. As Bill Bryson observes:[2]

> Clearly, some time ago makers and consumers of American junk food passed jointly through some kind of sensibility barrier in the endless quest for new taste sensations. Now they are a little like those desperate junkies who have tried every known drug and are finally reduced to mainlining toilet bowl cleanser in an effort to get still higher.

Without going any further into the culinary habits of Americans, suffice it to say that: (a) it continues to be one of the fundamental human needs, and (b) we're highly dependent upon various parts of the social infrastructure to provide, cook, and deliver food to us in a convenient manner.

And that brings us back to the theme of this book: What happens if a Year-2000 software problem interrupts this finely-tuned aspect of our social infrastructure? We'll first discuss how this might happen, and then revert to our standard categories of advice for two-day, one-month, one-year, and ten-year failures.

Delivery of Food

Our primary concern involves *deliveries*, both to the neighborhood grocery store, and to the fast-food outlets that some citizens have come to depend upon.[3] Fresh food, by its very nature, must be replenished and restocked on a frequent basis. Many other forms of food (including the hamburger patties at your favorite junk-food emporium) are frozen, and thus could presumably be stockpiled to provide ongoing supplies of food for months or years. But, both hamburger outlets and grocery stores operate on razor-thin profit margins, which requires keeping low inventories and using a "just-in-time" (JIT) delivery mechanism to restock on a daily or weekly basis.

While you might not be able to determine the inventory levels at your local MacDonald's or Burger King, you can certainly investigate the situation at your grocery store. Chances are you'll observe daily restocking in many departments, especially in the fruit-and-vegetable area, as well as meat and dairy products. Most of the non-perishable items, including those packaged securely in cans, boxes, or plastic containers, are restocked once or twice a week.

Next, take a look at the inventory levels. As part of your normal shopping, you may have occasionally encountered the out-of-stock phenomenon, but it's fairly rare in American stores. It's far more common that you'll take one loaf of bread off a shelf filled with what might seem, to the casual observer, an infinite quantity of loaves. But it's more likely to be a few dozen loaves, or perhaps a hundred at most. The same is true for most of the other items in the store; most of the store's inventory is right in front of you, on the shelves.

Now ask yourself a simple question: What happens if you and a few dozen of your neighbors all decide to buy a loaf of bread on the same day? And, what if you decided to buy a month's supply of cereal, instead of a one-week supply? The answer is pretty simple: The shelves would be bare, except for items like pickled kumquats and marinated pig's feet. However, in today's economy, *it doesn't matter*, because the shelves will be restocked tomorrow. And because everyone takes it for granted that that will be so, there's no need to get a month's supply of cereal; it's more convenient to buy enough to last for just a few days.

So, the bottom line is that precise inventory management, and a well-honed delivery infrastructure, are crucial for maintaining the well-stocked grocery store we take for granted. The same, by the way, is basically true for fast-food outlets. Most of them operate as franchises, and are obliged to replenish their supplies from the franchise-owner. This allows the franchise-owner to achieve economies of scale (by purchasing millions of pounds of beef at a time), and also allows the franchise-owner to maintain control over the proprietary nature of the junk food (e.g., the secret formula for Kentucky Fried Chicken, invented long ago by the fabled Colonel Sanders). Each franchise keeps careful track of the quantities of food sold, not only to maintain a reasonable reputation of providing hot, fresh junk food, but also to optimize the steady process of restocking by the franchise-owner.

The astute reader has probably anticipated where we are heading with this analysis. A Year-2000 problem can easily disrupt the delivery and inventory-management process. Inventory management is still done without computers in some establishments—you may have noticed grocery clerks manually counting the number of boxes of cereal on the shelves— but more commonly today, it's computerized. The same grocery clerk is involved, but now he or she carries a hand-held scanner that reads bar-code labels; sometimes the clerk keys in a few entries to indicate the quantity of goods left on the shelf. In theory, this should not even be necessary, because the cash registers at the checkout counter are connected to a central computer too, so that inventory management reports can be printed out in the store manager's office. However, the manual process is still important to keep track of spoilage, breakage, theft, and other forms of loss that might not be detected at the checkout counter.

Keeping track of how many boxes of cereal were sold, or how many Big Macs were consumed, is only the beginning of the inventory management process; what happens next is a *forecasting* computation to determine the likely number of days before the existing inventory will be completely exhausted, and whether the reorder quantity should be larger or smaller than usual to account for fluctuating trends and patterns. Indeed, this process has become enormously more sophisticated in recent years, with massive computer computations involving something known as "data mining" to look for trends that might not have been obvious to the human eye. A computer analysis might indicate, for example, that on Saturday nights, there's a strong tendency for purchases of beer to be accompanied by purchases of potato chips; this information might motivate the store manager to make certain that the shelves of beer are located next to the shelves of potato chips—or alternatively, to place the potato chips close to the checkout counter to accommodate the customer who visits the store on Saturday night for the primary purpose of buying beer, but who can then be persuaded to pick up an extra bag of potato chips if they happen to be easily visible at the checkout counter.

So there's a lot of computer intelligence behind the scenes, and—as you might have guessed—it's also Year-2000-sensitive. Indeed, dates and date calculations are essential to the

whole process of inventory management; the U.K. establish-
ment of Marks & Spencer has already run into Year-2000
problems because its computers are programmed to reject
incoming deliveries of food items if the "expiration date" indicates that the food has spoiled. Many food items packaged in
cans, boxes, or plastic containers have an expiration date that
is four years after the item was packaged; thus, an item delivered to the store in 1998 would have an expiration date of
2002. Unfortunately, if the inventory management system has
programmed its dates as two-year digits, it comes to the conclusion that the food item expired in 1902, not 2002.

Thus, we worry that inventory management systems, delivery scheduling systems, data mining systems, and much of the
"intelligence" that ensures the proper stockpiling of the proper
items at the proper time, may blow up on January 1; indeed, a
few of these systems are already blowing up. On the other
hand, there's already an automatic fallback mechanism. If the
shelves are empty, customers will complain vociferously, and
the store-manager (or the Burger King manager) will pick up
the phone and make a manual request for inventory replenish-
ment. An astute manager will notice the problem before customers inform him or her; if a manual inventory determines
that stocks are falling low, the same unscheduled phone call
can be made to the supplier.[4]

Nevertheless, we won't be surprised to see a moderate
amount of chaos and confusion while all of this is being sorted
out during the first few days, weeks, or months of the new
millennium. The problem experienced by Marks & Spencer
(and soon to be experienced by many other stores) is, in its
own way, a blessing in disguise—for it will force the stores to
fix their problems *before* January 1, 2000. But, there will be
many other computer systems in which the Year-2000 bugs

won't become evident until the stroke of midnight; and the result is that you will find some empty shelves in your grocery store during the early days of the new millennium.

But, this may not turn out to be the biggest problem. Assuming that the inventory control computer systems are working, there is still the issue of transporting food items from the farm, the fishery, the bakery, or the slaughterhouse to the store. This requires a vast, intricate network of ships, planes, trains, and trucks—all synchronized to deliver the right amount of food items while they're still fresh. We discussed the potential vulnerability of the transportation system in Chapter 4; it simply bears repeating at this point that transportation problems could quickly "ripple" into food delivery problems.

This is likely to be much more of a problem for urban centers than for suburban and rural areas for a simple reason: The rural areas are closer to food producing areas, and are thus not as dependent on trucks, trains, and planes. During the writing of this book, one of us spent the summer in a small town in rural Montana, at the edge of a large lake. If a Year-2000-induced food delivery crisis were to occur, there would be some hope of obtaining fresh fish from the lake, fresh vegetables from the local farm stands, and even fresh beef from the neighboring ranches. The area also produces large quantities of wheat, which could be used to supply the local bakery. Obviously, this represents only a small part of the rich, varied diets that Americans have come to enjoy, but at least the basics could be locally obtained.[5]

Urban centers, on the other hand, may face a serious problem. Consider New York City, where both authors reside. While there might be the odd backyard garden in Brooklyn or Staten Island, Manhattan is basically sidewalks and streets—unless one wishes to contemplate converting Central Park into a gigantic garden plot. Manhattan is an island, which means that no food will arrive unless transported by boat, plane, truck, or train from other parts of the country—and because a population of eight million people enjoy eating as a daily activity, large quantities of food must be delivered on a daily basis.

Some portion of this food is delivered by large companies (e.g, major dairy companies, or large companies like Dole and Heinz, etc.) to chains of stores throughout an urban region. Once the inventory control problems and generic transportation problems have been worked out, we would expect these deliveries to resume in the normal fashion.

But there are also numerous small food suppliers who deliver their goods to small, independent merchants—e.g., the local delis that populate nearly every street corner in Manhattan. And even in the case of the large companies, the deliveries are often made by independent truckers; this latter category is especially important, for even if food is brought to the edge of Manhattan by boat or plane, the final portion of the delivery is almost always made by truck, directly to the store or merchant.

Now consider the following scenario: You're an independent trucker, based in New Jersey or Connecticut or Long Island; you spend your days filling your truck with rutabagas and onions at the railroad depot in Newark; and, you deliver the fresh vegetables to a dozen small stores and delis in Manhattan. It's now January 10, 2000 and you've been having a hell of a time finding gas for your truck and figuring out how to avoid all of the delays at the bridges and tunnels that lead into Manhattan. Not only that, the onions and rutabagas that were supposed to arrive in Newark last week were delayed by a snafu in the train system. But all of that has now been overcome, and you're ready to make your delivery, as long as one thing can be assured—upon delivery, you'll be paid. Well, one other thing would be nice, too: having been paid, you'll be able to drive back to your modest home in New Jersey without being shot, hijacked, or robbed.

Indeed, the very prospects of payment problems and crime problems will be enough to keep some of the small, independent truckers from making such deliveries. And this creates a ripple effect of its own: The residents of Manhattan want to eat regularly, just like the residents of Brooklyn, Queens, Staten Island, and the Bronx. Not only have the food deliveries diminished sharply, but the welfare checks and food coupons, which some members of the city rely on, have gotten fouled up in the computers in Washington. Oil deliveries have been delayed because of some other snafu, and with an early-January temperature hovering near zero, the heat has been turned off. This combination of events would be enough to put anyone—including the well-heeled residents of Park Avenue on the Upper East Side, as well as the less-affluent citizens in other parts of the city—into a foul mood. So, yes, perhaps there will be a few more shootings, hijackings, and robberies than normal.

The interesting question is whether the legitimate concerns of the independent truckers might keep them from making deliveries *anywhere* in Manhattan, not just the neighborhoods they might normally associated with higher levels of crime. And if a problem like this exists in Manhattan, one could make a good argument that it will also occur in Boston (beginning with Roxbury), Chicago (beginning with the South Side), and a dozen other cities. Even without the issue of crime, the smaller cities may have a problem—for they will be served, more often, by smaller trucking firms who will insist on cash, gold coins, wampum, or some other credible form of payment before they unload their trucks.

Fallback Advice: Two-Day Failures

Planning for two-day disruption should be relatively easy; it simply requires stockpiling a couple days' food in the house. Keep in mind, though, that the food-related Year-2000 problems may not occur promptly on January 1; the kind of delivery problems we've outlined above could occur at any point during the calendar year 2000. Thus, it would be a good idea to ensure that, at all times, you've got a modest stockpile that could provide breakfast, lunch, and dinner if the stores shut down for a couple of days.

As we've noted throughout the book, residents of weather-sensitive areas of the country are quite familiar with this strategy. When they first hear of an impending hurricane or blizzard, many families drive to the local supermarket to stock up on milk, bread, bottled water, and various other essentials. They can then ride out the storm without any major inconvenience. It's the city dwellers who will need to begin practicing this kind of stockpiling. There's not likely to be a problem of cost; except for the people at the bottom of the socio-economic ladder in the U.S., virtually everyone can afford to buy a few days' worth of food in advance. The biggest problem for the city dwellers will be laziness or procrastination.

Fallback Advice: One-Month Failures

Obviously, a one-month disruption in the food supply is far more serious than having to coast on leftovers and peanut-butter sandwiches for a couple of days. Stockpiling a month's food is potentially expensive, and it's also inconvenient; since most Americans have *never* had the experience of being cut off from their food supply for a month, it will be difficult to convince them to plan for the eventuality.

Again, suburban and rural dwellers are at an advantage here, for they're more likely to have a freezer, cool cellar, and/or various other storage sites in which they can stockpile food. Those who are near hunting and fishing areas, and those with a backyard garden plot, may already be in the habit of canning or freezing a supply of food—not for disaster prevention, but simply to take advantage of the fresh food or meat when it's available. The city dweller, crammed into a small apartment, barely has enough room in the refrigerator for a two-day supply of food; the notion of a freezer for additional food supplies is out of the question.

Nevertheless, it may be necessary—and if one plans for it now, the logistical problems *can* be overcome. In virtually every city, and in almost all suburban areas, there are now "mini-warehouse" facilities that can be rented at a modest cost. Many families are already using these storage facilities to store leftover furniture and other items that would otherwise clutter up a small house or apartment. If you're determined to continue living in a large city, and if you believe (as we do) that a one-month disruption of food is indeed possible—*especially* in the big cities—then you should consider using such a mini-warehouse to stockpile a larger supply of food.

In this scenario, you probably won't have an opportunity to install a freezer; almost all mini-warehouses are unheated, empty spaces, with no electrical outlets or running water. Thus, you'll need to stockpile food that requires no refrigeration, but can also withstand cold (and possibly even freezing) temperatures. You won't stockpile a month's supply of fresh milk, but you might stockpile powdered milk, along with a supply of canned or freeze-dried foods. You may have sworn that you would never again eat the canned peas that you had to tolerate as a child; but, canned vegetables do have the virtue of remaining edible for reasonable periods of time.

It's not really difficult to organize this level of stockpiling; however, it may require as much as a few hundred dollars, depending on your taste for food. It may require a commitment for the rental of a mini-warehouse. It will certainly require a few hours of effort to think carefully about the combination of food that you and your family will find nutritional and at least minimally pleasant to eat. It may require several hours, and multiple shopping trips, to accumulate the supplies and store them away. But you've got nearly two years to do this; anyone who is serious—with the exception of those at the poverty level—can do it.

Meg Carter, who read the first draft of this book, offered the following valuable advice for those who are thinking of stockpiling food for the Year-2000 problem:

> *You used the blizzard model, which is very familiar to people in the northern and mid-western states. I grew up in Ohio, so I can remember stocking up on staples and baking while we were snowed in for a week at a time. Although transportation was stopped, the utilities rarely were: we still had heat and electricity. I now live in Northern California where we're on constant earthquake preparedness, and I think the earthquake model is more like a Y2K scenario, where the possibility of being without electricity, heat, fresh water and transportation for some period of time is likely.*
>
> *Here's what we're advised to do: stock up on canned and dried foods that do not need cooking and require a minimum amount of water to prepare. (Stock up on water, too, of course.) Pinto beans, for example, would not be a good choice because they require lots of water to clean, soak and cook and at least an hour of cooking time. But canned tuna would be good, as well as the sun-dried fruits and nuts that are available in health food and specialty stores in the fall and winter. A nationwide chain which specializes in dried fruits, nuts, trail mix, etc. is Trader Joe's.*

Also, stores that specialize in recreation have prepackaged freeze-dried meals that need only a small amount of boiling water to prepare. This type of food is used by backpackers and mountaineers, who have to trek all of their food and cooking supplies into the wilderness and then trek them out, so it takes minimal space and is easy to prepare, while being high energy. A nationwide chain which specializes in this type of food is Recreational Equipment, Inc. (REI).

For people who live in urban areas, there are ways you can grow small amounts of fresh fruits and veggies year-round indoors, or in windowboxes or atriums (if you live in the Western or Southern states). Many apartment dwellers already have "gardens" devoted to flowers. It would be quite simple to convert them to lettuce, onions, tomatoes, carrots, etc. You could also can or dry (by sun or with a food dehydrator) fruits and veggies from the summer harvest, no matter where you live.

The biggest problem that we see in this area is psychological: Stockpiling a month's supply of food forces you to acknowledge that you *are* serious about Year-2000 planning. Your family may disagree with you, and if you tell your friends and business colleagues, they may laugh at you. "What are you, some kind of end-of-the-world, gloom-and-doom nut?" they'll ask. No one wants to be branded a lunatic, and this level of stockpiling is likely to be the dividing line between normal caution and lunacy in the eyes of your friends and family.[6]

Ultimately, the decision here is a personal one, or one that is made by consensus within your family. Remember that a one-month supply of food is the best form of insurance: You can eat it if you don't need it. Indeed, that should be one of the major criteria for choosing emergency food in the first place: If it's so awful that you'll throw it away when the Year-2000 emergency passes (or if it fails to materialize), you shouldn't buy it in the first place.

Fallback Advice: One-Year Failures

If a one-month stockpiling effort is difficult, then the notion of a one-year food stockpile is likely to be entirely beyond the ability of most. Indeed, most Americans would have no idea how to go about such a task; it's not something we were taught in school, nor have we ever seen anyone do it.

Does it make sense at all? Can anyone imagine the local food stores being closed for 365 consecutive days? If such a catastrophe were to occur, it would drastically change the landscape of most urban centers; there would be food riots in the street for some period of time, and then everyone would leave—for while there might be a few ultra-conservatives with a one-year food supply, the overwhelming majority would have no such reserves. And assuming that the farms, fisheries, and ranches are still producing edible food (we haven't bothered exploring the possibility of Year-2000 problems so severe that this part of society breaks down, too!), then sooner or later food *will* show up in the cities, for whoever happens to be left. The same would presumably be true for small towns, suburban, and rural areas; the primary difference is that the people in these areas would have been somewhat more self-sufficient in the interim.

The point here is that we're not trying to suggest that a Year-2000-induced food distribution problem will completely eliminate the supply of food for a full, solid year. But, there's also no guarantee that the confusion and chaos will magically end on December 31, 2000; indeed, if food-distribution problems are combined with transportation problems, electrical problems, and problems in the various other areas discussed in this book, it's not at all unreasonable to imagine recurrent, unpredictable problems with the food supply over a period of 3-5 years, each one lasting for a day, a week, or a month. Thus, the notion of a one-year food stockpile would most likely be meaningful for those concerned about these long-term difficulties.

Building a one-year food stockpile is something that will be difficult for most Americans to accomplish without professional assistance. While some canned or bottled goods might last for a year, many of the items one would normally buy in a grocery store are simply not intended for long-term storage. Most food items are packaged in plastic, cellophane, boxes, or other containers that contain a certain amount of air; the air contains oxygen, and the oxygen contributes to a slow but steady spoilage of the food. There are some items in the store that are vacuum-packed (including junk food snacks like Pringle's potato chips, for example) or freeze-dried (including many varieties of coffee), but this accounts for only a small part of the overall diet that a normal family requires.

Thus, if you're going to pursue this level of protection against Year-2000 failures, you're probably going to need the products from one or more food-supply or food-packaging companies. You'll need to do some research in the library or on the Internet to find such companies, because many of them are relatively small; when we searched the World Wide Web to find a list of such suppliers, we discovered that fully a third of the ones listed had gone bankrupt or disappeared. However, here are three that you can contact for information:

- Walton Feed, 135 North 10th, PO Box 307, Montpelier, ID 83254; phone (800) 269-8563; Internet/Web address: http://www.waltonfeed.com

- Carol's Survival Foods; accessible via e-mail at survival@vegasnet.net; Internet/Web address: http://webcube.vegasnet.net/~survival/

- The Sallin Group; Internet/Web address:
  http://www.volcano.net/~good4u/ foodresv.htm

Most emergency food suppliers assume that a one-year supply will include a substantial amount of corn, wheat, rice, and
beans; thus, it's likely that to use these supplies, you'll need to
be willing to bake your own bread, as well as cook meals that
are probably much simpler than the meals you now enjoy.

As noted above, planning for this kind of Year-2000 contingency is not easy, particularly because it's likely to create scorn,
ridicule, and merciless teasing on the part of your friends and
neighbors. It's also more expensive—a one-year food package
for an individual adult is likely to cost $700-$1,000, depending on the supplier—and it obviously takes much more storage than the two-day or one-month options listed above. But
it *can* be done; the question is simply whether you feel the risk
warrants such action.

Fallback Advice: Ten-Year Failures

A ten-year disruption in the food supply only makes sense if
you're willing to assume that almost all of the other problems
areas discussed in this book have occurred in their most serious form. If the phone system, transportation system, governmental systems, electrical utilities, and all other aspects of our
socio-economic system were to utterly collapse because of
computer failures, we would be reduced to an agricultural
society reminiscent of America in the mid-nineteenth century.
There might be a few pockets of "advanced" civilization, but
in this scenario, everyone else would be back on the farm.
We're concerned, and occasionally pessimistic about the outcome of the Year-2000 problem, but not *that* pessimistic.

However, it does occur to us from time to time that this scenario describes the current state of China fairly accurately. Wouldn't it be ironic if China escaped most of the Year-2000 problems because of its agrarian society, and the U.S.—because of its extreme dependence on computers—was reduced to the level of China's economy?

Endnotes

1. Samuel Johnson, quoted in James Boswell, *Life of Samuel Johnson*, August 5, 1763 (published in 1791).

2. Bill Bryson, *The Lost Continent: Travels in Small Town America*, Chapter 3 (1989).

3. We should also note that the ripple effect might cause problems beyond those of food delivery. The August 8, 1997 issue of *Computerworld* reported that "a Michigan produce store has filed what is believed to be the first year 2000-related lawsuit because its cash registers freeze when customers use credit cards with year 2000 expiration dates. Produce Palace International in Warren Mich. recently sued Tec-America Corp in Atlanta and local service vendor All American Cash Register Inc.... claiming the companies sold a defective computer system they knew they couldn't fix."

4. However, it's becoming increasingly common to see EDI (Electronic Data Interchange) as the mechanism for communicating an order to a supplier. This is especially true for chains of stores, in which the items to be restocked are transmitted (by computer) from each store to a central headquarters; the aggregate order is then transmitted by computer to the supplier. As of autumn 1997, when this book was being finalized, the EDI software suppliers were still unsure about how they would handle the various details of standardizing and communicating Year-2000-compliant dates to one another.

5. Although Montana is not usually known for its wine or beer, it turns out that there's a vineyard on the shores of the same lake, which produces a decent Cabernet and Chardonnay; and, there are numerous local micro-breweries. Fortified with enough alcohol, perhaps one would not even miss the food delicacies from other parts of the country!

6. On the other hand, some religious groups have long advocated stockpiling food for unforeseen emergencies. Thus, at least a portion of the U.S. population may be well-prepared, even though they would never have guessed it was a Year-2000 computer problem that would be the source of the problem.

Year-2000 Impact
on Your Home PC

*Electronic aids, particularly domestic computers, will help
the inner migration, the opting out of reality. Reality is no
longer going to be the stuff out there, but the stuff inside your
head. It's going to be commercial and nasty at the same time.*

J. G. Ballard, interview in Heavy Metal *(April 1971;
reprinted in* Re/Search, *no. 8/9, San Francisco, 1984).*

Introduction

In preparing this book, we were intrigued by the number of
non-technical friends and colleagues whose first question about
the Year-2000 problem was, "What about my home PC?" We
were puzzled by the frequency of the question, because only half
of U.S. households have a PC at all, and in most cases, the PC is
used for games, children's homework, or for writing an occasional letter. While these are pleasant, and often even useful,
activities, they hardly seem as fundamental and important as
most of the other topics discussed in this book.

Nevertheless, people *are* interested in the potential impact
of Year-2000 problems on their home PC; perhaps it's just
because the PC represents a significant investment. Most people are vaguely aware that they really haven't learned how to
exploit all of the power and potential of their PC, and perhaps

they worry that it's their own lack of technical skills that will render their PC inoperable on January 1, 2000.

However, there are a few people—particularly the ones who use computers all day long in their office—for whom the home PC is just as important as the automobile. One of the authors uses his PC to organize most of his life, and often jokes that if the computer was stolen, he would have to commit suicide. Such people often have a backup PC in case of serious hardware problems, and are diligent about making daily backups of important data, and monthly archival backups that are stored in the local bank's safety deposit box, along with birth certificates and other important documents.

We'll assume that most readers of this book are not quite *that* fanatical about their computers, but we'll also assume that for more and more individuals and families, the home PC is becoming an important "appliance." Perhaps it's not quite as important as the family car, but its absence would create a moderate degree of discomfort. That being the case, let's turn to the fundamental question: Are home PCs vulnerable to the Year-2000 problem?

The answer is: "It depends." For those using relatively new computers (i.e., purchased within the last two or three years) and who carry out relatively simple, mundane functions (e.g., writing school reports with a simple word processor), there should be no problem at all. But for those using older computers, and also for those using very elaborate, sophisticated software applications on their PC, there's a much higher likelihood of Year-2000-related problems.

It's important to realize that the situation is *not* entirely black-and-white, even though many spokesmen for the PC industry have made unilateral statements to the effect that *nothing* about PCs is vulnerable to the Year-2000 problem.

Articles in popular magazines and newspapers have contributed to the confusion by strongly implying that Year-2000 problems *only* exist in mainframe COBOL programs written 25 years ago by Neanderthal programmers. The reality is that the problems can occur anywhere, anytime, on any machine; indeed, while this chapter was being written in the summer of 1997, a Year-2000 problem was reported in one of the very newest of PC-style programming languages, Javascript.[1]

In case you don't find this sufficiently convincing, consider the following commentary from Karl Fielder,[2] whose company, Greenwich Mean Time, specializes in Year-2000 work:

> *Greenwich Mean Time has now checked more than 4,000 microcomputer programs (including some on the shelves today) and has found some alarming figures:*
>
> - *28 percent of the programs with Year-2000 date failures were claimed by their manufacturers to be Year-2000 compliant.*
>
> - *21 percent of development tools were capable, in their normally installed configuration, of creating non-compliant programs.*
>
> - *20 percent of the programs use a date windowing technique to expand YY to YYYY, and these date windows are mostly different and are not changeable by the end user. [See Appendix A for a discussion of the "window" approach fixing Year-2000 problems.]*
>
> - *4 percent don't know 2000 is a leap year.*
>
> - *4 percent will only run during the 20th century*

To fully understand the range of Year-2000 problems that might affect your PC at home, we need to talk about the hardware, operating system, and application programs. The same areas of vulnerability exist on older mainframe computers, by the way, but we've concentrated our mainframe discussions throughout this book only on the application programs, since the hardware and operating system are largely "invisible" to the external user or customer. This is not the case for PCs. You're responsible for your own hardware; you may have a choice about which operating system you use; and you definitely have a choice about which application programs you use.

There are dozens, if not hundreds, of different types of PCs in the marketplace, but the overwhelming majority fall into two categories: Intel-based computers with DOS or Windows operating systems, and Apple Macintosh computers with the MacOS operating system. If you're still using an Apple II, an Atari 400, or a TRS-80 Radio Shack machine, you'll have to investigate the situation based on the guidelines and discussion below; but, there's a good chance that you're in trouble, simply because those machines are so old that they probably have not incorporated Year-2000-compliant features.

Hardware Vulnerability

The first area of Year-2000 vulnerability has to do with the hardware and "firmware" on your computer, especially the part which keeps track of the time. Almost all home PCs have an internal hardware time-of-day clock that "ticks" at the rate of once a second, or perhaps as frequently as 60 times per second. The clock can be accessed and/or updated by a low-level part of the computer called the BIOS (for "Basic Input-Output System"), and can then be used in whatever date calculations or displays are required by the operating system or other parts of the computer.

The problem is that the hardware clock and/or the BIOS logic in some of the older computers is *not* Year-2000-compliant. On January 1, 2000, the hardware clock (sometimes referred to as a "Real Time Clock," or RTC) will roll over, or "wrap around," to either January 1, 2000 or January 1, 1900, depending on the make and model of the computer. This may not be immediately apparent to you, because the calendar display on your computer screen may show 01-01-00; but internally, the date may be incorrect, and the problem will eventually manifest itself in the operating system or the various application programs on your computer.

As noted earlier, the hardware clock is accessed by the computer's BIOS. Karl Fielder, whose comments about microcomputer programs were cited above, has this to say about BIOS problems:[3]

> *GMT also checked some 500 different BIOSs and found:*
> - *BIOS test results vary from PC to PC, even between BIOS versions which seem to be identical in name and date.*
> - *Pre-1997 BIOSs failed in 93 percent of those machines tested.*
> - *1997 BIOSs failed in 47 percent of those machines tested.*

As mentioned earlier, this problem exists most commonly in the older computers, especially the Intel-based machines built prior to 1996. As far as we have been able to tell, none of the Macintosh computers have this kind of rollover problem at the hardware level (which does *not* necessarily mean that Mac applications are safe). As for the various other kinds of computers, you'll have to test them yourself. A common way of doing this (after you have safely backed up whatever files are important to you!) is to manually reset the system clock on your computer to 11:59 PM on December 31, 1999 and then wait to see what happens a minute later. If it appears that the Year-2000 rollover has worked correctly, then repeat the experiment—but turn your computer off after you've set the clock to 11:59 PM on December 31, 1999; wait a few minutes, and power the machine back on again.[4]

If it turns out that your computer does have a hardware and/or BIOS problem, you may be able to get a replacement at little or no cost. BIOS upgrades are typically available free from the vendor, and a replacement clock is likely to cost only a few dollars. The biggest problem will be that the hardware vendors are not very interested in servicing and repairing vintage 1983 PCs anymore, nor are the local computer stores. You may have to shop around, read through the back pages of various computer magazines, and talk to your friends. For obvious reasons, it's strongly recommended that you do this *now*, rather than waiting until December 29, 1999.

Operating System Vulnerability

As noted above, the hardware and associated BIOS logic in a PC can be interrogated to read the current time of day, and/or updated to change the date/time information stored by the computer. In most cases, this is accomplished by the operating system on the computer—e.g., MS-DOS, Windows, or OS/2 on an Intel-based PC; or MacOS on various Macintosh computers. Thus, even if the hardware and BIOS are Year-2000-compliant, the operating system may inject its own Year-2000 errors. As a corollary, since end-users (i.e., people like you and us) primarily interact with the operating system to accomplish the time/calendar functions, it's not always clear where the fault lies when a Year-2000 problem emerges. All you know is that the wrong date is showing on the display screen; you don't know (and probably don't care) where the problem originated.

That being said, here's the bad news: Most of the older versions of Microsoft's MS-DOS and MS Windows 3.1 operating systems will perform a Year-2000 rollover to January 4, 1980. The good news is that Microsoft Windows 95, Windows NT, and Apple's MacOS operating systems are fully Year-2000-compliant. Thus, if your home PC environment involves relatively new hardware (e.g., a Pentium-based computer or a Mac

PowerPC) and an up-to-date operating system, you're probably safe. But if you're still running on an old 286- or 386-class Intel computer, and if you're still running DOS or Windows 3.1, you may be in trouble.

What kind of trouble? Well, most of the problems will be manifested in the application programs that you run *on top* of the operating system—e.g., the word processor, spreadsheet, home accounting programs, etc. But it's possible that you could run into some problems at the operating system level, particularly with file manipulation commands. For example, suppose that on the morning of January 1, you fire up the word processor on your PC and dash off a few letters to your friends and relatives. Each of the letters would typically be stored on your computer as a separate file, and the operating system would automatically record the date and time that the file was created, as well as the date and time of last modification.

Perhaps you've decided to keep all of these word processing files in a directory (or "folder," depending on the vocabulary of your computer and operating system) called LETTERS. From time to time, perhaps you ask the operating system to display a list of all the documents (e.g., with the MS-DOS operating system, you would type a DIR command), so that you can clean up the contents of the directory/folder by deleting old documents. In fact, if you're a bit more clever than the typical home PC user, you might even have constructed a "script" or "batch file" to accomplish this clean-up operation automatically, each time you turn on the computer. The problem, of course, is that the Year-2000 problem causes a file whose *actual* creation date was January 1, 2000 to have an *apparent* creation date of January 4, 1980. Thus, your newly created files will appear older than the ones created in 1999—and they may thus be inadvertently deleted.[5]

If you do experience problems of this kind, don't expect a lot of sympathy from Microsoft, or from the company from whom you bought the computer. Their attitude is that you shouldn't be using an old computer and/or an old operating system. As far as they're concerned, they've solved the Year-2000 problem (and thus absolved themselves of any responsibility) by providing newer computers and newer operating systems. The fact that you can't afford to upgrade your computer, or that you don't want to upgrade your computer, is considered *your* problem, not *their* problem. *Caveat emptor!*

This may sound more critical of the manufacturers and computer stores than is appropriate, and we don't mean to imply that any of these organizations are malicious or dishonest. It's important to remember that the overwhelming majority of PC computers are sold to business organizations, not homes; and business organizations are far more likely to replace their computers every two or three years, thus creating the impression in the minds of the vendors that *everyone* does so. The individuals who work at Intel, Microsoft, IBM, Apple, and other computer organizations are generally well-paid technocrats; they replace their own home computers every couple of years (assuming their employer doesn't give them a new machine for free!), and they tend to assume that even a household with a modest income will do the same. While this might be the case if home computers cost only a hundred dollars, most middle-income families feel that a $2,000 investment in a home computer is *not* something they intend to do on an annual basis!

Remember also that we're talking about a problem that will manifest itself on January 1, 2000. While there might be a good argument for continuing to operate a DOS- or Windows 3.1 system in 1997 or even 1998, the argument becomes less and less persuasive as time goes on. An old Intel 386 computer purchased in 1992 with 640K bytes of memory and an ancient version of DOS will be quite antiquated by late 1999. Technically, such a computer *should* continue to work after the beginning of the new millennium; but the practical reality is that you won't get any sympathy from the companies who built that computer. It would be like complaining to Ford Motor Company that you're very upset that they don't stock replacement parts for their Model-T cars anymore.

Application Vulnerability

Though Year-2000 problems can certainly occur at the hardware, BIOS, or operating system level, any computer purchased in the latter half of the 1990s probably won't experience these problems. But the newer computers *are* still vulnerable because most of the computational processing is done at the "application level," above the operating system and hardware. That is, most end-users spend less and less time interacting with the operating system on their computer, and progressively more time interacting with their word processor, spreadsheet program, home banking system, or Internet Web browser.

Depending on the programs, and the underlying nature of the applications themselves, these applications may or may not be date-sensitive. Any application program that wants to deal with a date will typically do so by sending a request to the operating system (which interrogates the BIOS logic that reads the hardware clock); the application program might then display the date on your computer screen, or print it in a report, or store it in a database record. At this level, the variety of operations is as vast as in the mainframe world; it's hard to know whether you're vulnerable to a Year-2000 problem unless you investigate the various applications that you use on your computer. One of the authors, while working on this chapter, took a quick look at the contents of his PC, and found some 75 distinct application programs; any one of those programs might turn out to be non-Year-2000 compliant.

How could this happen? Quite simply, even if the operating system provides a legitimate date with a four-digit year field, there's no guarantee that an application program will use it. For reasons of efficiency, sloppiness, or downright ignorance, the programmers who created some of your favorite applications may have decided to truncate the high-order two digits of the year, and to carry out all subsequent processing with a two-digit year field—thus creating the famous Year-2000 problem.

In a recent article, consultants Joe Celko and Jackie Celko described the Year-2000 problems with the popular home-accounting system Quicken—specifically Quicken version 3 (which is not the latest version) running on MS-DOS version 6.[6] They also listed a few other culprits:

> Other PC applications known to exhibit the year 2000 difficulties include Microsoft Access, FoxPro, and Visual Basic; CA Clipper; Borland Delphi; Gupta SQLbase; and Oracle. Fixes or workarounds for many of them are widely available as freeware.

As with most things, the 80/20 rule applies here: Chances are that 80% of the activity on your computer involves only 20% of the application programs. It's likely to be your word processor, your home finance system, the e-mail program, and a few popular games that present problems. Those are the ones you should check first for Year-2000 compliance; and depending on the outcome, you can then determine how much disruption would be caused by Year-2000-related problems in those programs. This is a simplistic version of the "triage" strategy now being employed by large businesses. There are a few applications that may be absolutely essential to one's survival, though that is less likely for a home PC than for a business computer; in other words, there may be some applications that are "important," in the sense that we depend heavily on them, and would find it very expensive and difficult to do without. And then there are the non-essential programs, like the PC games. While one's children might suffer temporary withdrawal symptoms from being deprived of their alien-invader games, it's not likely to have any lasting consequences.

The one nice thing about this aspect of Year-2000 planning is that it probably won't cost you any money at all. As the Celkos note in their *Byte* article, fixes or workarounds can usually be obtained at no cost. The easiest way to get these solutions is from the vendor's Internet site (e.g., Microsoft's Year-2000 "frequently asked questions" page at http://www.microsoft.com/cio/articles/year2000faq.htm), but you should also be able to call the vendor's Customer Service department for assistance. However, there is a situation in which you won't be able to get away with a free update: If you have a very old version of the vendor's product, you may be instructed to upgrade to the latest (Year-2000-compliant) version; this is likely to cost $30–50, and it might even require additional memory or disk storage on your computer.

Things are worse, of course, if you call the vendor and find that the phone has been disconnected—i.e., they've gone bankrupt. This is particularly common with some of the older computer games; but, there are many other "standard" applications—word processors, spreadsheets, database packages, calendar programs, etc.—that were built by innovative little startup companies in the mid-1980s who finally had to concede that they couldn't compete against the software giants. If this happens to you, you'll be in a position to empathize more closely with the large corporate IT departments: this is exactly the problem they face, but on a larger scale. In your case, you have no option but to find a newer software package, produced by a company that will hopefully still be in business in the post-2000 years. The sooner you begin this process, the easier it will be.

We Have Met the Enemy, and He Is Us

There is one last category of Year-2000 problems to discuss here: applications written by end-users. For the millions of desktop and laptop computers within business organizations, this is where the *real* chaos will occur on January 1, 2000. The problems associated with the hardware, operating system, and "standard" applications from vendors like IBM and Microsoft are identifiable and manageable. But the budget-forecasting spreadsheets created in Excel or Lotus by a long-departed accountant, or the sales-territory database created in FoxPro or dBase-IV by a junior assistant in the Marketing department, are like mines left on a battlefield after the war is over. Nobody knows how many there are, or where they have been buried. All we know is that if anyone steps on them, it will be a terminal experience.

It's far less likely that we'll see a lot of problems of this sort for the home PC—except in the case of the PC being used to support a serious hobby, or a part-time business. If you're a stamp collector, you may have created a database of all your stamps using Microsoft Access or some other popular database package. If you're a freelance writer, you may have constructed a simple spreadsheet to keep track of your proposals, queries, payments, royalties, and related expenses using Microsoft Access or Lotus 1-2-3. And even if those vendor-supplied application packages are fully Year-2000-compliant, you may have innocently created your own Year-2000 problems by storing date-related information with a two-digit year.

This point needs to be emphasized: Not all of the dates in an application program are time-of-day information read from the computer's hardware clock; many of them are manually entered dates. Your database of rare stamps, for example, may include the date when you acquired the stamp and the date when you sold or traded it for some other stamp; chances are that those pieces of information will have been manually entered, rather than entered automatically. You may have informed the database program that a certain "field" of data was intended to contain date-related information (to prevent yourself from accidentally typing a telephone number into that field), and it's possible that the database program will then use that knowledge to force you to type in a date in YYYY-MM-DD format; but, it's just as likely that you were sloppy and provided no such clue to the database program at all (in which case, the field would have been defined as a "text" or "alphanumeric" field, which does provide the convenience of allowing you to express a date as "the day before Christmas, on the year before I got married").

Obviously, if you have this category of Year-2000 problem, nobody is going to be sympathetic; it is, in the final analysis, *your* problem. And the situation you face is similar to that being faced today by business organizations: You need to begin by investigating your own home-grown applications to see if they *are* Year-2000-compliant, and you need to fix them in the remaining months before the decade comes to an end. Most people have few, if any, such applications—and as a result, they may decide to wait until late 1999 to tackle the job. A few are beginning to realize that it's a big job, and that they'd better start now.

Fallback Suggestions—The Two-Day Failure

All of the advice above is proactive in exactly the same nature being carried out by business organizations facing their own Year-2000 problem: Analyze your hardware and software to see if the problem exists, and then take appropriate steps to upgrade defective components, or to replace defunct software with entirely new software.

But the whole premise of this book is that businesses won't be 100% successful, no matter how hard they try, because there are too many complexities and uncertainties. We could take a more optimistic stance towards home computers—simply because they're much less complex, and because you're likely to be much less dependent on them. However, for the sake of discussion, let's assume the "downside" scenario—suppose that even with the precautions described above, things go slightly haywire when you turn on your PC on January 1, 2000.

If it's a minor problem that prevents you from using the computer for two or three days, you probably won't be too concerned. The problem, though, is that if your computer begins spewing out gibberish on January 1, 2000, you may not be able to tell whether it's a minor problem that will require a day or two to fix, or a more serious problem of the kind discussed below.

Thus, the first piece of advice is: Make sure you have a backup of all your important data on a floppy disk, a magnetic tape cartridge, or some other reliable storage medium. Second, make a hard-copy printout of any information that you might need from your computer—e.g., copies of your resume, your favorite recipes, the mailing list of your family and friends, etc.

By the way, note that a problem of this magnitude could occur for a reason that's not the fault of the computer. As discussed in Chapter 3, electrical power might be out for a day or two. Thus, if you really *must* use a computer 8-hours-a-day, 7-days-a-week (which is definitely the case for one of the authors), you should also ensure that you have backup power, typically in the form of batteries, and that the batteries are fully charged. This may prove awkward for standard desktop computers, for which the readily available equipment provides protection against power surges and spikes, but not long-term power outage. Owners of laptop computers, though, may find their batteries to be especially useful during a brief Year-2000-induced power failure.

Fallback Suggestions—The One-Month Failure

Suppose the problem is more serious: An important program on your PC turns out *not* to be Year-2000-compliant, and because of the backlog and confusion, the vendor tells you that it will be a month before an updated version can be shipped to you. Or, it turns out that the BIOS in your computer is defective, and it will take a month to have it replaced with a new BIOS. What then?

If it's a software problem, and if you're dependent on that particular piece of software, you have no alternative but to wait. But, you might also have the option of switching to an equivalent software package that *is* Year-2000-compliant. You should have checked out all of these details *before* December 31, 1999, of course, but that advice will no longer be particularly useful as of January 1, 2000. Thus, some people may find, perhaps to their enormous surprise, that their favorite word processor no longer works; whether they like it or not (and people *do* become quite attached to version N of word processor X), they may have to switch. In almost all cases, this is nothing more than an inconvenience, because any competent word processing package can import documents produced by any other word processor. But if you're using a specialized program that creates its own database (e.g., a name-and-address mailing list database of your friends and business contacts), it might be more difficult to export that data to another program.

In any case, the biggest problem here is similar to that mentioned in the "minor" category above: If your computer is down for a month, you may not know whether it really *will* be up and running a month later, or whether things will deteriorate further into the one-year category. Maybe the software vendor will be so overwhelmed by its Year-2000 problems that it goes bankrupt; maybe the local computer store that promised to help you obtain and install a new BIOS will renege on its promise—and in the worst case, it too might go bankrupt, with your defective computer locked in its office.

So, if you think this level of difficulty could occur, our strong advice is to ensure that you have a *complete* backup of *everything* on your computer. You probably have a backup of all the programs—i.e., the original "master" copies of the programs, on CD-ROM or floppy disk, when you first purchased your machine. (If you've lost the floppies or CD-ROM, get a replacement now, while things are still relatively calm!) And you'll need to make a copy of *all* the documents, files, and data you care about, because you may need to "port" your entire computing environment to a brand-new machine, if things can't be fixed and restored within a month.

Fallback Suggestions—The One-Year Failure

The family that purchased a home computer as an amusing curiosity may not be particularly concerned about the prospect of a one-year disruption. The authors have friends who are already saying, "We bought that stupid computer for our kids to do their homework, but after they played a few space-invader games, they said it was more boring than the video games down at the local candy store. And we were planning to put our budget on the computer, but it turned out to be too much work, and the computer is too hard to use. So the damn thing is just sitting there, gathering dust." If that's the situation, then who cares if the mothballed computer has a serious Year-2000 problem?

But if you're using the computer actively—for school homework, household budgeting, e-mail, or for writing the Great American Novel—then a year is an unacceptable amount of time to wait for a repair. If you have followed our advice and backed up all of your programs and data before January 1, 2000, and if your computer has such serious problems that a one-year delay seems likely, then the most sensible thing to do is acquire a new computer that *is* Year-2000-compliant, and donate the old one to charity, assuming it ever works again.

We realize, of course, that this will be an economically unattractive option for middle-income families with tight budgets; for some families, the stark reality is that they'll have to retreat back to their pre-computing days, when people used typewriters, paper, and pencils. It's simply a question of priorities. For some families, the home computer has become almost as important and indispensable as the family car. If it breaks and can't be repaired in a reasonable time, then there's not much choice but to replace it.

Fallback Suggestions—The Ten-Year Failure

This last scenario is entirely irrelevant for most people in the U.S., and we've included it here primarily so that we can follow the same pattern you've seen in other chapters. However, in the computer field, it's common to hear technical people speaking of "dog years"—things change and improve so quickly that one year of calendar time in the computer field is almost like seven years in any other field.

The point to remember is that the newest home computers *do* have Year-2000-compliant hardware and BIOSs, and the latest versions of operating systems are Year-2000-compliant.[7] The application programs will eventually be updated to become Year-2000-compliant, even if a few companies go bankrupt in the process, and things will eventually get back to normal. Assuming that the manufacturing capabilities of the major computer companies hasn't been destroyed by their own Year-2000 problems, the computer industry will be happily producing Year-2000-compliant systems for all of us to buy. Even if we had to throw away all of our pre-2000 computers and start all over again, it would only take a few years—indeed, most businesses are already prepared to throw their computers away every few years, because the technology changes so quickly.

There's only one area where this argument makes no sense: the Third World and "emerging" countries that, in many cases, are using hand-me-down computers they've acquired from Western countries. The 10-year-old computer that most Americans would sneer at is still quite useful in much of Africa and other poverty-stricken regions of the world. It's sobering to realize that a university-educated computer programmer in India is likely to be making only $4,000 U.S. per year; thus, a typical, well-equipped home computer is likely to represent a substantial portion of a year's salary. Meanwhile, the school in a rural Indian village may have only installed electricity a few years ago, and barely has the budget to spend $100 for an old vintage-1986 computer that Americans would have thrown in their trash heap. In *that* kind of environment, if it turns out that the majority of "legacy" home computers are Year-2000-impaired, it's conceivable that a decade could go by before replacement computers could be afforded.

On the other hand, it's precisely *because* of this situation that many of these societies are perfectly capable of operating without computers at all—in the home or in the business. The abacus is still a widely-used computing device, and it doesn't require electricity! So the ultimate irony would be to find that the Third World countries actually survive better than we do, because they have no home computers to worry about!

Endnotes

1. "Javascript Hits Snag—Developers Face Year-2000 Headaches," *Infoworld*, July 10, 1997. The problem affects both Netscape's JavaScript 1.1 and Microsoft's Jscript. According to the article, "The InfoWorld Test Center tested date objects in JavaScript in Netscape's and Microsoft's [Web] browsers and found inconsistencies in the documentation and implementation of the scripting language."

2. Karl Fielder, "PCs Not a Problem—Think Again!" *Year/2000 Journal*, Vol. 1, No. 3, p. 6.

3. There is ongoing debate among Year-2000 technical experts about the consistency and credibility of some of the BIOS-checking programs. In addition to Mr. Fielder's organization, you can find additional information on BIOS-checkers on the Internet at http://www.rightime.com and http://www.solace.co.uk.

4. Before you do this, make sure that you have performed a backup of any important files and documents on your computer.

5. Les Holmes <designer@wsnet.com>, who was understandably annoyed when he found several glaring technical inaccuracies in the first draft of our book, responded to our concerns about the display of files in a computer directory: "If you bothered to try experimenting with the situation in Windows 3, you would find that (assuming you went to the terrible trouble of setting the RTC using the DOS DATE command [8 seconds or so]), while the file date display may leave

something to be desired, newly created files sort properly." We concede the point, but we're not convinced that many lay computer users will remember (or will know how) to use the DOS DATE command.

6. Joe Celko and Jackie Celko, "Double Zero," *Byte*, July 1997, p. 90.

7. However, if you're using the UNIX operating system, then you have another problem to worry about—the Year-2038 problem. UNIX keeps track of time with an internal memory register that is Year-2000-compliant, but it will roll over to zero sometime in the year 2038. We haven't bothered talking about it in this book because it's not relevant to most readers. However, it's just that kind of attitude—i.e., the problem is so far in the future that we don't have to worry about it—that caused the Year-2000 problem in the first place!

Year-2000 Impact on News and Information

The greatest felony in the news business today is to be behind, or to miss a big story. So speed and quantity substitute for thoroughness and quality, for accuracy and context. The pressure to compete, the fear somebody else will make the splash first, creates a frenzied environment in which a blizzard of information is presented and serious questions may not be raised.

Carl Bernstein, Guardian *(London, June 3, 1992).*

Introduction

During the writing of this book, one of the authors spent the summer in a small town in Montana, where "getting the news" meant watching the first seven minutes of the *Today* shows on television and reading the weekly town newspaper. The former consisted of brief sound-bites about events so far away they seemed irrelevant; and the latter consisted of front-page reports of the contestants in the annual rodeo.

Meanwhile, the other author spent the summer working in New York City, where news is considered as stale as yesterday's oatmeal when it's only a few seconds old. Not only does everyone in Manhattan seem to be both aware and concerned about the latest scandals, fashions, and sports events, but the Wall Street community experiences financial paroxysms within sec-

207

onds after the announcement of a change in the unemployment rate of Germany or the Japanese Prime Minister's
pronouncements about the strength of the yen.

In Montana, it's not clear that a Year-2000-induced disruption in the delivery of news would even be noticed, or that it
would have a great deal of impact on the day-to-day lives of its
citizens. By contrast, news is the lubricant that greases the
machinery of Manhattan; if the news stops, many of its citizens would have great difficulty carrying out their day-to-day
jobs. And since the news is carried on the same media as the
primary entertainment media—TV and radio—many of its
citizens would have no idea what to do with their time when
they got home from work in the evening.

Thus, it's hard to tell how much emphasis to put on Year-
2000 failures in this area of society; it matters a lot to some, but
only a little to others. The notion that there could actually be a
Year-2000-induced disruption in the delivery of news should
not be a large surprise at this point. We'll discuss briefly how this
could happen in the realm of TV and radio, as well as the substantially different medium of newspapers and magazines.[1]
Then we'll provide our usual list of guidelines for dealing with
two-day, one-month, one-year, and ten-year disruptions.

Television and Radio

At first glance, television and radio would seem to be
immune to the problems of many other utilities and services:
they're free, and they're delivered over the air-waves to anyone
who wants to tune in. Thus, it doesn't have to be addressed to
a specific person, and we don't have to worry about Year-2000-
vulnerable computers getting into trouble when they carry out
their billing operations.

There is one major exception to this optimistic view: cable TV. Whether it's associated with a satellite dish or a cable brought to the door, roughly 60 million Americans are dependent on the likes of TCI and other cable giants to bring a clear, sharp TV channel into the house.[2] We pay $20-50 per month, on average, for the privilege of having a set-top box and a remote-control unit that allows us to surf through hundreds of channels, so that we can watch Dan Rather *and* Tom Brokaw *and* Peter Jennings each night. If we don't pay the bill, the cable TV company shuts off our service; thus, the Year-2000 problems in this area will be similar to the ones discussed in Chapters 3 and 14.

For the remainder of this chapter, though, we'll assume that people are receiving their news broadcasts over "free" channels. Here are the other major areas where Year-2000 bugs could disrupt TV/radio news:

- *Broadcasting and distribution of the material*—The news is typically recorded by microphone or TV camera, mixed and edited in a control room, transmitted via satellite or telephone line to local stations, and then broadcast over a transmitter. Some of these operations are manual (after all, there were news broadcasts in the pre-1950 days when only the Defense Department had computers!), but many of them are heavily computerized. Much of the equipment contains embedded computers (which we'll discuss in more detail in Chapter 11), and much of the news content is "time-stamped" for archiving and retrieval purposes, and also so that it can be transmitted properly to areas of the country with different time zones. Thus, dates are very much involved in all of this, and Year-2000 bugs can certainly exist.

- *Bringing the news broadcasters into the studios—* We noted in Chapter 4 that airplanes can't fly without their crew; the same situation applies here. Entertainment shows can be "canned" and re-broadcast, as we all know, but most of the news that we watch or listen to is delivered by a live human. No human, no news.

- *Getting the news content from the "field" to the studio—*The authors sometimes wonder whether news broadcasters spend their entire lives in insulated broadcasting booths, inventing whatever news they feel like broadcasting—it certainly seems that way with weather reporters, who will tell you that it's sunny when a casual glance outside would confirm that it's pouring. In any case, aside from the occasional editorial commentary created in the studio by the news team, most of the "real" news occurs "in the field"—e.g., in Bosnia, Washington, or even Missoula, Montana. This has to be captured by on-the-scene correspondents, who transmit the appropriate information by telephone, satellite, telex, fax, or some other form to the studio. Many American citizens were awed by the live coverage provided by on-the-scene reporters in Baghdad during the Persian Gulf War in the early 1990s. This would have been impossible without the sophisticated satellite-supported transmission system. Recall the Chapter 4 discussion about the upcoming problems with the GPS navigation system; we can only hope these problems are fixed before the rest of the Year-2000 chaos engulfs us. In any case, the conclusion is simple and obvious: With no telephone or satellite connections, "live" news reports from the field become nearly impossible.

• *Managing the commercials that pay for the broadcasts*—It's no secret that what pays for almost all TV and radio broadcasting, including the news, is commercial messages from sponsors. It's true that most cities have a "public" TV station supported by contributions and government grants; and it's true that National Public Radio (NPR) provides a superb news reporting service without the usual commercial entanglements. But these are not the primary sources of news information, and we wonder how long they would continue receiving contributions and grants in a post-2000 world. In any case, the main sources of news are subsidized by commercial messages, which are marketed by the broadcasting organizations, and carefully scheduled and synchronized to fit appropriately into the rest of the broadcasting schedule. This entire activity, as you might have guessed, is also heavily computerized—and the software that manages it depends heavily on date calculations. The immediate consequence of a Year-2000 failure in this area might be commercial-free broadcasting, which most of us would consider a blessing; but with no commercials, there is no revenue.

And if there is no revenue, then the TV and radio stations can't afford to continue operations. A two-day disruption would be annoying, but not fatal; if the problems escalate to the one-month or one-year level, it probably *will* be fatal, especially for the smaller broadcasting stations.[3]

Newspapers and Magazines

Newspapers and magazines form the other major source of news for many of us; and while these "hard-copy" publications may seem rather low-tech, and thus impervious to Year-2000 failures, the reality is quite different.

Many of us receive such publications on a subscription basis. We pay in advance, and the publication arrives in our mailbox on a regular schedule. Thus, the Year-2000-related invoicing and billing problems that we've mentioned throughout the book could be relevant here. However, if *Newsweek* and the *New York Times* refuse to deliver their publications to us for alleged lack of payment, we always have the option of going to the local newsstand or magazine store to purchase a copy.

This assumes, of course, that the publishers can keep their distribution network functioning. As with the discussion of food distribution in Chapter 6, magazines and newspapers are delivered to retail outlets through a complex network of planes, trains, and trucks; if something goes wrong with this mechanism, the publications won't arrive. The situation is compounded by the fact that many publications—especially the larger newspapers like *USA Today* and the *Wall Street Journal*—are created in one location, and then broadcast electronically to various locations around the country (and around the world) for local printing and distribution. Thus, newspapers (and in a few rare instances, magazines too) are dependent upon the satellite and telecommunications network for distributing their product.

Magazines and newspapers are also dependent upon the telecommunications network for receiving news reports from the field. In this case, we're not dealing with quite the same degree of real-time immediacy that the television stations achieve—but if the satellites or telephone systems are down for a day, there may not be *any* news that the *New York Times* considers fit to print.

Similarly, magazines and newspapers depend upon advertisements for the bulk of their revenues, just like television stations depend on commercials. The advertising material is delivered in a variety of forms to the publishers, and much of this is also computer-dependent. As noted above, the issue of "immediacy" is a little different than it is for TV commercials; a newspaper might be able to hold its printing run for an hour or two until its biggest advertiser manages to deliver the copy and graphic layout for an expensive full-page advertisement. But whether it's a daily, weekly, or monthly publication, the degree to which the advertising "system" depends on computers determines the degree of vulnerability to Year-2000 problems.

Finally, there's the question of how newspapers and magazines will be affected in their production and printing operations. The era of manual typesetting has long since disappeared; today's publications are partially, if not wholly, dependent upon computers for phototypesetting, page composition, graphic design, and a host of other production details. For the larger publications, this often involves very expensive, specialized computer equipment. It would require a case-by-case analysis to determine whether these machines are Year-2000-compliant. On the other hand, it's intriguing to see how many magazines and smaller newspapers are composed and printed with the same desktop PCs and laser printers that many of us use in our office or at home. They may be somewhat bigger, and they may have more RAM, a bigger display screen, and a higher-resolution printer, but they still use the same operating systems and page layout systems (e.g., Quark Xpress, PageMaker, Ventura, etc.) that we use for the church newsletter that we produce on our home computer. As we saw in Chapter 7, these computers are indeed vulnerable to Year-2000 problems.

Finally, newspapers and magazines require large quantities of paper, ink, dyes, glue, and other materials. Some of this can be stockpiled, but in many cases (particularly paper), it's so bulky and expensive that the publishers acquire it on a "just-in-time" basis. This leads to another potential Year-2000 problem: If the paper companies and ink manufacturers can't get their raw materials to publishers in time, there will be no publications.

Fallback Advice—Two-Day, One-Month, One-Year, and Ten-Year Failures

As noted above, a two-day disruption in news delivery wouldn't even be noticed by some Americans, nor would it cause any serious inconvenience. Ironically, there might be an exception in the early days of the new millennium: If as many things begin breaking down as we've suggested in this book, it might become *very* important to get the latest news about disruptions in transportation, banking, government services, etc.

In any case, if the prospect of a two-day news blackout worries you, what should you do? Our advice is based on an optimistic premise that we can't prove: Not all sources of news delivery will be knocked out at the same time, or for the same period of time. If NBC is down for two days, perhaps ABC will still be running; if all the TV stations in your town are knocked out, hopefully radio will still be available, and so forth. In the worst case, we may need to depend on news broadcasts from Canada, Europe, or other parts of the world; conversely, their news broadcasts could be affected by the same Year-2000 problems, so they may be tuning in to our broadcasts.

Thus, the basic strategy for coping with news disruptions is to ensure that you have "redundant" sources. Most people have those already, but since they often depend on just one source (e.g., the TV news on CNN), they often let the others atrophy. There was a time when everyone listened to the radio in the household; now, many of us listen only to the car radio. In preparation for the Year-2000 problem, make sure that you *do* have a working radio in the home (and perhaps one that will operate on batteries); make sure that your newspaper and magazine subscriptions are up-to-date; etc. If you're really feeling paranoid, get a short-wave radio that can pick up overseas broadcasts.

Much the same advice applies for longer-term disruptions of a month, a year, or a decade. Conceivably, your local TV station could be out of operation for a month; your local newspaper could shut for a month, or even a year; and perhaps some forms of news delivery will disappear for a decade. But because they all involve different technologies, different transmission and distribution mechanisms, and different companies, the chances that there will be *no* news from *any* source for long periods of time is pretty close to zero. However, if your career, or your peace of mind, depends on timely, uninterrupted delivery of news, then the more redundancy you can provide for yourself, the better.

Endnotes

1. We've left the Internet out of this discussion, even though it's beginning to represent a major source of news for the "digerati," as *Wired* magazine calls the technically elite computer-savvy part of the population. Access to the Internet and World Wide Web depends, for almost all of us, on access to the telephone network; we'll discuss that in Chapter 13.

2. We are greatly indebted to Phil Govert (pgovert@aol.com) who read through the first draft of our book and then tracked down a December 11, 1995 FCC report entitled "Annual Assessment of the Status of Competition in the Market for the Delivery of Video Programming" (CS Docket No. 95-61), which states, in part, "The number of homes passed by cable grew from approximately 90.6 million at the end of 1993 to approximately 91.6 million at the end of 1994, which is 96% of all television households in the United States. The number of subscribers increased from 57.2 million to 59.7 million between the end of 1993 and the end of 1994. Penetration (i.e., the number of subscribers as a percent of homes passed) rose 3.3% from the end of 1993 to a penetration of 65.2% at the end of 1994." We think it's a conservative estimate indeed to prognosticate that by the end of 1997, as this book goes to press, the number of subscribers will have reached 60 million or more.

3. The absence of commercials will presumably cause a decrease in sales on the part of the advertisers, which will create a different set of problems; on the other hand, it's possible that some companies would find that their sales are unchanged, which might help eliminate the mystique and glamour of TV and radio advertising. In any case, this is all an example of the ripple effect discussed in Appendix B.

Year-2000 Impact
on Health/Medicine

*A sound mind in a sound body, is a short, but full description
of a happy state in this World: he that has these two, has little
more to wish for; and he that wants either of them, will be
little the better for anything else.*

John Locke, Some Thoughts Concerning Education,
opening sentences (1693).

Introduction

Some of the topics covered in this book may be regarded as
"necessities" for modern life, but if questioned closely, we
would have to agree that we can survive without television and
telephone for days at a time. If we lost our job and our bank
account, we could start over; if the utilities failed and our car
didn't work, life would somehow go on. But then there are the
real necessities, like food, water, and air—and, as we will discuss in this chapter, medicine.

Today's health and medical industry is supported by a vast
array of high-tech instruments and devices, in the laboratory
and the hospital and the doctor's office. And the industry is surrounded and controlled by a vast bureaucracy, which many feel
is on the verge of collapse even without an external perturbation
like the Year-2000 crisis. In any case, a moment's thought will
convince you that all of it—medical instruments and paperwork

bureaucracy alike—is heavily dependent on computers. We'll explore several specific aspects of Year-2000 vulnerability in this chapter; one reason for doing this is a September 1997 assessment from the Gartner Group that health care providers are far behind banks, insurance companies, and most manufacturing companies in their Year-2000 efforts.[1] However, it does appear that the industry is beginning to recognize the urgent need for action; one source of information on the Internet about current Year-2000-related activities in the medical/health-care is the Rx2000 Institute web site at http://www.rx2000.org.[2]

Interestingly, this may be one of several areas where the Year-2000 problem has generational overtones. Overall, Americans are a reasonably healthy lot, and the healthiest age group tends to be those in their teens through middle adulthood. Aside from an annual visit to the dentist, many young adults will tell you they've never been inside a hospital, and don't even have a "family doctor" they visit regularly. For this group, a Year-2000-induced disruption in the health/medicine industry would have no immediate impact—unless, of course, they sustained a sudden injury or illness.

Meanwhile, another segment of American society needs regular, constant medical attention. In addition to those of all ages who have acute illnesses, a significant part of the elder generation—typically those in their 60s, 70s, and 80s—are heavily dependent on Medicare, Medicaid, and various insurance programs to provide a regular supply of prescription medicines, as well as regular visits to their doctor or hospital. It has been one of the blessings of the late twentieth century that we have had the technology and economic prosperity to provide a longer and healthier life to so many Americans—but if the computers stop and the bureaucracy collapses, it will cause a significant crisis indeed. And while it may not get much immediate attention from those in their 20s and 30s, there is likely to be enormous and immediate political pressure from those most dependent on medical supplies and services.

Year-2000 problems may also exacerbate the tensions between rich and poor, particularly in today's era of HMOs and managed health care plans. Just as disruptions in the food supply may be visible in the poorer neighborhoods first, disruptions in the complex network of hospitals, doctors, and prescription medicines are likely to be felt in those same neighborhoods. Those in the affluent neighborhoods and the middle-class suburbs are more likely to have private practitioners they can turn to for help—at least in the short term.

Medical Devices and Hospital Systems

Let's begin with the computer-augmented medical devices that one sees in a well-equipped doctor's office, as well as most hospitals across the country. The familiar example, which most of us have seen on popular TV programs like *General Hospital* or *E.R.*, is the monitoring device that's attached to a patient who has just completed an operation. Complete with flashing lights, display screens, digital read-outs, and audible "beeps," these bedside monitors record and display a patient's heartbeat, blood pressure, temperature, and various other vital signs. More importantly, they *monitor* these vital signs, constantly watching to see that they remain within acceptable limits. If an indicator goes above or below a threshold, medication can be automatically administered through an IV; if the indicator goes significantly beyond its acceptable range, an audible alarm can be generated in the nurse's station.

Beyond the patient-monitoring systems popularized by TV dramas, there are dozens of additional devices that doctors, nurses, and medical technicians depend upon for both routine and emergency medical practices. Whether it's a CAT scan, MRI, heart-checkup, or one of the dazzling devices in the operating room, they're all computer-controlled, or computer-augmented. In most cases, they simply wouldn't operate if the computer shuts down.

And that brings us to the obvious question: *Could* they break down on January 1, 2000? The honest answer is: We don't know. We received an e-mail message from Dr. Paul R. Lindeman, an Emergency Medicine physician, who reviewed the first draft of our book and commented:

> *In a general sense, most routine bedside medical monitoring devices tend to be ignorant of the year and are as such probably (there's that word again!) immune from y2k. These devices include the ubiquitous "IV pumps" which deliver fluid and medication at precise rates, as well as the heart rate monitors which display waveform and rhythm/rate and perhaps a BP (and generally nothing else). Some of the more exotic devices found within the ICU may not be similarly classified.*

You can interpret that as "good news" if you have the luxury of standing outside the hospital on New Year's Eve with all of your friends and loved ones standing around you. However, it's not very reassuring news if you happen to be on the operating table at that moment, with cathodes and IV tubes connected to a device whose failure could kill you by commission (e.g., giving you an overdose of medication) or omission (e.g., failing to sound an alarm). Or they could simply shut down, as is likely to be the case with medical devices whose internal computer-controlled clocks mistakenly decide that they've operated too long without being serviced or re-calibrated.[3] While we were researching the material for this book, we came upon an e-mail exchange between members of a Year-2000 health care "user group," in which one individual offered the following assessment for his organization's medical systems:

I am the Y2K Project Manager for the _____ Medical System. We too are in the assessment phase, however, we are approaching this as a potential disaster because we don't know where the problems lie. We have 29 mission critical off the shelf clinical applications, over 15,000 medical devices from approximately 2000 vendors, another 2 to 3000 suppliers of goods and services, 5000+ PCs, plus the complete hospital infrastructure (elevators, security, chillers, heating & cooling, etc.). All of the above has to be verified and tested for Y2K compliance. Testing alone could take 6 months to 1 year. We have already had failures and know that at least 1 of our systems is two versions behind the Y2K compliant version. So I believe it is wrong to assume that this is a small problem.[4]

The potential Year-2000 vulnerability of all these devices is associated with both a very simple, and a very complex, aspect of computers. The simple part has to do with the nature of most "real-time data acquisition" or "process control" computer systems: they "sample," or read, a sensor at frequent intervals of time. In the case of an automobile computer, the sensor may be the internal temperature of the carburetor; in the case of a patient monitoring system, it may be the body temperature of the patient. The automobile computer might have to monitor the temperature 1,000 times a second to ensure a smooth combustion mixture of fuel and oxygen; the patient monitoring system might only have to sense the patient's temperature once a second. But in any case, it's accomplished with a hardware chip that measures the passage of time in appropriate units. If that hardware chip was acquired from a computer manufacturer that incorporated day, month, and year into the chip, and if the associated hardware and software logic is Year-2000-sensitive, then there is a definite risk that the chip will exhibit aberrant behavior on January 1, 2000.

In the case of the hospital system, it's highly likely that the time-sensing chip is part of a much larger system that includes some date-sensitive logic. Thus, the patient monitoring system that administers medication via an IV tube has probably been programmed not to administer the medication for more than 24 hours without a manual approval (and perhaps a "reset" of the device) by the nurse or doctor. Or it may have been programmed to administer a lower dosage at night, when the patient is sleeping; or it may have been programmed to store all of the sensor-readings in a database, to compare this patient's prognosis with other patients.

For example, in a recent Congressional hearing, Ms. Ann Coffou testified that:

> ...*every time a heart pacemaker detects an irregular heartbeat it sends a shock to the system and then records the time the event occurred. This information is regularly downloaded to a computer system so it can be analyzed by medical personnel. Whenever the information is downloaded, the pacemaker resets itself. The downloaded information is used by cardiologists to detect patterns and irregularities in the patient's heart rhythms. If the software in the receiving system starts recording faulty times for the shock deliveries, the cardiologist could misinterpret the results and administer improper medical care.*

> *The U.S. Veteran's Administration funded a project to interview the top five pacemaker manufacturers to see if they were aware of this potential problem. One company was aware of the problem and said they would have it corrected by the end of 1997. Two companies said that the problem would be fixed before the Year 2000, one before 1998. Finally, one company flatly refused to acknowledge the problem and when pushed declined to discuss the topic any further.*

> *A physician in a heart clinic in Spartanburg, South Carolina, related that a new shipment of heart defribulators the clinic received recently were recalled by the manufacturer. The defribulators use an embedded device that calculates the time since last maintenance similar to elevators. Like the el-*

evator, if the time since the last maintenance check surpasses a certain time frame, the defribulator will not operate, thereby reducing the possibility of malfunctioning on a patient. The manufacturer voluntarily recalled their products when they discovered they were not designed to handle the change in century.

The legal ramifications for these and other medical system malfunctions have the ability to become enormous, precedent-setting lawsuits, not to mention the backlash effect on physician malpractice insurance.[5]

Most of this programmed computer logic will have been written by the medical equipment companies that provide the patient monitoring systems and the various other kinds of medical devices. As with the software for electrical generators and nuclear reactors, this software tends to be written much more carefully, and tested much more thoroughly, than the business applications developed in a typical corporate IT department; indeed, the software (and the rest of the equipment) has to be approved by the Food and Drug Administration and/or other governmental regulatory bodies before it can be used at all. But this does *not* mean that the software is bug-free; completely independent of the Year-2000 problem, there have been several documented cases over the past decade where software bugs have caused serious medical problems—including a few cases where patients have been killed.

The FDA and government regulators now include Year-2000 compliance in their checklist of tests and audits required to approve a *new* hospital/medical device, but that won't eliminate the problem for the *existing* equipment—not unless every one of them is tested for Year-2000 compliance. Again, it's important to recognize that the Year-2000 problems can occur at several "levels": within the hardware and its associated BIOS logic for recording the time, within the operating system, within the programming language, within the database system, and/or within the application programs.

The problem is likely to be compounded by additional application programs written by the hospitals themselves. Almost all hospitals, except the very smallest, have a computer staff that deals with all the "business" programs for billing and insurance paperwork; they also install, maintain, and fix minor problems in the patient-oriented systems described above. But in addition to that, the larger hospitals have research departments developing their own computer systems; and they have doctors who often feel the urge to write their own computer programs for various medical activities they're involved with.

Colleagues of ours like to joke that doctors are lousy pilots and should never be allowed to handle small airplanes; their power in the operating room makes them feel God-like and they act as if they're omnipotent when coping with bad weather and other airplane hazards. Whether or not this is true, we can report from personal experience that doctors are lousy programmers (as are nuclear physicists and members of various other highly skilled professions). They have brilliant ideas, and they have the best of intentions when it comes to translating those ideas into computer programs. But, they're very impatient, and very unwilling to deal with the minute, niggling details of computer programming. Their testing is spotty, their documentation is non-existent, and their willingness to explain the details of their program to anyone else is roughly the same as their willingness to explain brain surgery to a kindergarten-age child.

Like all generalities, this characterization is flawed, and we realize that there are numerous exceptions. Nevertheless, we predict that a hospital whose medical devices and computer systems include a substantial amount of "amateur" programming by doctors is going to be even more susceptible to Year-2000 failures.

Doctors

Doctors, as we've discussed above, are active participants in the hospitals that we visit for operations and serious illnesses. But many of them also maintain a practice *outside* the hospital; indeed, that's the most common form of doctor-patient interactions that most of us experience.

A doctor's office is a small business unto itself. It may have two or three physicians, a few nurses and medical assistants, and a few secretaries, receptionists, and administrative assistants. As we've already discussed, a typical doctor's office will also contain computer-controlled medical devices; there won't be as many as there are in hospitals, and they may not be quite as sophisticated, but they're still computer-controlled, and they're still vulnerable to Year-2000 problems.

However, our main concern here is the vast amount of paperwork that doctors have to cope with these days. Some of this is still maintained in file folders, stored away in massive file cabinets; you've probably noticed this whenever you visit your doctor, for there's bound to be a manila file folder with all kinds of details about your medical history and your previous interactions with the doctor. Some of the information in the file folder consists of printouts from medical devices (e.g., EKG readouts when you had your last cardiac checkup), and some of it consists of reports and printouts from various computer systems in the doctor's office, from your hospital, from other doctors you've visited, or from a medical lab that reported on your cholesterol level. But at least it's all on paper, and in a well-managed doctor's office, it's been filed someplace where people can find it; if a Year-2000 failure knocks out all the computers, a permanent record of your medical situation still exists.

But, the ability of the doctor's office to function as a "business" is more and more dependent on computers. This is largely because of the billing and reporting bureaucracy associated with insurance companies, Medicare/Medicaid agencies, and various state and federal regulatory bodies that monitor the kind of medication and medical practices administered by doctors. Much of this, of course, involves money: if the doctor charges you $100 for your annual checkup, the bill might be paid by a combination of your employer's insurance plan, your personal insurance policy, Medicare, and your own personal finances (in the form of a check, cash, or credit card). Keeping track of all of this is a massive job, and during the past ten years—as desktop computers became cheap enough so that doctors could afford them—most of the details have become computerized.

In the early days of such computerization, it was often the doctors themselves who wrote the computer programs; a few of these legacy systems may still be in operation. For the most part, though, today's doctor's office is supported by a software "package" that can be purchased from professional software companies who specialize in this kind of application. But while some of this software comes from large, reputable companies like IBM, much of it comes from much smaller companies—some of whom are no longer in business, even though their software is still running in the doctor's office.

Thus, from a Year-2000 perspective, doctors are in the same position as many other small businesses who carry out their invoicing, receivables, payables, inventory control, payroll, and other business activities on a computer. Most of this software runs on standard, general-purpose desktop computers; in some cases, an ambitious doctor has augmented this by connecting several of his office computers in a network, and/or connecting the computer(s) to the nearby hospital via modem and the Internet. As we saw in Chapter 7, these computers are highly susceptible to Year-2000 problems, especially if they're more than a year or two old; to compound the problem, many doctors (who behave in the omnipotent/amateur fashion discussed above) are incredibly sloppy when it comes to backups and archives of their databases. Thus, it will be of little surprise to the authors if doctors begin reporting massive failures, disruptions, and data loss after January 1, 2000.

This may be of little immediate concern to you if you're the typical healthy American who only sees his or her doctor for an annual checkup. But if you depend on regular prescription medicine, and if the prescription has to be authorized by the doctor before the pharmacy will refill it, then you'll be *extremely* annoyed if the doctor tells you that he or she has lost all of your records.

Medicare, Insurance, and Hospital/Doctor Paperwork

We've already noted that doctors and hospitals are inundated with paperwork associated with medical practices and services. Twenty years ago, we would have pointed the finger of blame (to the extent that "blame" should be attached to something that virtually everyone regards as an onerous task) at the insurance companies; the patient, the doctor, and/or the hospital would file a claim for payment, in the hope that the insurance company would cover most, if not all, of the cost of the medical service.

Today, there's another entity whose paperwork requirements dwarf that of the insurance companies within the private sector: Medicare. Gary North, an eloquent and astute
observer of the Year-2000 problem, has recently drawn attention to a May 16, 1997 report to Congress from the General
Accounting Office entitled *Medicare Transaction Systems: Success Depends Upon Correcting Critical Managerial and Technical
Weaknesses*, authored by Joel M. Willemssen. North's conclusion: The anticipated volume of one *billion* insurance claims
and payouts of $288 billion in the year 2000 are highly imper-
iled by a combination of administrative and managerial fias-
coes that the likelihood of Medicare being Year-2000-
compliant is extremely low. Actually, his words are: "My conclusion: Medicare will *not* make the year 2000 deadline.[6, 7]

In a July 10, 1997 testimony before the GAO's Technology
Subcommittee,[8] Mr. Willemssen detailed a number of problems, including those associated with a massive effort currently
underway to replace 70 private firms that currently administer
Medicare's day-to-day operations with a single government-
run system. As Mr. Wilemssen points out:

> We also reported and testified this past May that the Health
> Care Financing Administration (HCFA)—a major compo-
> nent agency within the Department of Health and Human
> Services (HHS)—had not completed numerous critical as-
> sessment activities for the systems run by its contractors to
> process approximately $200 billion annually in Medicare
> claims. Specifically, HCFA had not required systems con-
> tractors to submit year 2000 plans for approval, and lacked
> contracts or other legal agreements detailing how or when the
> year 2000 problem would be corrected, or indeed whether
> contractors would even certify that they would correct the
> problem. We made several recommendations to HCFA to
> address its shortcomings in this area, including regular re-
> porting to HHS on its progress. HHS reported in May that
> it expected to complete the assessment phase last month.

If you're a gambler and a believer in miracles within government, perhaps you can find a way to read this report and still believe that everything will work properly on January 1, 2000. If you're a cynic, or a hard-nosed manager, your attitude might be, "Those jerks will run around in circles and get nothing done until the last possible minute, until someone cracks the whip over their heads and tells them to get to work. The result is that it will be *much* more expensive, and it will waste millions of the taxpayer's money." Ah, if only it were that simple! As we discuss in detail in Appendix A, software problems are not the sort of thing that can be solved by throwing massive quantities of money and people at them. Even professional software managers fall victim to this illusion from time to time, and we expect that professional politicians (if that's not an oxymoron) will march bravely forward with a strategy roughly equivalent to impregnating nine women to produce a baby in one month.

Prescription Medicines

Prescription medicines, by their very nature, are regulated. They're not like tomatoes or peaches, which you can buy from a neighborhood farm stand if the local supermarket shuts down. In addition to being regulated by the FDA and/or other government agencies, many of them are protected by patents—i.e., they represent highly profitable *proprietary* products invented by a drug or pharmaceutical company. The more highly regulated, and the more proprietary a product is, the more vulnerable it becomes to Year-2000 disruptions. We're not so concerned about a disruption in the supply of Anacin or cough syrup, but we are concerned about specialized medicines for the treatment of heart disease, cancer, AIDS, and various other diseases.

The first problem we worry about, of course, is a bankruptcy, shutdown, or serious disruption within a pharmaceutical company itself. These are companies with highly specialized manufacturing processes (not to mention the R&D processes, which are busily at work on the next generation of medicines), which are—no surprise—highly dependent on computers. And like any other business, pharmaceutical companies have elaborate business applications to manage their finances, their inventories, their payroll, etc. If the Acme Sausage company breaks down because of a Year-2000 bug in its mainframe computer, both employees and customers of the sausage company will be affected; but if the very same mainframe bug disrupts the computers of the Acme Miracle Drug Company, it could have far more serious consequences.

Another interesting comparison: A shut-down of the Acme Sausage company probably won't cause many lawsuits, if any Indeed, it would have to be a fairly serious flaw in the production process—e.g., mixing ground glass with the bratwurst—before we would expect to see any lawsuits at all. By contrast, the potential litigation associated with pharmaceutical failures could be massive indeed. We've already seen examples of multi-million dollar, if not multi-*billion* dollar, lawsuits against pharmaceutical companies in recent years. We have no way of knowing whether such lawsuits will emerge in the post-2000 days and months, but given the litigious nature of American society, it would be no surprise. And the point of this discussion is simple: It doesn't take very many mega-dollar lawsuits to shut a company down.

Finally, we note that drugs and medicines, whether "prescription" or "over the counter," must be delivered from pharmaceutical manufacturing facilities to doctors, hospitals, pharmacies, and retail outlets. In this regard, medicine is like food; and the potential disruptions fall into the same categories as those discussed in Chapter 6.

Fallback Advice—Two-Day Failures

If you're an optimist, then perhaps you'll believe that all of the problems described in this chapter will be identified in advance by the appropriate authorities, and that almost all of the problems will have been remedied *before* January 1, 2000. In this optimistic scenario, only a few problems will slip by the programmers, testers, and the government regulators, and the disruptions will require only a few days to fix.

Though some problems of this minor nature could occur all during the first year of the new millennium, the most likely period of difficulties will be the first few days of January. Thus, no matter how optimistic you're feeling, prudence suggests that you should avoid elective surgery until at least mid-January. For expectant mothers whose due date is January 1 or January 2, especially those with fetal complications, there is a real life-and-death decision to be faced: Should one hope that the medical equipment will continue functioning, or should one opt for a slightly premature Cesarean-section birth on December 30? We are in no position to offer advice to an unknown reader in this area; all we can do is ask you to think carefully about the tradeoffs if the situation applies to you.

What if your doctor is unavailable for a few days because of a Year-2000-induced disruption? If it's an emergency, you may not be able to wait that long; thus, you should take steps to provide a backup mechanism to contact your doctor, and perhaps even find some backup doctors that you can visit if you or your family have a medical history that includes occasional emergency situations. For those who find themselves dealing with HMOs or other managed-care forms of treatment, this will be difficult—for the relationship between doctor and patient is becoming more and more impersonal, which makes it more difficult to the attention one needs in an emergency. As recommended in our discussion of utilities in Chapter 3, it makes sense to cultivate a personal relationship with a competent doctor, to improve the chances of getting the necessary attention if a post-2000 problem develops.

The issue likely to be of concern for a much larger number of people is prescription medicine. Common sense suggests that you maintain a *minimum* inventory of two or three days of whatever medication you depend upon—and never let the inventory fall below that level. Indeed, given the reasonable cost and ample availability of most medicines, it probably makes far more sense to ensure that you have a 2-3 month supply, unless your physician or pharmacist specifically recommends against it.

Fallback Advice—One-Month Failures

While two or three days of Year-2000-induced disruptions in medicine is likely to be only a minor nuisance for most, a one-month disruption could be a serious problem for even those who consider themselves reasonably healthy. Again, it will be difficult to impress young, healthy adults of this problem, for they typically go several months between visits to doctor or dentist. But parents of young children should be more concerned, as should older citizens and anyone else with serious medical needs.

If your primary concern is access to prescription medicine, then the stockpiling suggestion mentioned earlier may still be applicable. It may be a little more expensive to maintain a one-month supply of blood pressure pills or insulin, but it shouldn't be a serious strain on the budget for most people; in any case, if you begin preparations now, you can spread the cost over a year or more. A more serious problem is likely to be that of the doctor and the pharmacist, who typically regulate the supply of prescription medicines to minimize the chances of misuse on your part. In addition, some prescription medicine is tightly controlled to prevent patients from giving it away to others. Such practices are particularly common if a medicine is expensive and if its costs are subsidized or covered by an insurance program; the insurance companies are legitimately interested in keeping their costs under control, and thus do their best to prevent you from building up a stockpile.

What if you're concerned about the possibility that a Year-2000 problem will prevent you from seeing your doctor, or will make it impossible to get appropriate medical care in a hospital? If you're dealing with elective surgery or non-critical illness, the advice is simple and obvious: Wait for a month, until the Year-2000 problem is overcome. But for those with acute illnesses or injuries, that option may not be available—and the only advice we can offer is to make the proactive decision to move to a less-populated area, where you're more likely to find doctors and nurses who have not been overwhelmed by the urban problems of Medicare and Medicaid.

Of course, Year-2000 software problems could occur in medical equipment regardless of the size of the city in which they exist. One could argue that urban centers are likely to have the latest, and most sophisticated, medical equipment—but as of mid-1997, when this book was being written, there was no indication that "current" medical equipment was any more likely to be Year-2000-compliant than devices built five or ten years ago. So the patient monitoring systems, life-support systems, EKG machines, and CAT-scan devices could just as easily fail in Missoula, Montana as in New York City. But we believe that you're more likely to get direct, personal, humane attention from a doctor in a smaller city than in a larger one; this isn't guaranteed to happen automatically, but it should be easier to *create* a personal relationship with a doctor, in advance, within a smaller community.

Paul Lindeman, whose observations were noted earlier, added:

> *Two types of patient bear specific mention, the diabetic and the patient on dialysis (all too often the same individual). Glucometers are handy little devices which diabetics use to monitor their blood sugar levels. Often times they rely on this information to determine how much insulin to give themselves. Many of these newer devices are capable of storing results and so contain date information. Most units display the date in mm/dd/yy format, and thus must be considered y2k vulnerable.*

> *Diabetics who must self-administer insulin have an additional concern, and that is refrigeration. All insulin must be refrigerated.*

> *In summary, then, diabetics ought to ensure a 3 month (minimum) supply of insulin, syringes, needles, and testing strips. They must also have a back-up plan for refrigeration of their insulin in the event of power disruption. They would also be well advised to contact the manufacturer of their glucometer and inquire about compliance.*

> *Dialysis patients rely on this technology for their very life. Many dialysis machines are rather old (some would say too old) and do not store date information. Newer machines however do store date information, primarily for use in reports, and are to some extent y2k vulnerable.*

> *Independent of the age and type of dialysis machine; each and every dialysis session requires a filter, be it disposable or reusable. Because this entails a pre-requisite flow of supplies in order to support the dialysis (replacement filters, solutions for washing reusables, etc.), this brings to bear issues of supply, distribution, transportation, ripple effect, etc., as discussed elsewhere in this work.*

Fallback Advice—One-Year Failures

Is it possible that hospitals will shut down, doctors will be inaccessible, and prescription medicines unavailable for a period as long as a year? Phrased in this way, it hardly seems likely; after all, the Red Cross manages to provide emergency medical services in situations far more extreme than the "serious" Year-2000 scenarios we've envisaged. In any case, we don't think it's a likely scenario for the more common aspects of medical equipment and services. However, it *is* a possibility for the more expensive, esoteric kinds of equipment and services.

If, for example, your hospital has a million-dollar medical machine used to diagnose and/or treat rare illnesses, and if that machine has a Year-2000-vulnerable computer system in it (which is not so difficult to imagine), then it could easily take a year for the hospital to get a replacement. In the best of all cases, the manufacturer of that medical device will ship some new software to the hospital, and the machine will be fixed within a matter of days. But in some cases, the offending computer equipment will have to be physically removed and replaced; and the waiting list for such replacement parts could be several months or longer. Indeed, in the worst case, the manufacturer will have suffered such traumatic Year-2000 problems of its own that it goes bankrupt; in that case, there will be no replacements until a new company pops up in the marketplace.

In any case, there's a point beyond which the stockpiling of medicines and the development of personal relationships with neighborhood doctors can protect us from such a calamity. If you envision this kind of serious Year-2000 scenario, then take whatever proactive steps you can: Stockpile a supply of medicine, take care of any optional/elective medical procedures before January 1, 2000, move to a more hospitable community, and engage in appropriate preventive practices to improve your health as much as possible. And then, hope for the best.

Fallback Advice—Ten-Year Failures

There's only one scenario that we feel worth mentioning in terms of a ten-year failure: the possibility of a collapse in the governmental agencies that subsidize and support medical care. While it may seem an exaggeration, the reality is that a substantial number of American citizens—not only the elderly, but also those in low-income brackets—are alive today *only* because of the financial support of Medicaid, Medicare, and similar systems.

We've already discussed the possible breakdown in the massive computer systems developed by the federal Medicare agencies; this could easily be exacerbated by Year-2000 problems in insurance companies, hospitals, and doctors' offices. The entire system barely works in today's environment, and many experts argue that it's already on the verge of collapse; a series of systemic Year-2000 failures could push the entire thing over the cliff.

And then what? Obviously, new government agencies could be created; new legislation could be passed; new forms and paperwork procedures could be designed and implemented. All of this would take more than a year, but it's difficult to imagine that it would take a decade—except for one thing: *politics.* President Clinton's first-term attempt to introduce a national health care policy is a good example, and one can find continuing examples in the ongoing debate about "reforming" the medical system at the local, state, and federal levels. Powerful lobbies and special-interest groups are involved, billions of dollars are at stake, and intense emotions are ignited whenever political debates about health and medical insurance are raised.

We're not so pessimistic that we would predict the debates going on for a decade—though a cynic might argue that they *have* been going on for a decade, without any satisfactory resolution of today's problems. However, if a serious Year-2000-induced problem caused the utter collapse of the Medicare/Medicaid bureaucracy and much of the nation's medical facilities, we assume that there would be enough sense of urgency to force some kind of political action within a matter of months…or perhaps a year.

The question is: What kind of policies and bureaucracies would emerge as a replacement for the current medical insurance system? Our crystal ball is no better than yours when it comes to predicting this aspect of a possible post-2000 future. However, it occurs to us that if Year-2000-related medical problems are combined with the various other Year-2000 problems discussed in this book, the political mood of the country *could* turn sharply to the right, in which case subsidized medicine could be sharply reduced, if not eliminated. Of course, one could argue the opposite as well: A newly-elected Class of 2000 in the House and Senate, together with a newly-elected President, could respond to the Year-2000 crisis in a fashion reminiscent of FDR's New Deal program. But even in that scenario, it's likely that jobs, banking, national defense, Social Security, and other issues might well take precedence over Medicare and Medicaid—at least for the first few years of post-2000 recovery.

Thus, if you're a pessimist, it's not at all difficult to imagine a Year-2000 scenario that marks the end of government-supported health care as we currently know it. It's a grim prospect indeed.

Endnotes

1. The report, which can be retrieved from the Internet at http://
cwlive.cw.com:8080/home/ online9697.nsf/All/970924gartner184E2,
observed that "Vertical industries that are leading the remediation effort include
financial services companies—including banks, brokerages and insurers—and
most types of manufacturers. At the bottom of the heap are health care providers—88% of all health care providers surveyed are at Level 1."

2. Also, consult the May 1996 white paper, "U.S. Government Year 2000 Issue,
Implications for public health Information and Surveillance" from the Centers
for Disease Control (CDC), which argues that, "It is vital that the public health
community begin aggressively addressing this issue to avoid serious negative
programmatic effects across public health." The CDC's perspective on the Year-
2000 problem can be found at their Web site at http://www.cdc.gov/y2k/.

3. You can find the full text of Mr. Wilemssen's testimony on the Internet at http:/
/www.house.gov/science/willemssen_7-10.html.

4. In a follow-up message to one of the authors, this Year-2000 project manager
provided these additional details:

We have 33 hosts representing a variety of the following:

• IBM ES-9000

• IBM RS/6000

• HP-9000

• DEC Vax

The platforms support seven different operation system architectures and
employ over 300 gigabytes of mass storage.

We use twenty-six mission critical applications which are Commercial Off-
the-shelf with few or no modifications. The data comm network is comprised of
approximately 6,000 desktop computers, 125 file servers and the normal number of routers and other equipment for a network of this size. The network
architecture is a mixture of Novell V3.11 and V4.11, Windows NT V3.51 and
V4.0 and varieties of UNIX. Desktop software is primarily Windows 95 or
Windows 3.11 with Microsoft Office V4.3. Although there is a standard suite
of software, Users augment their systems by providing their own additional software. Some of this software could turn out to be mission critical.

The numbers on the medical devices remained approximately the same with
the Clinical Engineering Dept. having responsibility for approximately 14,000
pieces of equipment representing approximately 2,000 vendors. The Radiology
Department is responsible for approximately 200 pieces of computerized equipment from approximately twelve vendors.

One of the areas everyone overlooks is the Physical plant. Systems within the physical plant are all commercially supplied and fall into the following thirteen general categories:

- Bulk storage of medical gasses/Surgical air pump system
- Energy Management and Thermostatic Controls
- Chilled H2O, Chillers and Controls
- Heating, ventilation and Air Conditioning, Distribution and Controls
- Electrical Distribution - High Voltage, House, Emergency and Un-interruptible Power
- Electronics - Fire Protection Sensors and Annunciators, Paging and Nurse Call Systems
- Beds and Bassinets - These are electronically controlled
- Security Systems
- Steam and Plumbing
- Heliport Operations and Fire Quenching
- Wireless Communications - VHF, UHF, Repeaters
- Vertical Transportation - Elevators, Pneumatic Tubes
- Telecommunications

We have approximately 3,000 suppliers of goods and services and have not yet determined the number of payers.

Ann K. Coffou, Managing Director, Giga Year 2000 Relevance Service, to the Subcommittee on Technology and Subcommittee on Government Management, Information and Technology, March 20, 1997, "Year 2000 Risks: What Are the Consequences of Technology Failure?" posted at <http://www.house.gov/science/couffou_3-20.html>.

5. Ann K. Coffou, Managing Director, Giga Year 2000 Relevance Service, to the Subcommittee on Technology and Subcommittee on Government Management, Information and Technology, March 20, 1997, "Year 2000 Risks: What Are the Consequences of Technology Failure?" posted at <http://www.house.gov/science/couffou_3-20.html>.

6. Gary North, "You Bet Your Life," *Remnant Review,* Vol. 24, No. 7, p. 2. North, who covers a variety of conservative economic issues in his newsletter, first began reporting on Year-2000 in 1996. Almost every one of the monthly issues in 1997 has focused on specific aspects of the Year-2000 problem. His newsletter is published by Agora Inc., 1217 St. Paul Street, Baltimore, MD 21202, phone 410-234-0691. He also has what we regard as the most informative and comprehensive Year-2000 Web site for the average citizen (as opposed to sites like http://www.year2000.com, which is populated primarily by computer professionals and Year-2000 vendors); we encourage you to visit it at http://www.garynorth.com.

7. You can find the full text of Mr. Wilemssen's testimony on the Internet at http://www.house.gov/science/willemssen_7-10.html.

8. You can find the full text of Mr. Wilemssen's testimony on the Internet at http://www.house.gov/science/willemssen_7-10.html.

10

Year-2000 Impact on Government

Now, as the millennium turns, as we have all seen from countless press reports, so do the dates on our computers. Experts are concerned that many of our information systems will not differentiate between dates in the 20th century and the 21st century. I want to assure the American people that the federal government, in cooperation with state and local government and the private sector, is taking steps to prevent any interruption in government services that rely on the proper functioning of federal computer systems. We can't have the American people looking to a new century and a new millennium with their computers, the very symbol of modernity in the modern age, holding them back and we are determined to see that it doesn't happen.

President Bill Clinton, Speech at the National Archives, *mid-August, 1997.[1]*

Introduction

Whatever your opinion of government, here is an important point to keep in mind: it was government that funded and acquired the first modern American and British computers in the 1940s, and it is government that owns and operates the largest amount of computer software today. Much of this has a military overtone. Not only the early World-War II computers, but even the technology that now forms the Internet, was funded by various branches of the U.S. Department of

Defense (DOD). And according to the Year-2000 metrics collected by Capers Jones, the military has more software than any other government agency or corporation within the private sector—with 6 million separate applications, 1,000 software sites, 200,000 software professionals, and 300 million function points of software[2] (approximately equal to 30 *billion* COBOL statements, though COBOL makes up only a portion of the DOD inventory).

Governments have been working with computers, accumulating vast stores of legacy programs, and building up enormous databases, far longer than most industries. Though punched cards have largely disappeared from computer installations today, the so-called "Hollerith card" was invented by Herman Hollerith in 1880 as a means of recording and retrieving information for the decennary U.S. census.[3] Since then, billions of dollars have been spent to acquire computers that can count, tabulate, compute taxes, and perform the myriad collection of bureaucratic activities that government is so often associated with. Combining the federal and state government agencies (but not including DOD), Capers Jones estimates an aggregate of 1,688,891 applications, 650 software sites, 95,000 programmers, and 96 million function points of software.[4]

We tell you this not to brag on behalf of government; indeed, quite the opposite. The point is that just as most large companies are bedeviled by ancient mainframe legacy programs that nobody understands anymore, so is government. But in the case of government, the software applications are likely to be much older. And there are more of them, written in a wider variety of programming languages. Many of these programming languages, especially within the DOD, are so obscure that they're not used anywhere else (with the possible exception of defense departments in a few other unlucky

countries); thus, it will be difficult to find and/or train programmers to examine these programs for Year-2000 problems.
Similarly, the phenomenon of tight budgets means that many
government computer systems are running on ancient hardware, with operating systems the rest of the civilized world
considers dead. It's not only difficult to find computer professionals who can work with these old computers (especially
because most of the younger computer professionals vastly
prefer working with the very latest and most powerful computers), but it's also difficult to get the computer vendors to
provide support for products they've abandoned years, if not
decades, ago.

Then there is the procurement problem. The standard procedure for many government computer projects (as well as a
wide variety of other engineering projects, construction
projects, etc.) is to document the requirements in a massive
tome known as an RFQ (Request for Quote) or RFP (Request
for Proposal), and make it available to vendors in the private
sector who want the dubious honor of winning the contract
for the project. The process of writing the RFP can take
months; the bidding, evaluation, and award process can take
several more months; and to further complicate things, the
losing vendors sometimes sue, complaining that they were
evaluated unfairly. Somewhere in the midst of all this, the
budget must be estimated, documented, justified, and then
sent up the political hierarchy for approval. A common joke
among the "Beltway Bandits"—the mini-industry of defense
contractors, engineering firms, and computer software organizations whose offices are located near the Interstate "Beltway"
surrounding Washington, DC—is that most government
agencies won't even be finished with the procurement process
for their Year-2000 projects until 2001. It's not quite as bad as

that, in reality... but it's close enough to the truth that the joke receives loud gales of laughter from Year-2000 software organizations.

There is one last problem to point out: In general, the competence, organizational ability, and level of motivation of software project teams in the various branches of government is at the opposite end of the spectrum from what you would expect at Microsoft, IBM, Hewlett-Packard and other familiar companies in the private sector. No doubt this is an unfair criticism of some programmers, some managers, and some government project teams; and the reason we make the observation is not to offer a gratuitous insult, but to add an additional item for consideration when estimating the likelihood that a government-oriented Year-2000 project will finish on time.

Part of the problem is that government attracts both the best *and* the worst of the computer programmers, software engineers, database designers, and related computer specialists. We suspect that this is true for other professions, too, but our own personal, substantial experience in the computer field confirms it for software development. It's important to emphasize that there are men and women of extraordinary talent, energy, dedication, and enthusiasm who are attracted to various branches of the government because: (a) they want to work on projects far larger than would ever be attempted in the private sector; (b) they want to work on leading-edge projects, such as Star Wars or NASA; (c) they have a sincere desire to contribute their efforts to the betterment of society; or (d) they want the career stability supposedly associated with a Civil Service grade. These people occasionally accomplish miracles, either because of their individual efforts, or because they inspire the others on their team to levels of performance that would otherwise not have occurred. To these men and women, we offer our gratitude, respect, and admiration.

Unfortunately, even the most dazzling superstar can be buried in the bureaucracy and political intrigue so often associated with government organizations; the same thing happens in the private sector, to some extent, but it's positively Byzantine in government. And to compound the problem, the relatively small number of government-employed superstars are out-numbered by people who are average, as well as an even larger number whose lack of talent and skill, and whose utter lack of energy and enthusiasm, would certainly prevent them from being hired in the private sector.

Even in the best cases, many of the Year-2000 projects are going to require long stretches of 7-day work-weeks and 16-hour work-days during the next two years. This is "business as usual," in companies like Microsoft, during the final stages of developing a new product; and though it's not what most banks, insurance companies, and other private-sector organizations normally expect of their programmers, it's also not an alien experience. Again, it's not our intention to needlessly insult government workers, and we're sure that some will be working just as hard as their private-sector counterparts; but on the whole, we expect to see the typical Year-2000 government programmer working an eight-hour day. As one such programmer confided to one of the authors, "Listen, *every* computer project in this organization is late, and *every* project is screwed up. Always has been, always will be. I don't care what kind of official statements they make, this Year-2000 stuff is *not* going to finish on time. No project we've ever done in this organization, in the 20 years I've been here, has *ever* finished on time. So if that's the way it's going to be, why should I get ulcers and ruin my life? I'm going home in the 4:42 carpool, and that's that."[5] Time will tell—in only a very few months from now—whether this programmer's cynical assessment is accurate or not.

On the assumption that it *might* be accurate, we think it's a good idea to look at some of the government agencies whose Year-2000 failures could affect our lives. Arguably, *every* government agency could have some impact on us, but some are more visible, and have a more immediate impact on us, so we'll focus on only a few. Then we'll proceed with our standard categories of advice for minor, moderate, serious, and catastrophic forms of Year-2000-related problems.

Social Security

Let's begin with one of the largest and most visible government agencies, and one that happens to be farther ahead than any other federal agency in its Year-2000 conversion efforts: the Social Security Program (SSA). SSA was signed into law on August 14, 1935 as part of FDR's New Deal program, and until recent years, it was almost universally accepted by American society as the agency that guaranteed a modest, but viable, retirement income to all Americans, regardless of background or social class.

In recent years, there has been increasing emphasis on the financial plight of SSA, with dire predictions of bankruptcy when a generation of Baby-Boomers reach retirement age in the early part of the twenty-first century. This has been accompanied by massive amounts of political rhetoric from both political parties, together with proposals and campaign pledges to "save" SSA, "re-finance" SSA, etc. Analyzing and discussing the economic viability of SSA is a complex and controversial task, and is entirely outside the charter of this book. However, if SSA experiences severe difficulties, or a partial collapse, because of Year-2000 problems (or any other technical problems, for that matter), it could well be used as political ammunition by leaders in power in 2000 to justify whatever political changes they felt appropriate.

Meanwhile, ordinary men and women of retirement age are receiving monthly checks, and are depending on them just as heavily as were the retirees of the 1970s, 1960s, 1950s, and 1940s before them. And the ordinary men and woman of *less* than retirement age are continuing to find that larger and larger portions of their paychecks are disappearing into a tax category called FICA; if nothing else, they need to be reassured that their FICA contributions have indeed been credited to their account, and that if Social Security does still exist 10 years from now, then they'll get their fair due.

All of this is imperiled by the Year-2000 problem, of course. It's hard to imagine an application more date-sensitive than the various programs within SSA. When were you born? When did you begin working? How much of a FICA contribution did you make in each of your income-generating years? When did you stop working? When did you begin drawing Social Security payments? On and on … all of this information involves dates, and much of the computational logic within SSA involves date arithmetic. Dates and date arithmetic are embedded in a portfolio estimated at 30 million lines of code, which SSA began working on in 1991.[6]

Stop for a moment and take a look at that date: *1991.* That's roughly five years before most private industry organizations began focusing on the Year-2000 problem, and light-years ahead of the other government agencies. It's also before most of the automated computer tools had appeared from Year-2000 software vendors to help mechanize the process of scanning, analyzing, and converting the programs; thus, much of the work in the early years of SSA effort was carried out manually, or with home-grown tools. That probably explains why, as of June 30, 1996, 400 SSA programmers assigned to the Year-2000 project had only converted 6 million of the 30 million program instructions in its overall portfolio. If one extrapolated those figures forward, it would be easy to conclude that SSA won't finish the job on time; however, far more sophisticated tools are now available, and far more programmers have been assigned to the Year-2000 effort in recent months. As a result, the agency has been publicly proclaiming that it *will* be finished in time, albeit just barely.

But this optimistic assessment almost certainly ignores the "systemic" Year-2000 problems discuss in Appendix B. Many of the checks produced by SSA and other government agencies are now deposited directly into the recipient's bank, rather than being printed out and mailed through the postal system. This means that there are at least two computer systems within SSA (one that was developed originally for computing and printing retirement checks, and a newer one to siphon off a subset of those payments and transmit them to the bank, via magnetic tape or telecommunications link), plus at least one computer system within the banks to process the incoming payments and funnel them into the proper account, plus one or more computer systems that support the "inter-bank" financial transfers between all manner of financial institutions. Thus, even if SSA does its job correctly, there's no guarantee that a retired widow will find that her monthly check has landed in the right account at the right time.

Welfare, Food Stamps, Medicare, etc.

In Chapter 9, we noted the possibility that the vast Medicare system could encounter serious difficulties because of

Year-2000-related computer problems. The likelihood of this occurring increased, in our opinion, when the government decided in September 1997 to cancel a computer modernization project that had been outsourced to an external contractor.[7] A similar situation exists for food stamps, welfare, unemployment payments, Veteran's benefits, farm-assistance subsidies, education grants, low-income housing assistance, and myriad other programs that provide payments to specific industries, companies, or individuals. The few that we've listed here are among the more obvious ones, but our basic advice is: If you get a check (or any other form of payment) from any government agency, you're vulnerable. The details will vary, but all of these computer applications are date-sensitive, if for no other reason than they are scheduled to be made on a periodic basis (weekly, monthly, quarterly, or annually).

If you're *not* a recipient of any government subsidy, payment, or assistance program, your natural instinct is to ignore the issue. But remember the ripple effect. The fact that large numbers of *other* people are experiencing problems can eventually bounce back to you. An interesting example of this popped up in the newspapers while we were writing this book during the summer of 1997. An article discussing the impact of welfare and food stamp reductions in New York City made the interesting point that as much as 80% of a store's business can be conducted with food stamps in the Southside section of Williamsburg, Brooklyn.[8] If the distribution of food stamps is disrupted for a month because of a Year-2000 problem, a number of grocery stores in low-income areas around the country will find it difficult to survive. But that could turn out to be a small problem compared to the consequences of having a lot of hungry people in these same neighborhoods.

Internal Revenue Service

You know who these folks are, and it won't come as a surprise to learn that their computer systems are date-sensitive,
and thus vulnerable to Year-2000 failures. Here's how the IRS
describes the size and scope of its computer operation:

> *The Information Systems (IS) organization of the Internal
> Revenue Service (IRS) is a huge enterprise—employing in
> excess of 7,500 personnel across the United States, budgeted
> in excess of $1 billion annually and responsible for the design
> development and ongoing support of a highly complex and
> vast array of technologies which, taken together, comprise the
> technology-based engine that powers the IRS. A $1.4 trillion
> Financial Services Program, IRS business enterprises are un-
> precedented in size and scope—a Fortune One company—
> with service centers, district offices and regional office opera-
> tions, staffed by more than 100,000 employees, largely de-
> pendent on highly automated processes as well as the
> currency, comprehensiveness and availability of vast store-
> houses of computerized data.[9]*

And here are a few things that you might not know about
the IRS:

- The portfolio of computer applications within the
  IRS consists of approximately 50,000 computer
  programs, comprising roughly 100 million program instructions. Thus, the software inventory is
  about three times larger than that of SSA, but
  about 4 times smaller than the largest banks.[10]

- The IRS has had ongoing difficulties for several
  years with its aging and overtaxed (no pun intended) computer system. In early 1997, it essentially abandoned a troubled $4 billion
  modernization program and began developing
  new plans for review by the GAO and various

Congressional oversight committees. Whatever the reason for its past difficulties, the track record of the IRS in working on large, complex computer projects has been mediocre-to-abysmal. That obviously raises serious questions about the likelihood of it successfully completing what will almost certainly be a far more difficult effort to accomplish Year-2000 projects with a fixed deadline. But even more important, the IRS is now proposing to outsource its modernization project to an external vendor, *and that modernization project includes some of the Year-2000 conversion work.* That might be good news if the external vendor had been hard at work for the past few years, but the IRS schedule calls for reviewing proposals and carrying on negotiations from October 1997 to the end of September, 1998; the contract is scheduled to be awarded in October, 1998. That's incredibly late in the game to begin doing any Year-2000 conversion work on such a large, complex system.

- In April, 1997, the Chief Information Officer (CIO) of the IRS told Congress that he planned to move 300 IRS programmers away from other work, to focus on Year-2000 projects. An observation: This is fewer people, and a later starting date, than SSA.[11]

You can draw your own conclusions from this. From our perspective, it's difficult to draw any other conclusion than the obvious one: The chances that IRS personnel will be celebrating New Year's Eve, 1999 with smiles on their faces is close to zero. Indeed, it's interesting that the IRS reported to Congress in mid-June 1997 that it would need an additional $258 million in 1998 to become Year-2000-compliant, a figure that was increased to approximately $600 million in September 1997, with indications that the figure would continue climbing. But given the IRS' dismal track record in using previous computer-related appropriations successfully, there is some doubt as to whether these funds will indeed be approved by Congress.[12] We share Congress' concern, since we also have some personal knowledge of previous IRS computer projects; on the other hand, without such an appropriation (and, most likely, another one of a larger magnitude in 1999), it's virtually certain that the IRS will *not* be Year-2000-compliant.

And, there's an interesting point to keep in mind about the IRS's Year-2000 problems—problems which are not yet widely known, but almost certainly will be as the deadline approaches. While most people sincerely hope that the banks, insurance companies, telephone companies, and other components of society will find a way to solve their Year-2000 problems, they're much less likely to feel so kindly about the IRS. Indeed, it's hardly an exaggeration to suggest that a substantial percentage of the tax-paying public would be thrilled if the IRS collapsed under the weight of its computer problems, and was never heard from again.

Whether or not that's a rational way to view the situation is a topic for a separate discussion, one likely to be colored by one's political opinions about taxes, government bureaucracy, etc. But the point we want to emphasize here is that the *anticipation* of severe Year-2000 problems in the IRS could lead to additional problems. Obviously, it would be inappropriate (if not illegal) for us to suggest that anyone avoid paying their taxes, and we have no intention of doing so. However, that won't eliminate the almost certain tendency of some taxpayers to engage in wishful thinking along the following lines: "Hmmm, if I liquidate my stocks and engage in various other highly profitable activities in 1999, it won't have to be reported, and the taxes won't have to be paid to the IRS until April 15, 2000. But by then, there won't *be* an IRS. For that matter, if I don't file my estimated taxes and withholding taxes in the fourth quarter of 1999, there won't be an IRS to come after me in calendar year 2000."

We have no idea whether such a daydream is at all realistic; for all we know, the government has contingency plans for mobilizing the National Guard to collect taxes (that's intended to be a joke, by the way). What we *do* know is that the current tax system, as implemented by the Internal Revenue Service, depends heavily on voluntary compliance. If that compliance disappears because of real and/or perceived Year-2000 computer problems, the political consequences would be enormous.

The Defense Department

As noted earlier, the U.S. Department of Defense (DOD) has at least two unique problems as compared to other government agencies. First, it has far more software than any other federal or state organization—more, even, than entire industries in the private sector; current estimates of the aggregate military software portfolio are in the range of 30 billion program instructions. Second, its software has been written in dozens of arcane programming languages that are no longer in current use—including high-level languages like Jovial, and low-level assembly languages for computer hardware that's no longer being manufactured.

And there's a third obvious problem: Some, though not all, of the DOD software is embedded in weapons, for which the

consequences of a Year-2000 software bug could be catastrophic. Planes, missiles, bombs, tanks, satellites, ships, air-
defense systems, and devices whose existence DOD has never
admitted in public—all of these and more are controlled by,
scheduled by, or interact with, date-sensitive computers.

Aside from the weapons, DOD is a massive human organization, employing (in a manner of speaking) millions of men
and women in the U.S. and dozens of countries abroad. Thus,
there are massive computer systems for dealing with payroll,
housing, insurance, retirement benefits, scheduling and logistics of people and equipment, and so forth. These systems are
similar to the business applications in private-sector organizations, and they are vulnerable to the same kind of Year-2000
problems.

To further complicate matters, DOD is not a single organization with a simple hierarchical management structure. The
Army, Navy, Air Force, and Marines all have their own separate computer systems, in addition to some that they share on
an inter-agency basis. Then, too, there are the computer systems of the CIA and NSA, as well as other defense-related
organizations. And most of the weapons and equipment used
by the military agencies—along with the associated computer
systems—are built by aerospace companies and defense contractors. Thus, it's not entirely unreasonable to say that the
military is Year-2000-compliant, only if the Boeings, Lock-
heeds, TRWs, and several hundred other private-sector companies are Year-2000-compliant, too.

Notwithstanding these problems, DOD is now beginning
to address the Year-2000 problems with considerable energy
and financial resources; indeed, as of March 1997, the Army
announced that Year-2000 repairs had become a top priority.
But progress is slow, and DOD's estimated completion date is

dangerously close to the ultimate deadline. In a May 15, 1997 report submitted by Franklin D. Raines, Director of the Office of Management and Budget (OMB), entitled "Getting Federal Computers Ready for 2000,"[13] the OMB estimated that DOD would finish its assessment work (i.e., determining which of its computer systems needed Year-2000 repairs, and how much work would be involved) by December, 1997; the "renovation" work (which we've referred to as "repairs" throughout this book) is scheduled to finish by December 1998; "validation" is scheduled to finish in June 1999; and "implementation" (i.e., installing the Year-2000-modified computer systems) is scheduled to finish by November 1999. The only two federal agencies whose estimated implementation dates are later are the Veteran's Administration and the Department of Transportation.

Unfortunately, DOD is famous within the computer industry for projects that are years behind schedule, millions of dollars over budget, and ultimately useless when delivered. While this may sound like a blanket criticism of everything DOD does, we should also point out that the requirements and constraints of DOD software and DOD computer projects make banking systems and other corporate business applications look like child's play by comparison. Not many systems are involved with saving lives, defending lives, and destroying enemy lives on the scale that DOD attempts. But while we sympathize with the difficulty and complexity of DOD's work, the fact remains: The Year-2000 work that DOD faces will, by far, be the largest and most difficult project it has ever undertaken. Frankly, we think the odds of it finishing all of its work on time are virtually zero; the only hopeful note is that DOD, far more than any other organization we've discussed in this book (with the possible exception of the medical industry) *truly* understands the meaning of triage. We assume that DOD is concentrating its resources on the weapons systems and appropriate support systems that are truly crucial.

On the other hand, reports like the one excerpted below from the GAO certainly don't improve one's confidence in the DOD Year-2000 effort:[14]

> *If CCSS cannot correctly process dates on and after January 1, 2000, military equipment, such as tanks, artillery, aircraft, missiles, munitions, trucks, electronics, and other supporting materials for the soldier, in all likelihood, will not be ordered, stored, transported, issued, paid for, or maintained. Mobilization plans and contingencies would be significantly impaired if materiel is delayed. However, LSSC has yet to resolve several critical problems associated with the assessment phase to ensure that (1) systems are adequately tested, (2) contingency plans are developed, and (3) interface partners are fully aware of LSSC's Year 2000 plans. Furthermore, during the same time that LSSC is addressing the Year 2000 issue, the agency is also working to implement considerably more software projects than it has in the past. This unprecedented workload is compounded by a reduced staff level and LSSC's basic lack of a mature software development and maintenance process. Together, these factors raise the risk level of the Year 2000 project beyond what is normally expected of a software modification effort of this magnitude. Until these problems are resolved, LSSC is not well-positioned to move forward into the more time-consuming phases of renovation, validation, and implementation. As a result, we believe LSSC will find it increasingly difficult to prepare CCSS in time for the arrival of the year 2000.*

Other Federal Agencies

Of course, the government consists of more than the IRS, SSA, and military services. There are dozens of other agencies, and it would require an entire book to discuss them one by one. The "scorecard" published independently by Capers Jones[15] in the summer of 1997, and by Congressional Representative Stephen Horn's Congressional subcommittee in September 1997,[16] are two interesting summaries of the overall state of affairs:

Table 10-1

Federal Agency	Grade: (Jones, Horn)
International Aid	A, F
Office of Personnel Management	A, D
Small Business Administration	A, B
Social Security	A, A-
Education	B, F
Nuclear Regulatory Agency	B, D
Department of State	B, C
Department of Defense	C, C-
Treasury Department	C, D-
National Science Foundation	C, B
Department of Agriculture	D, D-
Department of Commerce	D, D
Environmental Protection Agency	D, C
Health and Human Services	D, B-
Housing (HUD)	D, C
General Services Administration	D, B
Veterans Affairs	D, C

Table 10-1 (Continued)

Federal Agency	Grade: (Jones, Horn)
Department of Justice	D, D
Department of Interior	D, C
NASA	D, D-
Federal Emergency Management Agency	F, C
Department of Labor	F, C
Department of Energy	F, D
Department of Transportation	F, F

The grades shown above were intended to mimic a student's report card; but in the context of Year-2000, a "D" means "behind schedule," and an "F" means "dangerously unprepared."

State and Local Agencies

While state governments are obviously much, much smaller than the federal government, their Year-2000 tasks are also daunting—especially in such large states as New York, California, and Texas. Even the city governments can be critical. Consider the consequences of a severe disruption in welfare, police, and other services in cities like Chicago, Los Angeles, or New York.

There are, of course, 50 states; and within those states, there are several hundred medium- and large-sized cities, plus thousands of smaller towns and villages. The states are all working on Year-2000 projects independently; at the time this book was being written, it appeared that California and Florida were making good progress in their Year-2000 efforts, and another eight states have made some progress.[17] But most have not—either because of lack of awareness, or lack of budget authority. As Bob Violino reported in March 1997:

> *Many states are off to a slow start. Only 13 of 44 CIOs said their states were in the implementation or testing stage of year-2000 fixes, according to a survey conducted by the NASIRE year-2000 working group. Twenty respondents didn't know how many lines of code they needed to convert; 11 hadn't set a target completion date for conversion; and 20 didn't have an estimate of how much year-2000 fixes would cost.*[18]

Some of the problems with budgeting for Year-2000 repairs in state government organizations are: (a) budgets are limited in the best of cases; and (b) the estimates for Year-2000 work are often hysterically optimistic to begin with, and then escalated dramatically shortly thereafter. A good example is North Carolina. The state legislature had allocated approximately $7 million dollars for Year-2000 repairs as of the spring of 1997, but the State Controller reported, at about the same time, that the current estimate for repairs was $300 million.[19] In a report compiled by Steve Davis, the Budget Manager of Montgomery County, Maryland (see http://www.erols.com/steve451/impact.htm), the estimated aggregate *salary* cost for fixing the Year-2000 problem at the state level is $75 billion. For states that are already squeezed for budget appropriations, this is going to be difficult; if nothing else, we can be reasonably sure that it will provoke prolonged (i.e., time-consuming) debates before the funds are allocated. Meanwhile, the clock is ticking.

Bottom line: We expect that California, Florida, and a few other states will come through the Year-2000 problem in reasonably good shape; a dozen others will do a moderate-to-mediocre job. But that leaves quite a number of states (and their associated county and local governments). According to a report compiled by the U.S. Department of Health and Human Services in April 1997,[20] two-thirds of the states had not even completed the "assessment" stage of their Year-2000 projects; we doubt very much that they will be finished.

What Is Government Doing About the Year-2000 Problem?

In a nutshell: Lots of bluster and hot air in Congressional hearings, lots of frantic activity within the federal government agencies, less activity in the state agencies—*and virtually nothing from the President or Vice President*, aside from Bill Clinton's four brief sentences quoted at the beginning of the chapter.

Reports from the GAO and OMB, and presentations to various technology-related Congressional committees and subcommittees, have at least served the useful purposes of creating some public exposure and providing some credibility to what otherwise might have been dismissed as paranoia on the part of a few computer freaks. The first major hearing of this kind occurred in September 1996, and there have been a number throughout 1997, as this book was being written.[21] We expect more in 1998, and things will probably build to a fever pitch as we move into 1999. But it's important to remember that nothing *happens* in these committee hearings; experts are invited to present a speech, government officials wring their hands and agree with one another that the situation is dangerous, and several government agencies are still woefully unprepared for Year-2000. And then the hearing is over, and everyone goes home.

Meanwhile, activity proceeds—with varying budgets and degrees of intensity—within the various agencies. As we've already pointed out, the IRS, SSA, and military services are hard at work; in earlier chapters, we've also noted the Year-

2000-related activities of the FAA, Nuclear Regulatory Agency, and others. There are several inter-agency committees and task forces that may provide some degree of coordination and sharing of information. But as of September 1997, several major federal agencies had missed their deadline for assessing the size and scope of their Year-2000 work; those agencies included the Treasury, Defense, Transportation, and Agriculture departments.[22]

In terms of national leadership—i.e., in the House, Senate, and Executive branch of government—there has been an ominous silence. A few Congressional Representatives and Senators have expressed concern (it should be remembered that there are a few technically-literate members of the House and Senate, including former executives of computer companies); of these, the most senior and best known is Senator Daniel Patrick Moynihan. Moynihan introduced a bill (S.22) into the Senate on January 21, 1997 "to establish a bipartisan national commission to address the year 2000 computer problem"; the bill was read twice (we can't help wondering if that was necessary because some of the attending members were hard of hearing, or perhaps sound asleep) and then referred to the Committee on Governmental Affairs. At the time this went to press, the bill was still in a state of limbo, though Senator Moynihan continues to be one of the most outspoken advocates for serious attention to the Year-2000 problem.

Neither of the authors have the kind of first-hand political reporting experience that P.J. O'Rourke exhibited so eloquently:[23]

> *The government is huge, stupid, greedy and makes nosy, officious and dangerous intrusions into the smallest corners of life—this much we can stand. But the real problem is that*

government is boring. We could cure or mitigate the other ills
Washington visits on us if we could only bring ourselves to
pay attention to Washington itself. But we cannot.

But we can make some reasonable guesses about the likely
actions from government both before and after New Year's
Eve, 1999. We can also offer some thoughts about what government leaders *should* be doing, though we seriously doubt
that any of this advice will be followed.

Before the Year-2000 deadline occurs, we expect to see a
steadily rising level of rhetoric and activity in Washington—
and, to a lesser extent, in the various state capitols. Here's what
it's likely to consist of:

- *Exhortations, edicts, and regulations*—Congressional committees will continue to proclaim, in
  ever-louder terms, just how serious the situation
  is, and how important it is to do something.
  Agencies that have any power to enact regulations and restrictions on products, services, and
  activity in the private sector will begin doing so;
  indeed, the FDA *has* already begun doing so.
  Perhaps more interesting was the mid-Septem-
  ber 1997 statement from the OMB, which publicly threatened to restrict future IT expenditures
  in four of the agencies (Agriculture, Transportation (which includes the FAA), Education, and
  Aid for International Development) because
  "they missed completion dates for assessing systems, did not show measurable improvement
  since the May report, did not keep to their
  schedule for completion of the phases for best
  practices and failed to update their information,
  because they had not met their own published

schedule, and were not demonstrating adequate progress in their Year-2000 plans."[24]

- *Committees, commissions, and task forces*—Senator Moynihan's bill calling for the creation of a national commission is a noble gesture—but it's highly unlikely to accomplish anything, even if it is approved. Technical committees that establish computer interfaces for exchanging post-Year-2000 data will be helpful,[25] but committees that provide yet another opportunity for the Democrats to yell at the Republicans (or vice versa) won't delay the Year-2000 deadline by even a second.

- *Massive last-minute funding*—During the early-to mid-1990s, when money could have been productively used to pay for Year-2000 programmers or Year-2000 computer tools, budgets have been tight; in February 1997, the Office of Management & Budget (OMB) warned Congress that it could not count on the government to come up with extra money for Year-2000 projects. But that will change as the calendar moves into late 1998 and early 1999. Political leaders, being even more oblivious and pig-headed than senior corporate managers about the realities of software development, will announce emergency appropriations to solve the Year-2000 problem. They'll expect applause from citizens, and a sigh of relief from beleaguered agency officials. But computer programmers across the land will look at one another and whisper,

"Brooks' Law: Adding more programmers to a late software project just makes it later."

Notice the fundamental, unspoken premise that underlies all of this: Political leaders assume that this is "merely" a technical problem, and that by definition, technical problems can be solved. It's just a matter of exerting the appropriate level of authority, finding the appropriate amount of money in the budget, and *commanding* that the problem will, by God, be solved. With that perspective, one could argue that gravity is a "technical" problem. But no amount of money or authority or eloquent speeches is going to change the law of gravity; and while the Year-2000 problem doesn't involve something quite as absolute as gravity, it does share the common property that it cannot be coerced by political persuasion. As a result, most of the pre-2000 political activity concerning Year-2000 is likely to be about as effective as rearranging deck chairs on the *Titanic*.

What happens *after* January 1, 2000? That depends, obviously, on the severity of the Year-2000 failures that emerge. If it turns out that *all* of the consequences are nothing more than a few sporadic, unrelated, two-day disruptions, political leaders will proudly announce that it was their brilliant foresight that saved the day (2000 is an election year, after all!), and no further activity will be required. It's instructive to note, for example, that Senator Moynihan's S.22 bill calls for the dissolution of the national Year-2000 commission on December 31, 1999.

But suppose the problem is worse; suppose the problems are systemic, interrelated, and long-term in duration. Suppose the stock market goes into a free fall reminiscent of October 1929, and a thousand banks fail during the first six months of 2000. Suppose the lights go out for a month in a dozen major cities, and armed warfare breaks out in the streets because of the failure of food, food-stamp, and welfare check distribution. Suppose the airports shut down for six months because the FAA has far worse Year-2000 problems than anyone has imagined. Obviously, it would be far better for everyone if none of these things happened—but suppose God is in a bad mood after December 31, 1999, and several of these things *do* happen. What should we expect the federal government (and in a similar vein, the various state governments) to do?

Obviously, we don't know—nor does anyone else. And if you could get a competent politician to talk about it today (off the record, of course!), whatever he or she told you would be a "best guess," depending on the specific nature of the crisis, and also depending on the political mood of the moment. Nevertheless, the history of political reactions to previous crises leads us to make what we feel are some plausible predictions:

- *Finger-pointing and cover-your-ass speeches*—The first instinct of a politician will be to ensure that he or she cannot be blamed for having caused the Year-2000 problem, either through omission or commission. Corporate leaders are worried about this too, and they have the additional concern about stockholder lawsuits, class-action lawsuits, and even criminal liability because they are in a position of fiduciary responsibility. Political leaders will probably be able to wiggle out of this; it's unlikely we're going to see a Year-2000 version of the Nuremberg trials. But political leaders have their own form of Judgment Day—usually called Election Day. As noted earlier, 2000 is an election year, and any politician with a survival instinct will be trying to show ev-

eryone that he or she did his/her best to warn
Congress of impending doom. Though we
staunchly believe that Senator Moynihan is sincerely concerned about taking steps now to prevent the Year-2000 problem, it must have
occurred to his aides, if not to himself, that his
proposed S.22 legislation would help ensure his
reelection in the post-2000 years.

• *Enormous amounts of debate and wrangling over
  the steps to be taken—with a high risk that the
  wrong steps will be taken*—This is a reasonably
  safe prediction, for momentous decisions about
  difficult problems have always caused massive
  debate. Keep in mind that the Year-2000 problem, if it turns out to be serious, is not going to
  be a situation like Pearl Harbor. There won't be
  a reasonable excuse for Bill Clinton (who, in the
  normal course of events, will still be President
  when the clock chimes midnight at the end of
  1999) to convene a joint session of Congress, as
  FDR did after the December 7th "day of infa-
  my," and declare war on a tyrannical enemy.
  How can you declare war on a bunch of invisible
  software bugs in computer programs? Perhaps
  that won't stop Mr. Clinton; perhaps he'll declare war on the Year-2000 problem, just as recent national leaders have declared war on
  inflation, drugs, apathy, and racial tension. It
  could make for a stirring speech, but before any
  decisions could be made, Congress and the Senate would have to argue about it until they're

blue in the face. If there's one thing that almost all historians and economists agree about the situation immediately after the Great Crash of 1929, it's that government took far too long to do anything, and then generally did the wrong thing for quite awhile before taking some significant action. We see no reason to be more optimistic about government's reaction to a Year-2000 disaster.

• *Public statements of optimism and earnest appeals for calm*—We have a picture in our mind's eye of a Fireside Chat, televised from whatever room of the White House still has fireplaces, in which Mr. Clinton tells us that we have nothing to fear but fear itself. Business leaders will tell us the same thing in the early days of a serious post-2000 crisis, because they don't want their banks to close, their businesses to fail, and their stock holdings to evaporate. It is a tribute to FDR's leadership qualities that a significant percentage of Americans apparently *did* believe that there was nothing to fear; it remains to be seen whether Mr. Clinton will be able to evoke such confidence and support in a serious Year-2000 crisis. Since the Year-2000 problems are likely to be *worse* in government agencies than in the private sector, it's hard for us to imagine why any rational citizen would believe anything that a political leader said during the post-Year-2000 aftermath—but in any case, the barrage of opti-

mistic statements, and appeals for calm, are virtual certainties in the post-2000 years.

- *Frantic efforts to apply a "quick-fix" to Year-2000
  mistakes, and to complete any unfinished Year-
  2000 conversions*—If food stamps, unemployment checks, Medicare payments, and Social Security checks can't be generated by computers in
  the aftermath of a Year-2000 problem, the idea
  may well occur to politicians that they can be
  written by hand. The volume of transactions will
  probably make such a desperate attempt totally
  unworkable, but it will look good politically; we
  can envision televised reports showing thousands of government bureaucrats frantically
  writing checks by hand. Meanwhile, the efforts
  to fix and finish the Year-2000 projects that
  should have been finished long before December
  31, 1999 will be doubled, and redoubled, and
  redoubled again. Programmers will collapse
  from exhaustion (if they haven't had the good
  sense to quit long before things reach this stage),
  but new ones will be drafted.

- *Emergency legislation will be enacted*—When a truly *serious* crisis occurs, political leaders either become paralyzed, or they invoke emergency powers
  to restrict and curtail the policies and procedures
  that operate under normal circumstances. The details depend on the severity of the crisis and the
  political climate, but the most likely actions we
  would see in a severe Year-2000 crisis would include currency restrictions (e.g., you can only

withdraw $100 a day from your bank account); rationing of critical resources; price freezes; massive intervention by the Treasury Department to prop up the stock market and major banks; and perhaps even martial law. We say this not to be alarmist; we simply observe that in the past, severe crises have led to severe actions.

What *Should* the Government Be Doing About Year-2000?

We are not political leaders, elected representatives, or appointed officials of any government agency; thus, we offer the suggestions below with the greatest humility and modesty. But we do feel very strongly that there is a fundamental question that must be addressed before any intelligent discussion about preferred government actions can take place. The question is: *Do you believe that serious Year-2000 problems and consequences can be completely avoided through concerted efforts on the part of business and government?*

If you believe the answer to this question is "Yes," then the logical advice about governmental action (as well as advice to corporate leaders in the private sector) will be *preventive* in nature. Spend more, work harder, plan better, etc. The premise of the Year-2000 optimist is that, with enough work, money, people, and dedication, the problem *can* be solved. And, for whatever it's worth, that is the universal tone of the articles that laymen and professionals will find in the newspaper and magazine articles being written in 1997.

If *we* believed that the answer to our question was "Yes," we would not have written this book—for in that case, what would be the point of imagining scenarios in which critical services were disrupted for a month or a year? So our advice about appropriate governmental action is predicated on the assumption that *Year-2000 efforts will fail,* despite the best efforts of hundreds of thousands of dedicated, hard-working people. Yes, of course, most of the computer systems will be converted; but if you've understood the arguments we've presented in this book, you'll know why we think that some Year-2000 problems will slip through the cracks. Not just one or two, and not just the minor ones—but a sufficient number of major problems that we will see serious, systemic disruptions in the economy and nation's infrastructure.

So our first piece of advice to the government is: Take this book, and any other information you can find, as a starting point for your own scenario planning. Develop your own predictive models to determine the possibility of major disruptions of the kind described in this book. If you feel there's a non-trivial chance of such disruptions occurring, then *invest money in post-Year-2000 disaster planning,* including such things as:

- *Creating emergency contingency plans, to be implemented with Army or National Guard troops*— We've already suggested that riots could break out in the aftermath of a Year-2000 problem. Why not prepare emergency food and shelter in advance, just as authorities would do for an approaching hurricane?

- *Provide disaster-planning advice and guidelines for citizens*—The ideas in this book could be a starting point, but more detailed checklists and guidelines will be important. How should city dwellers plan on heating their apartments if they lose their oil heat and electricity, especially during winter periods? What steps should be taken in the event of disruptions in the food supply? How should people plan to communicate in the absence of a telephone system or Internet connection?

- *Plan damage control* before *January 1, 2000*—We will probably be accused of being isolationist in nature, but it seems to us that American troops would be much better utilized protecting American cities than Bosnian cities in the days following January 1, 2000. And if a scenario-planning exercise confirms that things could be as bad as the worst-case scenarios we've outlined in this book, then various systems and organizations should be shut down *before* New Year's Eve, 1999. Bring the troops home, shut down the Year-2000-sensitive military systems, and shut down whatever part of Washington is virtually guaranteed to fail after January 1, 2000. In the context of a Year-2000 disaster, *no* action from government may be better than *wrong* action.

- *Provide a realistic assessment to citizens of how bad the Year-2000 situation is, and how long it's likely to last*—This assumes that government leaders can exhibit characteristics of honesty and forthright, direct communication; it also assumes they will treat the public as mature, intelligent adults. These assumptions are obviously somewhat naïve, but it seems to us that most intelligent citizens would prefer to hear an accurate assessment of the situation, and an honest estimate of how long the crisis is likely to last. Faced with this information—unpleasant as it might be—we could then make whatever plans we felt appropriate.

We could elaborate on these points, for there's obviously a great deal of detail that would be required to implement them effectively. But we won't do so, for a very simple reason: Everything we've suggested in this section of the chapter contradicts common behavior and practice in the political environment of the U.S. and every other country we're familiar with. In the ideal world, a government planning department would have written this book; we could have devoted our energies instead to solving the Year-2000 problem, rather than warning people about it. It's depressing to note that one of the agencies given an "F" by Capers Jones on the Year-2000 scorecard (see Table 10-1) is the Federal Emergency Management Agency (FEMA).

Fallback Advice—Two-Day Failures

If the various government agencies we've discussed in this chapter should go into a tailspin for no more than a couple of days, we would consider it a miracle. In many cases, no one would notice. It's relatively uncommon to find anyone who requires day-to-day access to, and interactions with, the SSA, welfare, unemployment, and food stamp agencies.

However, there *is* the possibility that the day or two of disruption could turn out to be the day your monthly retirement check was supposed to be mailed, or the day you were supposed to pick up your unemployment check from the state unemployment agency. Many of the computer systems run in monthly cycles—e.g., everyone whose surname begins with an "A" has his or her check generated on the first day of the month, everyone with a "B" has his or her check generated on the second day of the month, etc. Given the nature of the first two days of January, 2000, the "A" and "B" folks would run the risk of being told by a frazzled clerk that their checks didn't get generated. In the best of all cases, the check would be generated a few days later, when the government agency corrected whatever minor blip caused the problem; but given the volume of processing involved, it's also possible that the "fallback" strategy within the agency would be to wait until the first day of the *next* month, at which point two months' worth of payments can be made. Thus, even a minor problem, which affects only a small percentage of the constituency served by the agency, could have month-long consequences.

There are other aspects of government service for which even a short-term breakdown could be serious; in particular, we're concerned about the services provided by police, fire departments, Coast Guard units, etc. Obviously, there's not much the average citizen can do to influence this, and the only reasonable advice we can think of is to maintain a low profile during the first few days of calendar year 2000.

Fallback Advice—One-Month Failures

If the Year-2000 problem turns out to be significant enough to shut down one or more government agencies for a month, there are likely to be serious social and political consequences— both of a direct nature, and of a secondary, ripple effect nature.

To the extent that you depend on government for financial support, it means that you'd better have a "buffer" of a month's emergency funds. The unfortunate paradox, of course, is that the people who would be most seriously affected by a month-long disruption in food stamps, welfare checks, etc., are precisely the same people who lack the means to set aside a month's living expenses. But, there are others whose financial situation is less extreme—e.g., the majority of Social Security retirees—for whom the advice of stockpiling a month's financial resources might not be so absurd. We have no "instant cure" solution for this problem, and the only optimistic observation we can make is that it's better to be aware of the prospect of a serious problem two years in advance than it is to be taken entirely by surprise. If a problem of this magnitude develops sometime in the first few months of 2000, there are bound to be a lot of angry people— both middle-class retirees, as well as low-income welfare recipients, who sputter indignantly, "Why didn't someone warn us about this in advance?" If nothing else, you should consider this book to be your warning.

A more serious concern is that of a major social collapse in various urban centers if government services are disrupted for a month. It could take two or three months of non-delivery of Social Security checks before people begin marching on Washington; but it could take much less time for riots and looting to break out in urban ghettos if food stamps, welfare checks, and other forms of financial assistance are disrupted. The situation could be compounded by Year-2000 problems in the police, fire department, and other civil services; New Yorkers, for example, could look forward to the possibility of a shutdown in garbage-collection services, as well as the subways and city-financed schools.

America's cities, alas, have some experience with riots, looting, and various other forms of urban unrest. They've often been triggered by individual events—e.g., the Rodney King incident in Los Angeles in 1994, or the electrical blackout in New York City in 1977—and they have often required substantial police force to bring them under control. In this case, the "trigger" could be the disruption in welfare checks or food stamps, but there is likely to be much more of a "systemic" nature to the problems that motivate hungry, unemployed, and generally disgruntled people to take matters into their own hands. If the Year-2000 disruptions go on for a month, there's no reason to believe that the riots will last only a week; indeed, we could well find a situation where government authorities have no alternative but to impose martial law.

All of which leads to a basic question: Do you want to continue living in an urban center under circumstances like these? Even if you have a one-month supply of TV dinners in your refrigerator (and a generator to power the refrigerator in the event of electrical failures), it may not be safe on the streets for weeks at a time. The prospect of this kind of Year-2000-induced social breakdown might not be enough to persuade you to sell your home and move out of the city *now*, but it should be enough for you to make "fallback" plans to leave your urban residence for a month-long sabbatical if things get bad.

Our assumption is that the situation would not be as bad in the suburban and rural areas, but this could turn out to be a dangerous assumption indeed. For example, both federal and state government agencies sometimes turn out to be major employers in smaller towns and suburban areas; whether it's a regional processing center for the IRS, or an administrative center for the state unemployment agency, it could well turn out that a significant number of people are furloughed by a Year-2000 shutdown that lasts more than a few days. We don't expect that furloughed IRS workers are going to indulge in looting and rioting, but the point is that if these agencies represent a major part of the economy in a small town, the effect of the disruption could be significant.

Fallback Advice—One-Year Failures

What if the Year-2000 problem is sufficiently serious that food stamps, unemployment benefits, Society Security checks, and other government services are disrupted for a year? If you're financially dependent on any of these organizations, the unavoidable reality is that you're going to have to change your lifestyle. The likelihood of the average citizen taking this seriously, and making some proactive decisions now, is fairly small; it's such an unpleasant prospect that most people would prefer to simply cross their fingers and hope that the Year-2000 problem will somehow be solved at the last moment, just as we've come to expect in most "disaster" movies. And as we've already noted, the low-income, unemployed, and welfare-class part of the population has little, if any, ability to make proactive decisions about its economic future.

So this part of the discussion must be aimed at the reader who has some degree of flexibility for proactive Year-2000 planning, even if the potential choices all seem unpleasant. If you're a retirement-age person in reasonable health, you'd better find a "backup" form of employment—even if it's flipping hamburgers at McDonald's. If you're a farmer or small business owner who has been able to take advantage of government subsidies and benefits, you've got two years to restructure your business so that it can survive, if not prosper, on its own. And if you're concerned about the dangers of living in an urban center whose low-income residents have been cut off from food stamps and welfare for a year, then you should move to a safe area now—while you can. And while you're thinking about this, keep the ripple effect problem in mind. In addition to disruption in government services, we've already discussed the possibility of disruptions in utilities, transportation, banking, communications, news, and your own job.

The alternative is to cross your fingers and hope for the best—which is what we expect 90-95% of the population to do. But in that case, events are out of your hands, and you're no longer in control. The low-income, unemployed, and welfare-class citizens might shrug their shoulders and remind you that they've never had much control over their situation; but the middle- and upper-class elite in most urban centers have traditionally had the luxury (or perhaps the illusion) that they *are* in control. Thus, the consequences of a systemic Year-2000 disruption could be quite a psychological shock, in addition to everything else.

Fallback Advice—Ten-Year Failures

Will government vanish from our lives for a decade? Will the police and fire departments vanish from cities for ten years? Will we have to wait for a decade for a new Thomas Paine to write a *Post-2000 Common Sense* that will galvanize a new generation of leaders to create a new Constitution?

Such an apocalyptic future is far beyond anything we can imagine, despite the rather gloomy nature of everything else we've written in this book. Presumably, some form of current government will survive; presumably there will still be a Congress and a Senate, and our political leaders will still find a way to raise taxes to pay for the army and the bureaucracy.

But the devil is in the details. While our three-branch, representative form of government will presumably survive, the balance of power between the states and federal government could shift substantially. Even if there's a Congress and a Senate, there may not be a Social Security Administration, or an IRS, or a Medicare. Changes like these would be revolutionary in nature, at least from the perspective of the segment of society whose entire lives have been influenced or controlled by these government agencies. As John Kenneth Galbraith observed about revolutions:

> *All successful revolutions are the kicking in of a rotten door. The violence of revolutions is the violence of men who charge into a vacuum.*[26]

The important thing to remember here is that while faulty technology may be responsible for creating a serious Year-2000 crisis in various government services, technology won't be responsible for the long-term disappearance of those same services. If, for example, all of the computer systems and all of the computer programmers of the Social Security Administration implode into a black hole, along with every other employee and every piece of furniture, the whole thing could be reconstructed within a few years—if government and society felt strongly motivated to do so. The problem (or the opportunity, depending on your perspective) is that leaders in government, as well as various lobbying groups, and ultimately the voting public itself, will be saying, "Since we have a chance to start with a clean slate, we should organize Social Security in an entirely different way...let's do it this way..." The debate would continue for months, if not years, and the ultimate decision would be a political decision, not a technological decision, to re-build Social Security exactly as it was before, or in a radically different way, or not to build it at all.

If someone predicted that the sun was not going to come up on January 1, it would be a terrific shock. Assuming you could get past the "denial" stage and sincerely believe the prediction, it would still be a terrific shock; after all, a great deal of your life is predicated on a regular, predictable separation between night and day. While it may seem a bit of an exaggeration, a substantial number of citizens have a similar reaction to the prospect of their favorite government service disappearing.

This would not have been the case a century ago, because the average citizen was far less influenced by and/or dependent upon government services; indeed, this entire chapter would have been reduced to a paragraph or two. It's also intriguing to note that the two generations represented by the authors of this book are relatively blasé about the prospect of Social Security collapsing at some future date, and *not* being a reliable source of post-retirement income—simply because we've been warned of this possibility on a regular basis for the past twenty years. The problem is that warnings of a Year-2000-induced collapse of Social Security or any of the other government services discussed in this chapter have only begun this year—and for the most part, the average citizen has not heard the warning, or has decided not to believe what he or she hears.

If you've read this far, then consider yourself warned again. Social Security could disappear. Food stamps could disappear. Farm subsidies could disappear. Unemployment and welfare assistance could disappear. Student loans and low-income housing assistance could disappear. All of these things, and more, could disappear for a decade or for the rest of our lives, beginning in January 2000—not because it's technologically impossible to build entirely new computer systems, but because the political reaction to a Year-2000 crash might banish them from the landscape forever.

How do you plan or prepare for such a contingency? The words are easy, but the actions will be difficult. The words are: Become self-sufficient, remain flexible, and don't assume that the government services you depend upon are as eternal and as reliable as the daily rising of the sun.

Endnotes

1. The entire speech by President Clinton, together with a related speech by the First Lady, was posted on the Internet at http://www.whitehouse.gov/Initiatives/Millennium/announcement.html#president.

2. Capers Jones, *The Year 2000 Software Problem: Quantifying the Costs and Assessing the Consequences* (Addison-Wesley), 1997, p. 52.

3. Later, Mr. Hollerith founded the company that became IBM. This, too, is a common pattern: Government often provides the funding and/or the justification for a computer project; it then moves in various ways into the private sector.

4. Capers Jones, *op cit.*, p.52

5. Similar comments can be heard from first-level and second-level managers, whose frustration with the bureaucracy has embittered them over the years. The interesting thing is that even if a mid-level manager made such a statement in public, and even if one could somehow prove that the Year-2000 project failed because of the manager's lack of enthusiasm, there would probably be no legal recourse. Year-2000 projects are being spurred on in the private sector partially because of fears of massive litigation from angry customers; but with rare exceptions, citizens are not allowed to sue their government.

6. For details on this, see http://www.cio.com/forums/091596_socsec.html.

7. We have no way of knowing whether the contractor was doing a good job or a bad job, or whether he or she deserved to be fired from the project. The point is that such abrupt changes in the middle of any large, complex software project almost always create delays and disruptions, even in the best of cases; in the worst of cases, such a change is the straw that breaks the camel's back. It remains to be seen what happens with the Medicare project.

8. Joe Sexton, "Merchants with Stubborn Hopes," *New York Times*, July 19, 1997, p. 1, 20.

9. This can be found surfing at both http://www.ustreas.gov/treasury/bureaus/irs/prime/primerfc.htm on the Internet, and by selecting "Request For Comment No. TIRNO-97-H-0010". It's a 116-page Adobe Acrobat document describing the new IRS modernization program. It describes a complex system on the verge of collapse, and a staggeringly complex plan for modernizing it.

10. An e-mail message from an IRS programmer sent to members of a Year-2000 Internet mailing list claimed that the figure was closer to 62 million lines of code. But other IRS documents have strongly implied that nobody is quite sure what the number is—for there are an unknown number of computer programs, spreadsheets, and databases that have been developed on personal computers spread throughout the vast IRS organization.

11. Bob Violino and Bruce Caldwell, "And Now For The Bad News," *Techweb*, April 21, 1997. You can retrieve this article from the Internet at http://techweb.cmp.com/iw/627/27iuyr4.htm.

12. See "IRS Seeks $258M more for Year 2000 solution," by Elana Varon, *Federal Computer Week*, June 23, 1997 (available on the Internet at http://www.fcw.com/pubs/fcw/1997/0623/fcw-newbudget-6-23-97.htm).

13. You can retrieve this from the Internet at http://www.cio.fed.gov/yr2krev.htm.

14. "Defense Computers: LSSC Needs to Confront Significant Year 2000 Issues." GAO report AIMD-97-149. 21 pp. plus two appendices (6 pp.), September 26, 1997. Available on the Internet at http://www.gao.gov/new.items/ai97149.pdf.

15. Capers Jones, *The Year 2000 Software Problem: Quantifying the Costs and Assessing the Consequences* (Addison-Wesley, 1997), p. 83.

16. Stephen Barr, "Year 2000 Report Flunks 3 Agencies; Lawmakers Urge Special Aide to Handle Looming Computer Problem," *The Washington Post*, September 16, 1997; p. A15.

17. In "Two More States Claim Year 2000 Compliance," (*Information Week*, July 7, 1997), reporter Bruce Caldwell reports that Illinois, Wyoming, Arkansas, California, Georgia, Missouri, Oklahoma, Michigan, and Oregon claim that their financial management systems are now Year-2000-compliant. That leaves *lots* of other systems to worry about, and lots of other states.

18. Bob Violino, "50 States of Alert," *Information Week*, March 24, 1997. You can retrieve this from the Internet at http://www.techweb.com/se/directlink.cgi?IWK19970324S0054.

19. See Patrick Thibodeau, "Squabbling agencies endanger year 2000 work," *Computerworld*, April 21, 1997.

20. See Patrick Thibodeau, "Squabbling agencies endanger year 2000 work," *Computerworld*, April 21, 1997.

21. A particularly sobering report was provided by Sally Katzen, the Administrator of OMB's Office of Information and Regulatory Affairs on July 10, 1997 (see http://www.house.gov/science/katzen_7-10.html), in which Ms. Katzen reported that "71 percent of the 7,649 mission-critical systems ... must be repaired or replaced"—meaning that such repairs had not yet taken place.

22. As Dave Barry would say, "We aren't making this up." This deadline information comes from David Braun, "Feds Face Y2K Disaster, GAO Warns," *Techwire*, July 10, 1997. To retrieve this from the Internet, see http://www.techweb.com/wire/news/jul/0710year2000.html. For a related report, see Rajiv Chandrasekaran, "Government Said to Move Too Slowly on Year 2000 Computer Problem: Partial Crash Possible if Machines Aren't Able to Recognize Date, Specialists Warn," *The Washington Post*, July 10, 1997 (available on the Internet at http://washingtonpost.com/wp-srv/WPlate/1997-07/10/087L-071097-idx.html), which quotes Joel C. Willemssen, Director of Information Resources Management at GAO as saying, "It's becoming increasingly clear that agencies are not going to be able to correct everything before the year 2000. We're going to have to start making priorities among all the systems we view as critical."

23. P. J. O'Rourke, *Parliament of Whores*, "The Mystery of Government" (1991).

24. Nicole Lewis, "Feds signal deepening Y2K crisis," *Federal Computer Weekly*, Sept. 22, 1997.

25. For example, the computers at the IRS and SSA exchange tax-related information; both agencies are busily trying to convert their respective systems, and it's highly likely that a "windowing" approach will be used for at least some of

these systems. Thus, the computer programs will be modified so that any two-digit year will be assumed to exist within a century-wide "window." But if the IRS decides that its newly-defined window runs from 1940 to 2039, while the SSA uses a window stretching from 1910 to 2009, then any date-sensitive data passed between the two agencies would be interpreted in an inconsistent fashion. Agreeing on a common windowing convention between all of the government agencies would be a massive job, and could best be accomplished by keeping the politicians away from these committees.

26. John Kenneth Galbraith, *The Age of Uncertainty*, Chapter 3 (1977).

Year-2000 Impact on Embedded Systems

The world is divided into two categories: failures and unknowns.

Francis Picabia "L'Humour Poetique," in La Nef, no. 71–72 (Paris, Dec. 1950—Jan. 1951; reprinted in Yes No: Poems and Sayings, "Sayings," edited by Rémy Remy Hall, 1990).

Introduction

In several of the earlier chapters of this book, we mentioned the possibility of Year-2000-related failures in "embedded systems." Because there are so many different kinds of embedded systems, and because they affect so many other parts of the social infrastructure, we'll discuss them in a more general fashion in this chapter.

First, what do we mean by an "embedded system"? Historically, the term was used within the computer industry to describe a small "micro-computer" that was literally *embedded* within some larger piece of engineering equipment or industrial product. The embedded system provided the intelligence associated with "process control" systems (e.g., the control of mixing machines and heating vats in a chemical refinery) or "data acquisition" systems (e.g., a smart radar unit that performs on-the-fly analysis of both friendly and enemy aircraft).

As an example of the kind of problem that computer software professionals are worrying about within plants, refineries, and manufacturing organizations, consider the following excerpt from the January 8, 1997 issue of *The Dominion*, a Wellington, New Zealand newspaper that reported on the consequences of a non-Year-2000 date calculation problem:[1]

> *A computer glitch at the Tiwai Pt [in South Island of New Zealand] aluminum smelter at midnight on New Year's Eve has left a repair bill of more than $1 million [New Zealand Dollars]. Production in all the smelting potlines ground to a halt at the stroke of midnight when the computers shut down simultaneously and without warning. New Zealand Aluminum Smelters general manager David Brewer said the failure was traced to a faulty computer software programme, which failed to account for 1996 being a leap year.*
>
> *The computer was not programmed to handle the 366th day of the year, he said. "Each of the 660 process control computers hung up simultaneously at midnight," Mr. Brewer said. The same problem occurred two hours later at Comalco's Bell Bay smelter, in Tasmania [Australia]. New Zealand is two hours ahead of Tasmania. Both smelters use the same programme, which was written by Comalco computer staff. Mr. Brewer said the cause was difficult to trace and it was not till a telephone call in the morning from Bell Bay that the leap year link was made. "It was a complicated problem and it took quite some time to find out just what caused it."*
>
> *Tiwai staff rallied through the night to operate the potlines manually and try to find the cause. The glitch was fixed and normal production restored by midafternoon. However, by then, the damage has been done. Without the computers to regulate temperatures inside the pot cells, five cells over-heated and were damaged beyond repair. Mr. Brewer said they would have to be replaced at a cost of more than $1 million.*

Twenty years ago, these specialized computer systems were very expensive, and were thus used in a relatively small number of sophisticated factories and engineering installations. But in the past decade, computer chips have become dramatically smaller, cheaper, and more sophisticated—so that the term "embedded system" now encompasses almost any device that has "built-in" computer logic. Thus, the sophisticated oil refineries and radar systems still have embedded systems (for which the consequences of a Year-2000 failure could be disastrous, as illustrated in the above example), but we now have a similar kind of technology embedded in consumer appliances ranging from microwave ovens to VCRs to digital wristwatches to automobiles. A more dramatic example of "embedding" is the modern pacemaker that's literally embedded into a patient's body to help monitor and regulate his or her heartbeat.

A total of 3.5 *billion* microprocessors (the "chip" that constitutes the embedded system) were sold in 1995, and 7 *billion* were sold in 1997. It's reasonable to expect that equally large numbers will be sold in 1998 and 1999; thus, we're likely to have an aggregate of 25+ billion of these little machines floating around the planet on New Year's Eve, 1999. As we'll discuss below, only a small percentage of these chips are likely to be "year-sensitive," and only a small percentage could be described as "mission-critical" (in the sense that a failure could cause severe economic consequences and/or loss of life)—but even a small percentage of a small percentage can be a large number when we start with a population of 25 billion chips.

The vast quantity of these embedded systems is one of the key issues that you need to keep in mind. There are simply not enough programmers, not enough repair technicians, and not enough time to repair and/or replace them all; even if only one tenth of one percent of the 25 billion chips are Year-2000-defective, that still leaves us with 25 million repair jobs.

The problem is compounded by the nature of the embedded system. The "logic" carried out by the system is "burned into" the computer chip and, in most cases, cannot be changed. This is fundamentally different than the situation with your home PC and with the typical business computer system, where a Year-2000-defective software program can be modified and re-installed on the same computer. Thus, if it turns out that the word processor on your home PC is Year-2000-defective, you can ask Microsoft or Corel (makers of the two most popular word processing programs) to send you an updated/corrected version of their word processor, and you would never dream of throwing the entire PC in the garbage can. On the other hand, if your digital wristwatch turns out to be Year-2000-defective, chances are that you'll have to throw it away and buy a new one.

In some cases, the manufacturer can extract the microprocessor chip from the device in which it's embedded and insert a replacement chip. That might be a viable option for an expensive household appliance like a VCR or a fancy phone/fax/answering machine device. But in many cases, the manufacturer never planned for such replacements, and has no replacement chips available; this is particularly likely if the device is more than a few years old. The cost of such a replacement is going to be staggering, because it's labor-intensive work, and because large volumes are involved; thus, it will often turn out that the most practical solution is one of replacing the entire device, rather than attempting to replace the defective chip within it. Indeed, even this option may not be convenient, as in the case of the following apocryphal story quoted by *The Times of India*:[2]

> *Robin Guenier, the man charged with solving the "single most expensive problem in history", tells a story.*

"The micro-chip controls when the bank vault can be opened and closed. It allows the jackpot vault to be opened during the working week, but keeps it closed at weekends. For security reasons, it has been buried inside the 20-ton-door of the vault, and can only be inspected by removing the whole door.

"The big problem arises because the bank building has been built around the vault, again for security reasons. So to inspect or change the micro-chip requires half the building to be demolished and the door removed. The people who built the chip, the vault and the bank never imagined that the chip would have to be removed in the lifetime of the building," he added.

"But at midnight on December 31, 1999, something they never foresaw will happen. The chip has been programmed to read only the last two digits of the year, and assumes the 19 prefix. So it believes that it is back in 1900. That would make no difference, except that January 1, 2000 falls on a Saturday, while the same date in 1900 was a Monday. The vault will open on Saturday and Sunday, but not on later working days. So, to ensure depositors have access to their deposits, the bank building has to be demolished. That sums up the millennium problem."

This hints at another problem common to the industrial-variety of embedded systems: It's often very difficult to locate, identify, and manipulate embedded systems. The embedded systems in satellites are an obvious example; indeed, that's the essence of the problem with the Navy's GPS satellite system discussed in Chapter 4. Similarly, embedded systems submerged underwater in oil drilling platforms won't be easy to retrieve and fix.

Obviously, none of this is relevant unless embedded systems are vulnerable to Year-2000 failures. In some cases, it's fairly easy to tell, but in many cases, it's almost impossible for even a trained computer professional to predict the Year-2000-related behavior of an embedded system, and this has led to enormous debate within the computer industry. A relevant example: Is a typical automobile vulnerable to Year-2000 problems—and if so, how would we know in advance? The obvious solution would be to get a definitive statement (complete with a legal warranty) from the automobile manufacturer about the Year-2000-compliant status of its products; the fact that none of the auto manufacturers have made such a statement as of the time this book was being written, is sobering.

Several computer professionals have suggested a common-sense way of analyzing the situation: If an embedded system does not provide a human operator, or end-user, with a means of setting "current year" information, or changing that information, then it's unlikely that the embedded system is aware of, or dependent on, the year. In other words, it won't know that the year has "rolled over" from 99 to 00, and it won't care; it's not Year-2000-vulnerable. One can imagine a scenario where a chip *is* year-aware, even though the year can't be set by the end-user; the manufacturer may have "burned" a starting date into the chip corresponding to the year in which the chip was created. It's possible, but unlikely—so, for most people, the simple guideline will be: The newer the device (and thus the more sophisticated its internal micro-chip is likely to be) and the fancier its operating characteristics are, the more likely it is to be year-aware, and thus Year-2000-vulnerable.

For example, one of the authors spent the summer of 1997 writing this book with the assistance of coffee produced by a newly-purchased Mr. Coffee automated coffee-maker. The device allows the end-user to set the time of day, and can distinguish between AM and PM; but, it won't allow the user to set the day, month, or year. Ergo, it probably doesn't keep this information internally, and won't care about the Year-2000 rollover. The typical newly-purchased VCR, on the other hand, *does* allow the end-user to program year-sensitive dates into the device to specify when a specific TV show should be recorded in the future. Hence it *is* highly likely to be Year-2000-vulnerable, and there's no obvious way of knowing whether the device is indeed Year-2000-compliant.

In some cases, the situation may be a little more subtle. For example, the owner of today's modern automobile will probably discover that while he or she can set the time-of-day on his/her auto dashboard clock, he or she cannot set the day or year. But when he or she takes his/her car into the highly computerized service station for an annual tune-up, the auto mechanic can attach a diagnostic computer to the car; this enables the mechanic to read and/or update various "parameters" within the car's embedded systems (including, for example, a mileage counter that tells the auto owner how many miles remain before the car is due for its next servicing—an item that the mechanic forgot to reset when one of the authors last brought his Jeep into the shop for a tune-up!). The interesting point here is that there are embedded systems within the car that the owner may not even be aware of; for example, Jim Rivera made the following observation on a recent Year-2000 Internet discussion group:[3]

> There is a federal (U.S. gov) standard for a car's emissions control systems logging any failure conditions of the components, for example a fuel injector being open longer than it is supposed to due to some dirt in the fuel. The name for the logging system is OBD2 (On Board Diagnostics 2).
>
> This next is informed speculation. Suppose there is date-time logging for the failure. Suppose that the date routine for some of the software is (surprise) not Y2K compliant. Suppose the failure mode is either to lockup or refuse to run the car (unlikely but not impossible). I have seen statements in both directions - that some automotive engine control processors will or will not fail after The Day. It seems to me that it is likely

*that those who know (because they wrote the software) are
probably contractually bound to keep quiet. The rest of us are
just guessing.*

Of course, the fact that an embedded system is year-aware
and Year-2000-vulnerable does not necessarily mean that it
will fail on January 1, 2000; it simply means that we should
take steps to find out *in advance* if it will fail, and what the
consequences of a failure might be. The sense of urgency associated with this advance investigation depends on the nature
of the system itself. We might not bother checking the Year-
2000-compliant status of a $19.95 digital wristwatch, but we
probably should check the status of our car. To put it another
way: suppose the public-relations office at General Motors,
Ford, or Chrysler (or for that matter, Toyota, Honda, or
BMW) responds to your inquiry with the comforting assurance, "don't worry about your car's computer being Year-2000
compliant; the engine will run just fine after January 1, 2000."
But if you're hurtling down the highway at 80 m.p.h. on New
Year's Eve, 1999 and your engine suddenly dies at the stroke of
midnight, it won't be very easy to track that PR representative
down and ask for a refund.

The natural assumption is that automotive engineers would
design hardware-oriented failsafe mechanisms, *independent of
the onboard computer*, that would prevent an abrupt shutdown
in the event of a computer failure. And it's easy to imagine that
the worst consequence of a Year-2000-related computer failure
would be an annoying red alarm light on the auto dashboard
that says, "This car needs to be serviced *now!*" But the question is: *Are you willing to bet your life that it won't be any more
serious than that?* Unless you have a legally binding warranty
from the auto manufacturer, it seems to us that the best way of
testing the Year-2000-compliance of your car is to park it in
your garage or driveway on New Year's Eve 1999 and wait

until the morning of January 1 before turning on the ignition to see what happens.

Here's a summary of the situation we'll all be facing with regard to embedded systems that are "year-aware"—and both business organizations and government agencies will have similar situations. A good example of a high-risk embedded system for a business organization is its PBX telephone system; if it fails, then there's no telephone service even if AT&T continues functioning smoothly. As discussed in Chapter 9, medical electronic systems are "high-risk" for both the patient and the hospital. So are the elevators in high-rise office buildings.

Table 11-2

	Non-Year-2000 compliant	Year-2000 compliant
High-risk embedded system	Dangerous	Safe
Low-risk embedded system	Nuisance, but not dangerous	Nice, but somewhat irrelevant

Other systems—including many household appliances—fall into the category of low-risk embedded systems. As we've mentioned, many household appliances are not even aware of the year, and are thus not vulnerable to Year-2000 failures; it's the fancier and more sophisticated devices that may be vulnerable. If it turns out that your VCR fails, and you're unable to tape the *Seinfeld* show, chances are that you'll find a way to survive. But if you have an office at home and your integrated phone/fax/copier/answering machine stops working, it could have more serious consequences.

To prepare for this aspect of the Year-2000 rollover, you need to begin by making a list of the embedded systems that you depend on and/or interact with during your normal day-to-day life. For many people, this will require some careful attention, and even some detective work—for it simply doesn't occur to us that computers are embedded in almost every device that we use. If your household appliance, office machine, or apartment-building elevator has an LCD display (e.g., a bright green or bright red display that tells you the temperature of your oven, or the phone number being dialed on your office phone, or the floor number of your elevator), then it probably has an embedded system. If the LCD display shows the calendar date, it's a dead giveaway that it's year-sensitive, and thus Year-2000-vulnerable. And even if it doesn't display the date, it may be Year-2000-vulnerable.

The other thing to ask yourself is: *Does the device exhibit intelligent behavior?* By "intelligent," we don't necessarily mean the full-blown artificial-intelligence kind of behavior exhibited by IBM's Deep Blue chess-playing computer or HAL in the classic movie *2001*. What you need to look for is a device that responds in different ways to different environmental conditions—and in particular to different time-oriented schedules. The reason we're concerned about elevators in high-rise office buildings, for example, is that many of them are programmed to behave differently on weekends than they do on weekdays. As in the case of the Year-2000-defective bank vault mentioned above, a Year-2000-defective elevator could erroneously conclude that January 1, 2000 was actually January 1, 1900—which was a Monday. In that case, it might revert to its weekend behavior on Thursday, January 5, 2000—which could leave office workers stranded on the top floor of the building while the elevator stubbornly parked on the ground floor.

Many of us have come to accept "intelligent devices" as commonplace, and we don't even stop to think about it anymore. Thus, the prospect of a Year-2000 failure requires us to pay much closer attention to the engines, appliances, and devices that are so much a part of our lives. Indeed, sometimes the intelligent behavior is truly hidden from the end-user, as in the case of the fuel ignition and braking systems of a sophisticated modern automobile. Fortunately, the manufacturers of these devices and appliances are prone to brag about such features—for the next two years, it's worth paying attention to TV commercials and newspaper ads to see whether the manufacturer is indirectly warning us of potential Year-2000 problems.

Fallback Advice—Two-Day Failures

From the perspective of an embedded system, there is no such thing as a Year-2000-related two-day failure—the device either works or it doesn't work. As we've already pointed out, defective Year-2000 logic in an embedded device is essentially part of the hardware, not part of the changeable, modifiable software; thus, we don't have the option of calling in a programmer to make a few changes and thereby remedy the problem.

Thus, for household appliances and other devices that are under your direct control and ownership, there is a simple reality: Once the device has failed, it has failed for good. In a few rare cases, you might be able to order a replacement micro-chip from the manufacturer and replace the defective chip within the appliance unit; but in the majority of cases, you'll have to replace the entire device. If you're willing to pay for the replacement yourself (and if the stores are open, the lights are working, your credit card is operational, etc.), you might be able to find a replacement within a day or two. But if you send the device back to the manufacturer for an upgrade/ repair, it's likely to be months before you get it back.

The only scenario where the concept of a two-day disruption is relevant is the embedded device that's *not* under your direct control, but is instead controlled by a business or government agency that might have the resources to achieve a relatively quick replacement or repair. Thus, you might ask yourself: *What happens if the elevator in my apartment building has a Year-2000 failure and it takes the elevator company 2-3 days to replace the defective computer? What happens if the security system in my office building is defective and nobody can get into the office for 2-3 days?* In most cases, the consequences won't be immediately life-threatening; the important thing is to plan for such contingencies in advance, so that you won't be taken by surprise.

Fallback Advice—One-Month Failures

Because a Year-2000 failure in embedded systems requires the replacement of a computer chip, we believe that most failures will indeed take much longer than 2-3 days to repair. Household appliances can be replaced in 2-3 days, even if it requires the expensive option of buying a new appliance at the local store. But that's not a viable option when we're dealing with elevators, office security systems, and other expensive, sophisticated industrial-oriented embedded systems.

There are several areas where bottlenecks and delays are likely to occur. First, a "field" technician must be available— after all, we can't pull the elevator out of the office building and ship it back to the manufacturer, so a repair technician has to visit the office site to make the repairs. Ironically, the reason that many of these embedded systems will fail on January 1, 2000 is that even though the manufacturers already know that

their products are defective, there aren't enough repair technicians available to fix them in advance. The problem won't get
any better in the days immediately after January 1, 2000.

Second, the embedded system must be located and
"acquired" so that the repair work can be done. There's no
problem locating the elevator in an office building, though
there might be some minor problems "acquiring" it if it's stuck
mid-way between two floors. The situation described earlier
with the Year-2000-defective bank vault is a good example of
the problem some companies will face; similar problems exist
with embedded systems on the ocean floor, in satellites, or
submerged underground.

Third, a Year-2000-compliant replacement chip must be
available. In the case of elevators and other sophisticated high-
risk embedded systems, there's a very good chance that such
chips will have been manufactured and stockpiled in advance.
But this is less likely to be the case for the lower-risk, less-
expensive devices, especially office machines and household
appliances. Because the micro-chip industry is extremely competitive, and because the technology has been changing very
rapidly, new chips are introduced on an annual basis, and
sometimes even more frequently. Thus, if you have a vintage-
1992 VCR device that turns out to be Year-2000-defective,
there's a very good chance that the manufacturer will politely
explain that: (a) it's no longer under warranty; (b) it's obsolete;
(c) the chip manufacturer from whom they acquired the chip
to provide the VCR with its programmable intelligence has
discontinued that chip because it has a newer one that's ten
times faster and three times cheaper; (d) the new chip is
installed in all of the current-vintage VCRs; and (e) the new
chip won't work in the old VCR. Bottom line: You're screwed.

Thus, there is the distinct possibility that some of the embedded systems that you depend on will be out of service for a month or longer—until they can be replaced or upgraded with a Year-2000-compliant micro-chip. If it's an embedded system that belongs to you, you'll have to decide whether it's worth replacing with a brand-new unit, which will probably be done at your own expense. Perhaps you can tolerate the absence of your phone/fax/copier/answering machine for a couple of days, but you simply can't operate your home business for a month without such a device. The proactive strategy, of course, is to find out *now* whether the device is Year-2000-compliant, so that you can remedy the problem (ideally at the manufacturer's expense, rather than your own) *before* January 1, 2000. But if that turns out to be impractical, then the post-2000 strategy for one-month disruptions of personally-owned embedded systems is likely to be simple, straightforward, and expensive: be prepared to spend money for replacements.

A one-month disruption in a corporate- or government-owned embedded system is obviously a different matter; as a private citizen, you don't have the option of replacing a Year-2000-defective elevator in your apartment building. If embedded system failures occur within the office environment, it could lead to a month-long shutdown of your employer's business; thus, you may be faced with the unemployment scenarios that we discussed in Chapter 2. A month-long embedded system failure in hospitals could render some medical devices inoperable; this could lead to the scenarios we discussed in Chapter 9. And, embedded system failures in the security, heating, air-conditioning, elevator, plumbing, and other environmental systems could render modern apartment buildings unsafe or unlivable for a month at a time. As we've discussed in previous chapters, you may need to plan for a vacation to a tropical island where you can live in a grass hut for a month.

Fallback Advice—One-Year Failures

Severe backlogs, delays, and associated problems could conceivably cause year-long disruptions for some of the embedded systems we've discussed. Again, this is not likely to be the case for simple household appliances. If the manufacturer of your VCR is unable or unwilling to provide a replacement, you can always buy one from a competitor. Household appliances, digital watches, and many other examples of embedded systems are *commodities* today, and while there might be a temporary shortage created by Year-2000 problems, we don't expect that it will last for a year.

But, the expensive, sophisticated, industrial-strength embedded systems are *not* commodities, and it's conceivable that delays in their repair could last well beyond a month or two. In addition to the bottlenecks and delays already discussed above, the ability of, say, an elevator manufacturer to cope with all of the required upgrades and repairs of elevators that it has installed all over the country could be further impaired by the various ripple effect problems we've discussed throughout this book. Indeed, Brand-X elevator company could go bankrupt six months after the onset of Year-2000 problems; the remaining elevator manufacturers could easily take the position that they're unable and unwilling to repair the products of their former competitor; and, they might insist that the elevator be completely replaced with one of their own products. Given the other problems and delays associated with the overall Year-2000 phenomenon, it could well take a year before the Brand-X elevator is replaced by a Brand-Y elevator.

Unfortunately, it's simply impossible to predict in advance where, when, and how such year-long Year-2000 problems might occur. The only thing that we can be sure about is that if it *does* occur, it will necessitate an entirely different response, on your part, than a month-long failure requires. Thus, your fallback plan should be of a similar nature to the one-year disruption plans that you have for your job, your bank account, and other important aspects of your life.

Fallback Advice—Ten-Year Failures

As with the other aspects of Year-2000 problems, it's hard to imagine anything having such a devastating impact that a full decade would be required to get things back to normal. The technology required to produce Year-2000-compliant micro-chips already exists, and some vendors are already producing Year-2000-compliant embedded systems with them. Even if some go bankrupt, and even if a substantial number of non-Year-2000-compliant "legacy" chips must be replaced, it wouldn't take more than a couple of years. So what's the problem?

Clearly, we're not concerned about long-term problems with household appliances; and when it comes to decade-long consequences, we're not even concerned about elevators in high-rise office buildings. What we *are* concerned about is the embedded systems in underwater oil-drilling rigs, or embedded systems in nuclear reactors, or embedded flight-control and guidance systems in military satellites and guided missiles, or embedded process control systems in a natural-gas refinery located at the edge of a city. These are a few such scenarios where a Year-2000-related failure could involve radiation leaks, massive oil spills, or significant loss of life.

Obviously, these systems are beyond the control of ordinary citizens. You might want to write letters to your local community leaders and your Congressional representatives; if you're really concerned, you might want to participate in some lobbying efforts. But for the most part, we all have to hope that our business leaders and government officials are focusing their efforts on the high-risk problem areas of this kind, rather than wasting precious time and energy to ensure that everyone's $19.95 digital watch remains Year-2000 compliant.

Endnotes

1. The important thing to remember about this example is that there are additional opportunities for leap-year miscalculations on January 1, 2000. If a year is divisible by four, it's a leap year, unless the year is evenly divisible by 100 (e.g., the year 1900), in which case it's not But there's an exception to the exception: If the year is evenly divisible by 400, it *is* a leap year.

2. Frank Kane, "Moving to Millennium Meltdown," *The Times of India*, May 18, 1997.

3. Jim Rivera, "Re: cars an Y2K?" comp.software.year-2000 USENET newsgroup, Tue, 29 Jul 1997, 23:32:48 -0700.

Year-2000 Impact
on Education

*It is an axiom in political science that unless a people are ed-
ucated and enlightened it is idle to expect the continuance of
civil liberty or the capacity for self-government.*
Texas Declaration of Independence, *March 2, 1836.*

*People commonly educate their children as they build their
houses, according to some plan they think beautiful, without
considering whether it is suited to the purposes for which they
are designed.*
*Lady Mary Wortley Montagu, Letter, 19 Feb. 1750, to her
daughter Lady Bute (published in* Selected Letters, *edited
by Robert Halsband, 1970).*

Introduction

In earlier chapters, we drew the analogy between Year-2000
disruptions and blizzards that can shut down a city for a few
days. If you mention this to a school child, he or she will leap
to the obvious inference: "A blizzard means no school. Do
Year-2000 problems mean no school, too?" To extend the
analogy further, our answer might be: It's a question of degree.
Just as a one-inch snowfall rarely closes a school, we can imagine a variety of minor Year-2000 problems that would not
interrupt the educational system. A twelve-inch snowfall probably would close most schools for a day or two, except in those
regions of the country that experience heavy snow on a regular

basis. And a three-foot blizzard, accompanied by gale winds and sub-zero temperatures, might keep schools closed for a week. We can easily imagine the equivalent degrees of serious Year-2000 problems; the most serious Year-2000 scenarios could close schools for a month, a year, or even longer.

The nature of a Year-2000 impact on schools is similar to much of what we've discussed in earlier chapters. If electric power and/or other utilities (gas, oil, water, etc.) are disrupted, the schools have no alternative but to shut down. If there's no telephone service for a few days, it's questionable whether schools will continue operating. The same is likely to be true if food supplies (for school lunches) are disrupted, if the teachers can't travel to the schools because of breakdowns in the transportation systems, or if the school buses are unavailable to bring the children to the schools. School is a "job" for a number of adults, and thus it's vulnerable to the kinds of problems we discussed in Chapter 2; but the point we want to emphasize in this chapter is that school is a "job" for children, too. If schools shut down, then the children are out of "work" just like their parents.

Large school districts and universities often have computer systems as complex and widespread as the medium-sized business; school lessons, homework assignments, student-teacher communications, research, and scheduling of administrative activities are all driven by computer programs. Of course, not every school is computerized, and not every school depends heavily on its computers; in some cases, the computers sit quietly in a "lab," to be used for the once-a-week "computer appreciation" courses. But it's quite different in most universities and in some of the leading high schools; these schools are so thoroughly "wired" for computers that if the computers are shut off, the administration might as well turn off the lights too. If the computers stop, the school comes very close to shutting down.

Another example of a heavily computerized school application is that of assigning students to classes, and assigning teachers to classes. The computer programs that carry out the scheduling assignments—which can be enormously complicated for high school and college students—are definitely date-sensitive, and possibly Year-2000-sensitive. In the simple case, the scheduling program might ask the school administrator to type in the day, month, and year of the beginning of a school semester; if the year is recorded as two digits, the scheduling program might decide that its computations should be carried out for the year 1900, rather than 2000. As we noted in Chapter 11, the problem is that January 1, 2000 is a Saturday, while January 1, 1900 was a Monday. Thus, the Year-2000-defective scheduling program might erroneously schedule children for Saturday and Sunday classes, which would obviously cause some confusion.[1]

While businesses have to worry about the Year-2000 impact on their customers and their revenues, schools have a somewhat different perspective. Their "revenues" come from a local school district, which is augmented by monies received from state and local governments. Ultimately, all of this is derived from taxes: property taxes at the local level, and income taxes at the state and federal levels. In addition, there are numerous forms of grants and subsidies—for school lunches, student loans and scholarships, grants to teachers, etc. None of this is likely to be affected in the first instant of January 1, 2000—but as we discussed in Chapter 10, government agencies at all levels are extremely vulnerable to Year-2000 problems, which means that their ability to continue providing the stream of payments (by whatever name they're called) to schools, students, and teachers could be impaired within a matter of weeks or months. Thus, while schools might have sufficient funds in the bank (assuming the banks are still operating normally!) to last through the first half of 2000, a serious Year-2000 problem in the government arena could keep the schools from opening in the fall of 2000.[2]

It's important to note that there are some differences between school-as-work and jobs-as-work. For one thing, we wouldn't want to expose our children to the kind of physical discomforts and dangers that an adult might have to tolerate in the event of a Year-2000 disruption. To remain employed, adults might be willing to put up with a lack of heat in the office, or a lack of public transportation to travel to and from the office; it's far less practical to envision such a scenario for an eight-year-old child.

Another point to remember is that school serves as a surrogate babysitter for most parents. While children look forward with eager anticipation to "snow days" when they can stay home, parents find the experience doubly annoying: not only do they have more trouble getting to work, but they have to find a backup mechanism to take care of the children while they're home playing in the snow. High school and college students can look after themselves, of course, but one of the serious side-effects of a moderate, month-long Year-2000 disruption is that parents will have to cope with the equivalent of a second summer vacation.

Finally, remember that a month or a year in a child's life has a different meaning than a month in an adult's life. A one-month Year-2000 disruption would obviously be unpleasant for an adult, but it would probably be treated as "putting your life on hold" for a month. But a month-long disruption in the school schedule means that the required curriculum might not be fully covered; as a result, the school year might have to be extended. A more serious disruption of 6-12 months would mean that many students would have to repeat a year of school; among other things, this raises some interesting questions about tuition payments for colleges and private schools. University and private school tuition payments for the first half of 2000 will be due and payable in December 1999, if not earlier. Thus, if a serious Year-2000 disruption forces the school/college to shut down for an entire semester, a lot of grumpy parents will want their money back.

Thus, the impact of Year-2000 computer problems on the field of education may not be as fundamental and serious as the impact on other parts of the economy or social infrastructure—but it's serious enough that it ought not to be ignored. In particular, it *can't* be ignored by parents of young children, since a shutdown of the schools would eliminate the surrogate babysitting service upon which they rely.

Fallback Advice—Two-Day Disruptions

As with most of the previous chapters, there isn't a strong argument for planning for two-day disruptions in the educational infrastructure. While such disruptions could theoretically occur at any point during 2000, it's most likely that they will occur during the first few days of January. College students are likely to be enjoying their Christmas break at that point, since most colleges and universities don't resume classes until mid-January or later. But it's possible that high school and elementary school students will be scheduled to return to school on Monday, January 3. Be prepared to keep the kids home for a couple of days.

Fallback Advice—One-Month Disruptions

If Year-2000 problems turn out to be somewhat more severe, students may be faced with a one-month sabbatical. As noted earlier, this can cause problems in households where both parents work; if you anticipate this level of Year-2000 disruption, it would be a good idea to plan for backup babysitting or child-care services in advance. Don't depend on government-sponsored day-care centers; they're likely to have problems of their own. Instead, make arrangements to have older siblings, grandparents, or neighbors look after your children. Just as many adults have found it beneficial to car-pool, they may find it useful to pool their babysitting and child-care services. The details will obviously vary from family-to-family, but the key point is to create a network of sympathetic and like-minded parents or family members *before* January 1, 2000.

As noted above, a one-month disruption in the educational schedule may cause problems with the school's requirement to cover a minimum educational curriculum (a requirement often imposed at the state level, in return for certification and eligibility for funding). If schools are shut down for the month of January, 2000, it's possible that the school year will be extended an extra month into the summertime; but it's also possible that school districts will expect children to catch up on homework, reading assignments, and written reports on their own. Thus, if you're concerned about the possibility of your child falling behind, you should meet with the child's teachers in late 1999 to get as much information as possible about upcoming educational topics and work assignments. Since month-long Year-2000 disruptions could occur at any point in 2000 (e.g., if the school budget is exhausted in the spring of 2000, and state and federal agencies are unable to provide their normal funding), you may need to continue meeting periodically with the teachers to ensure that you're always a month ahead of your child's current assignment.

Keep in mind that you'll probably be coping with your own Year-2000 disruptions during this period. If your office shuts down and you have to stay home for a month, then you'll have plenty of time to deal with your child's school problems. But it's also possible that you'll be spending longer-than-normal hours traveling to and from work, as well as dealing with the extraordinary problems of providing food, shelter, and clothing for your family in the post-2000 days. Thus, advance planning to cope with your child's problem will be all the more important.

Fallback Advice—One-Year Disruptions

A one-year disruption sounds almost unbelievable—after all, how difficult can it be to get the lights back on and the children back in school? But remember that many of the schools in crowded urban areas are already facing disruptions—budget problems, union problems with custodians, overcrowding, asbestos and other health problems, violence and crime in the classroom, and so forth. There is very little in the way of a "reserve buffer" to deal with extraordinary problems, and Year-2000 could well turn out to be just such a problem. If the school district's payroll computers break down, for example, or if the banks experience severe problems, then the teachers, custodians, and administrators won't get paid; and in a school district where there's already a lot of union-management strife, it won't take long for the affected workers to go on strike. Combined with the various other problems that the schools may be facing, it won't take more than a month or two of disruptions before some schools will simply declare that they're closed for the semester—or until the beginning of the following year's school term.

Obviously, no one wants this to happen, and we think the chances are relatively small; if it does happen, it's likely to be on a community-by-community basis. But it *could* happen—and if it does, the situation will be qualitatively different than a one-month vacation or a two-day holiday. College students and high school students might spend the year working (assuming the economy hasn't collapsed a la the Great Depression), or finding ways to help their parents cope with the strain of a severe Year-2000 disruption—but what can you do if your elementary school child has no school to attend for the entire year of 2000?

The straightforward strategy is to extend the backup babysitting mechanism discussed above, so that a relative or trusted neighbor continues to look after your children. But this is a lot to ask, unless there are grandparents available on almost a full-time basis to take on the burden of child care. Perhaps more important, the typical American parent would be deeply concerned about "wasting" a year that could be, and should be, spent educating the child in the traditional reading-writing-arithmetic skills. We can imagine some lively debates among educators and parents about how a child's mind will stagnate after a year away from the traditional classroom—but it's a safe bet that many parents will consider it unacceptable.

The possible solution, if you're truly concerned about this, is home-schooling. Approximately 1.1 million students are already acquiring their elementary and/or secondary school education in this fashion[3]—either for religious or political reasons, or because they (or their parents) feel that the locally available schools are inadequate. Accredited home-schooling institutions already exist, and appropriate educational materials can be acquired at a moderate cost; if you're interested in pursuing this option, a good starting point is The Home School Resource Center on the Internet at http://www.rsts.net/home/ home.html, or the National Home School Association at http:// www.alumni.caltech.edu/~casner/nha.html.

Fallback Advice—Ten-Year Disruptions

If you've been following the line of thinking that we've documented in previous chapters, you can probably anticipate the nature of our ten-year concern for education. We're not concerned that the "physical plant" of the schools will collapse if they're shut down for a few months, or even a year. We're not concerned that teachers are going to commit mass suicide and vanish from the face of the earth; and we're not concerned that books will be burned, or that the supply of pens and paper will disappear. Schools that are highly dependent on computers today—especially the ones that depend on computer-based training, as well as networked interactions between students and teachers—might have an adjustment period if a severe Year-2000 problem rendered all of the existing computers unusable. But the adjustment wouldn't take more than a year or two—and we suspect that a large number of teachers would be secretly overjoyed to get rid of computers and return to the "old-fashioned" approach to teaching.

So what's the problem? It's simple. As noted above, most schools survive because of funding provided by three levels of government bureaucracy. And that's only the direct funding; some schools survive only because of the proliferation of grants, scholarships, and funding sent to students and parents to enable a child to attend school. We've already noted in previous chapters that the current form of Social Security, unemployment benefits, food stamps, Medicare, and welfare benefits could disappear in the event of a severe Year-2000 crisis—and by the same argument, the same could happen to the current mechanisms for funding schools and subsidizing students. This is not as radical and far-fetched as it may seem. After all, there are ongoing debates about the ineffectiveness of the education-oriented spending and initiatives at the federal level, with periodic proposals that the Department of Education be eliminated entirely. At the state level, many states—including, for example, California—have been faced with steadily shrinking budgets, which in turn have forced cutbacks throughout many of the state universities whose attractiveness is at least partly due to the low tuition costs enjoyed by state residents. Even at the local level, there continue to be battles over funding, with scattered incidents of budget cutbacks.

Even with a severe, long-term Year-2000 crisis, we don't think for a moment that American parents would decide to stop educating their children. But they might well find that the government bureaucracy has been paralyzed, and that Senate/House leaders voted into office in November 2000 want to focus their emergency aid activities on more pressing issues of providing food and jobs. As a result, control *and* funding of the nation's school system could revert entirely to the local level, at least in the short- to medium-term. And while that might be a welcome change for some neighborhoods—especially the affluent neighborhoods that could acquire funding directly from the parents and local property owners—it could be a disaster for the urban ghettos and rural areas whose school systems are heavily dependent on government funding.[4]

In the long run, a severe Year-2000 crisis could be the catalyst that causes the nation's educational system to be completely re-examined and overhauled. Perhaps the year 2010 will see a nationwide school system with a uniform curriculum and testing standards for both students and teachers, administered by a newly-chartered federal agency. Or perhaps we will see the opposite end of the spectrum in 2010: Perhaps a national consensus will conclude that the federal government should play no role at all in deciding how our children should be educated, and that even the states should play a minimal role, with far less funding authority than they have now. In the long run, perhaps the educational system will be transformed into something far better ... or something far worse.

In the long run, of course, we'll all be dead. And in the "long run" of ten years, a child of eight will have become a young adult of 18, at which point any discussion of reforming the elementary and high schools is moot—at least for that child, and for the generation of his or her peers. Thus, if you're not planning to have any children until 2005, you can afford to wait and see how things turn out, assuming that we're halfway through a severe Year-2000 crisis at that point. But if you have young children now, you don't have the luxury of waiting a decade—children can't be put into a cryogenic freezer, to be thawed when the crisis passes.

As with the other "severe crisis" scenarios we've postulated, there's nothing specific that we can recommend at this point. The likelihood of a crisis so severe that it essentially paralyzes the current educational system for a decade is sufficiently small that 95% of the parents in this country would probably reject any serious proposal to remove their children from the public school system in 1999, with the intention of providing the remainder of their education at home.[5]

But it's important to note that parents won't be forced to make such an extreme decision in the early days of January, 2000. If the Year-2000 crisis does turn out to be severe, it might be a matter of months, if not more, before the reality becomes widely accepted. Indeed, one of the paradoxes of the ripple effect that we've discussed throughout this book is that there might be *no* Year-2000 crises within the schools themselves, but apparently unrelated Year-2000 crises in business or government could eventually trigger the kind of economic crisis that could lead to severe budget cutbacks and policy changes. Thus, in this worst-case scenario, it might not be until 2001 or 2002 that the trends became unmistakably clear; but at that point, it might be too late to begin making plans for alternative education schemes.

We've deliberately avoided offering our personal opinions about the state of the current educational system, or what the best possible outcome might be. From the perspective of the Year-2000 phenomenon, our personal opinions and your personal opinions don't matter much at all. If a catastrophic Year-2000 disruption occurs, it will create an entirely new, unique—and unmistakably alien and frightening—environment, in which old political opinions will be radically altered and new ones created overnight. As we've suggested throughout this book, when discussing the possibility of severe Year-2000 disruptions, flexibility and self-sufficiency will be extremely important for weathering the storm. It's difficult enough for adults to do this; it's all the more difficult when trying to plan for the education of one's child.

And perhaps this is a good way to wrap up the message of this chapter: Even if you don't feel like making Year-2000 contingency plans for your own sake, do it for the sake of your children. No matter what happens, and no matter how bad the Year-2000 crisis may be, it will be today's children that will carry our culture and civilization into the decade of 2010 and 2020.

We need to protect them and prepare them as best we can, even if our own lives are exhausted in the process of doing so.

Endnotes

1. This may turn out to be one of the examples where a technique known as the "28-year rollback" might work. It turns out that 1972 has the same cycle of days-of-the-week and leap year as 2000 (and 1971 has the same characteristics as 1999, etc.). Thus, if the scheduling program is told to prepare a schedule of student assignments for 1972, it should produce the same results as if the program had been Year-2000-compliant in the first place. This strategy doesn't always work (for reasons that are too obscure and technical to bother describing in detail here), and most computer professionals regard it as a temporary strategy, at best.

2. One university professor responded to this paragraph in the first draft of our book with the comment, "At some universities like mine, Federal Assistance is important for enrollment. No Federal Assistance for our students and no enrollment. Will the Department of Education be ready? Who knows—but students may not get student aid and not be able to attend." Unfortunately, the prognosis as of September 1997 was not very encouraging. As we pointed out in Chapter 10, the Education Department was one of four federal agencies that was given a flunking grade by the Congressional committee overseeing Year-2000 preparation efforts.

3. See Karl M. Bunday, "Homeschooling Has Been Growing Rapidly in Recent Years," available on the Internet at http://www.concentric.net/~kmbunday/homeschool_growth.html.

4. An example will help illustrate this point. One of the authors has a friend whose role as a single parent is more difficult than most of us experience. His children are physically handicapped, and without personalized, expensive assistance from specialists within the school system, their education would suffer enormously. After months of investigation and analysis, and several more months of difficult personal changes (changing jobs, selling his house, etc.), our friend moved his family from California to Nevada. The reason: California's budget cutbacks have severely curtailed the availability and quality of special assistance his children need, while the lucrative gambling profits of Nevada's casinos have helped to create a generous state educational system, which *does* provide a superior level of educational assistance. Fortunately, our friend's children will have finished their schooling before January 1, 2000; the planning and decision-making process would have been enormously complicated if it had been necessary to take Year-2000 into account. Our friend is a computer expert, so he is fully aware of the Year-2000 problem. The point is that such

decisions need to be made carefully, and in advance, for once having been made, they are extremely difficult to change at a moment's notice.

5. The study by Karl Bunday, cited earlier, indicates that approximately 1.1 million students, out of a total of 46 million students nationwide, are already receiving their education through various forms of home-schooling. That's slightly more than 2% of the student population already, so it's not entirely unreasonable to suggest that advance warning of a Year-2000 crisis in 1999 might cause a lot more parents to pull their kids out of the public school system.

Year-2000 Impact on Telephone and Mail Services

Transport of the mails, transport of the human voice, transport of flickering pictures—in this century as in others our highest accomplishments still have the single aim of bringing men together.

Antoine de Saint-Exupéry, Wind, Sand, and Stars, Chapter 3 (published in Terre des Hommes, 1939).

Two prisoners whose cells adjoin communicate with each other by knocking on the wall. The wall is the thing which separates them but is also their means of communication. It is the same with us and God. Every separation is a link.

Simone Weil, Gravity and Grace, *"Metaxu," (1947; translated 1952).*

Introduction

When we began writing this chapter in August, 1997, the nationwide UPS strike was entering its third day. Reporters estimated that 5-7% of the nation's Gross Domestic Product (GDP) moves through UPS, and each night's TV news showed small businesses and individuals whose lives were already being affected. Such is the impact of one communications-oriented service provider that lasted a total of 16 days.

Obviously, we would have preferred that the strike didn't occur—but we couldn't help observing that it had one unexpected positive result: It demonstrated quite vividly how dependent society is on the smooth functioning of a complex, interconnected infrastructure. It may be difficult to accept the possibility of the banking failures or power-grid failures we've discussed in this book, and the comparison between a Year-2000-related computer failure and a blizzard may seem too academic for some readers. But the UPS strike was very real and very recent, and since UPS moves 12 million packages a day, it didn't take long before everyone was affected.

UPS and its competitors—Federal Express, DHL, etc.— provide one form of communication. And while the recent strikes illustrated the importance of these service providers, an even more critical form of communications is also threatened by the Year-2000 problem: telecommunications. We'll begin this chapter by discussing the impact of Year-2000 problems on the telephone, fax, electronic mail, and Internet services; then we'll discuss the mail services. This will lead to our now-familiar set of guidelines for coping with minor, moderate, serious, and devastating Year-2000-induced disruptions.

Telephone, Fax, and E-mail

Along with banking and the electric power grid, the nation's telecommunications network is part of what a colleague, Steve Heller, refers to as the "iron triangle." If any component of the iron triangle fails in a Year-2000 collapse, the other two are likely to fail quickly too. And if the iron triangle goes down, most of what we refer to as "modern society" goes down with it.

Obviously, we could survive for awhile without the social use of telephones—e.g., the phenomenon of teenagers spending hours on the phone each evening with their friends. And obviously, some businesses can get along without phones: the corner newspaper stand, and many other mom-and-pop businesses might still expect their customers to show up in person to transact business. But, Wall Street cannot function without telephones; nor can the vast majority of large businesses carry on their day-to-day operations with customers, suppliers, partners, and vendors.

Similarly, a shutdown of the telephone system means, for all practical purposes, that the Internet and the World Wide Web, and the pervasive phenomenon of electronic mail, grinds to a halt.

This sounds alarmist in nature, and it's important to realize that we are *not* trying to construct an end-of-the-world scenario. We're not trying to suggest that all phones, everywhere in the world, will fail permanently on January 1, 2000. But we *are* suggesting that some phone companies could stop providing service to their customers for a few days, or perhaps a month ... or possibly longer. Again, we remind you that a few days of a UPS strike caused significant discomfort across the country—what would be the impact of a three-day outage on the part of AT&T, MCI, or Sprint? What happens if a combination of network switching problems, billing problems, and bureaucratic snafus shuts down the phone system in your company for a month?

There are three aspects of telephone service that concern us: the network switches, the "private branch exchange" (PBX) systems that control the internal telecommunications in most large offices throughout the country, and the financial/administrative systems within the "carrier" companies.

Network switches are the devices that establish the connection between your phone and another phone whenever you make or receive a call; indeed, several switches are likely to be involved in a telephone conversation, unless both parties live in the same local neighborhood. The switches are manufactured by companies such as Lucent Technologies, Inc. (formerly Bell Telephone Laboratories), Nortel, Inc., and Siemens AG. Until the mid-1960s, the switches consisted mostly of massive electromechanical relays, with relatively little software-based intelligence; but starting with products known as ESS-1 ("Electronic Switching System 1"), Bell Labs began introducing computerized switches that were faster, cheaper, smaller, more energy-efficient, and far more sophisticated. Combined with the computer systems provided by the carriers (AT&T, Sprint, MCI, GTE, etc.), the switches support call-forwarding, call-waiting, caller-ID, and a variety of services that simply didn't exist 25 ago.

Although the switching systems are not responsible for billing or any of the other accounting and finance applications within the phone company, they play one vital role vis-à-vis Year-2000 problems: they record the starting time and ending time of a telephone call. And because a phone call can cross the "boundary" between one day and the next, or one month and the next, or one year and the next (e.g., a 10-minute call originating at 11:55 PM on New Year's Eve), the switch has to record the year, date, hour, minute, and second of the beginning and ending of the phone call.

What makes the situation particularly difficult is that long-distance calls and overseas calls almost inevitably involve multiple network switches, which may have been manufactured by several different vendors. Thus, if some switches are Year-2000-compliant and others are not, the phone call may not get through. A recent article in a British computer newspaper[1] highlighted the problem:

> Telecoms users and operators fear a collapse of the global network unless there is an international effort to co-ordinate millennium bug fixes. The chairman of the Telecoms Man-

agers Association has slammed the Department of Trade and Industry for not responding to its three letters asking for help to tackle the year 2000 problem in the telecoms industry.

And BT has criticized the International Telecommunications Union for not responding to calls that it should act as a central body co-ordinating the millennium activities of telecoms companies worldwide.

Association chairman Martin Hart said his director-general David Harrington wrote to the government on 4 April to highlight the issue of the millennium problem on telephone switches. He asked the department to put pressure on suppliers to publish lists of compliant equipment.

The letter was followed up by a reminder in June and another this month, but there has been no response. "We will not let the department off the hook," said Hart. "Unless it gets suppliers to address the issue immediately, telecoms equipment could stop functioning on 1 January [2000]. This could mean we won't be able to make any calls outside the UK.

Hart said efforts to solve the millennium problem in the PC industry are not being mirrored for telecoms equipment, although he stressed that the problem is exactly the same. "If anything, it's more pressing," he warned. "Networks and telecoms equipment tends to hang around longer and get replaced less often than standard PC equipment." Mili Lewis, corporate relations manager for BT's year 2000 project, fears a lack of co-ordination between different countries could lead to post-millennium chaos for international traffic.

Since all of the switching manufacturers are aware of the Year-2000 problem, and most (if not all) have already produced Year-2000-compliant versions of their products, our optimistic assumption is that all of the major carriers will have upgraded or replaced any faulty switches by the end of the decade. But as the British telecommunication authorities have warned, we also need to worry about the Year-2000 compliance status of international telephone companies. And closer to home, we need to worry about the status of the hundreds of smaller telephone companies that have sprung up in the current environment of deregulation. One of the authors, for example, spent the summer of 1997 working on this book in northwestern Montana; telephone service in the region was provided by such tiny companies as the Blackfoot Telephone Cooperative, the Ronan Telephone Company, and PTI Communications—*not* the major regional "Baby Bell" companies. If these tiny telephone companies turn out to be non-Year-2000 compliant, the local residents won't get much solace from the fact that AT&T and MCI have upgraded their computers.

The problem faced by many of the telephone companies is that in addition to updating their own computer systems, and their own connections to standard network switches, they're also faced with the need to establish more and more links with new telecommunication vendors spawned by the current environment of deregulation. Connections to cellular vendors, "personal communication service" (PCS) vendors, Internet vendors, and startup telecommunication vendors has created a small degree of chaos within the telecommunications industry, which further complicates the Year-2000 problem.

One of the most important kinds of telecommunications switches is the PBX system installed in many medium- and large-sized companies, as well as government agencies. The Year-2000 problem is particularly significant for "call centers" that handles tens of thousands of calls each day for reservations, telephone mail-order centers, customer service and inquiry hot-lines, etc. A recent article in a computer trade magazine estimated that "as much as 25% of installed call center equipment may need to be replaced to handle the year 2000."[2] One of the reasons for this is that approximately half of the companies with PBX systems don't upgrade their technology regularly, and "most of the installed base [of customers] is at least two software releases behind [the current version.]" And this raises the obvious question: Are the network switching computers Year-2000-compliant? The answer is that most, if not all, of the major switch vendors, have been offering Year-2000 compliant switch products since the mid-1990s. But even the most reputable manufacturers will acknowledge that their older products had problems:[3]

> *The R2 Call Management System, provided by Lucent and based on AT&T's old 3B2 computer, will not function because the 3B2 does not recognize the year 2000 as a valid date. "It really breaks, and we recognized that up front," admits Tom Nash, call-center offer manager for Lucent, the former AT&T unit that now supports the R2. Lucent recommends that R2 customers upgrade to newer equipment. The customers will get a 20% discount from the normal upgrade price of $40,000 to $75,000. Lucent guarantees that any of its products introduced after Sept. 30, 1996, will be year 2000-compliant—or Lucent will pick up the tab for making the products compliant.*

While all of this is being discussed openly and candidly in the computer trade magazines, it's quite likely that many smaller companies are completely unaware that their PBX phone systems are vulnerable. Others have heard of it, but are procrastinating because of the cost of an upgrade. And if these companies suddenly decide to upgrade their systems in late 1998 or 1999, they may find it's too late—because, as we discussed in Chapter 11, the PBX systems, like most embedded systems, require a field service technician to visit the office and install the upgrade. One of the authors has a colleague who is a nationally-recognized Year-2000 expert; during an e-mail dialogue, the expert offered the following observation:

> *My problems with the electrical and telephone companies is that without them, nothing else works. Clearly, banking and finance is next. My guess is that finance is in better shape*

than the other two, especially because of this wall of silence.
I don't have a lot of information on the subject, except for a
friend of mine who used to be the head of the GTE Y2K
project. His estimates are that it will take about 1/2 day to
fix each of their switches and they have 500,000 switches!
The problem is numbers here and everywhere else.

If this estimate is correct, it would require an army of approximately 1,000 people, working full-time for a full year, to fix all of the switches. Lucent, Mitel, Nortel, and the other vendors are dealing with similar numbers; all of these vendors are likely to face increasing backlogs of upgrade and repair work as the calendar moves into 1999.

Finally, we need to mention the "business applications" in all of the telephone companies—including not only the vendors of switching systems, but also the major carriers like AT&T and MCI, as well as the regional operating companies (NYNEX, Southwestern Bell, etc.) and smaller local telephone companies. These computer systems handle the billing, record-keeping, scheduling of phone installations and repairs, as well as the internal marketing, administrative, and financial operations of the company. Industry experts estimate that AT&T has 500 million lines of code to analyze, and Sprint has 100 million lines; MCI has not publicly disclosed the scope of its Year-2000-related software portfolio.[4]

As we've discussed in previous chapters, Year-2000 problems in this software could lead to billing problems, erroneous decisions to block calls or shut off service, and various other customer-related difficulties. Thus, in the worst case, your phone could be shut off even though the switching network is operating perfectly.

Mail and Parcel Post—FedEx, UPS, DHL, and the U.S. Postal Service

The 1997 UPS strike demonstrated that disruptions can come from human causes, in addition to the Year-2000-related problems we've discussed in this book. The strike also provided some interesting statistics about the size and importance of the shipping industry. In 1996, the combination of domestic air shipments, domestic ground shipments, parcel, and air exports amounted to 4.7 billion shipments and $65.3 billion in revenue. UPS currently holds 63% of the market share (and 80% of ground shipment of packages), while Federal Express has 13%, and the U.S. Postal Service comes in third with 4%.[5]

Another interesting tidbit from the strike was the size of the air fleet that UPS uses to move its packages. The company has 200 of its own aircraft, plus approximately 300 chartered airplanes, which serve 400 airports in the U.S. and 200 airports in other countries. The strike by 185,000 UPS workers was further exacerbated by 2,000 pilots who are members of the Independent Pilots Association, and who refused to fly during the strike.[6]

One last item: Because of early threats and predictions of the UPS strike, some companies made contingency plans in advance—just as some companies will be doing if there is a Year-2000-induced disruption in the shipping industry. As the *New York Times* reported:

> *Some of America's biggest businesses, especially those that do a heavy mail-order trade, had seen the strike coming and made contingency plans, arranging for their products to be shipped by Federal Express and other air express companies or through the United States Postal Service. But the extra load on those services was a burden as well as a boon. U.P.S.*

*normally handles 80 percent of packages shipped by ground
nationwide, and transportation experts say FedEx and the
postal system cannot take up all the slack. [7]*

While the UPS strike focused attention on parcel post packages and overnight courier mail, we must not forget "ordinary"
mail, which is transported primarily by the U.S. Postal Service
(USPS) as first-class, second-class, bulk-rate mail, and various
other categories. The USPS interacts with seven million customers daily, in 40,000 post offices, and processes an average
of more than 600 *million* mail pieces daily, of which approximately 14 percent is carried by air.[8] Because it deals with
stamps, money orders, and various other financial functions,
as well as an enormously complex mail-sorting and logistics
operation, its computer systems are as complex as most of
those in the major federal government agencies we discussed
in Chapter 10.

What does this tell us about the Year-2000 situation? Simply that if a disruption similar to the 1997 UPS strike should
occur, it will have a noticeable impact almost immediately. If
the disruption lasts more than a few days, or if it hits more
than one carrier, businesses across the country will find it
increasingly difficult to ship products, contracts, and other
packages.

It's easy to understand how a union strike can bring a major
shipping carrier to a halt. But what kind of problems would a
Year-2000 software bug cause? Here are a few:

- A substantial number of cross-country and international shipments; all of the major carriers have
  their own air fleet, though not as large as the
  UPS fleet. We've already seen in Chapter 4 how
  Year-2000 problems could ground the country's
  air traffic; this could affect not only the passen-

ger airlines, but also the cargo and package transport flights.

- UPS, FedEx, and other shippers (including the USPS) have sophisticated computer systems to schedule, route, and control the movement of packages from pickup to delivery. Along the way to its destination, a package will typically spend part of its time in a pickup truck, a delivery truck, local offices in the city of origin and the city of destination, one or more airplanes, and one or more dispatching centers. The computer systems that schedule and coordinate all of this are extremely complex; if they suffer Year-2000 disruptions, packages can be lost, misrouted, or left stranded en route.[9]

- Like other businesses, the shipping carriers have elaborate billing, marketing, and other business applications. Individual packages shipped by "retail" customers are generally invoiced and paid for (by the person making the shipment) before the package is accepted; but corporate customers are more likely to maintain an ongoing account with FedEx or UPS, with monthly invoices that cover all shipments made during that period. A Year-2000 problem in these systems probably wouldn't cause the shipper to shut down right away, but it could cause billing problems and other administrative problems.

Fallback Advice—Two-Day Disruptions

As we've pointed out several times in this book, Year-2000 disruptions won't necessarily occur *en masse* on January 1, 2000; depending on the nature of the computer problems and the associated bureaucratic snafus caused by those problems, we might see the equivalent of the UPS strike in August 2000. But if you're a gambler, the "safe bet" is that January 1, 2000 is the most likely time that disruptions will start to be noticed; and just as businesses were able to make plans in advance of the August 1997 UPS strike, so it will be possible to make plans in advance of a possible January 2000 disruption.

The main thing, of course, is to ensure that any important business packages are shipped substantially before January 1. The Christmas season is busy enough under normal circumstances, and there may be a number of cautious people trying to avoid potential problems as New Year's approaches; thus, you should make sure that you've allowed a few extra days. If you wait until Monday, January 3, 2000 to ship a critical package to a client or a customer, you have nobody to blame but yourself if you find that the shippers have been grounded.

Beyond that, there is no obvious "silver bullet" strategy. Given the nature of Year-2000 problems, it's quite possible that FedEx might be grounded while UPS is operating, or vice versa. It's quite possible that the disruptions will be localized and sporadic; we may simply have to accept that the claims by shipping vendors that a package will "absolutely, positively" arrive overnight are no longer quite as dependable.

As for two-day disruptions in the telephone system, the same kind of preparations are appropriate. If you live in a suburban area, you may already have experienced occasional telephone outages—e.g., during the aftermath of an ice storm, tornado, or blizzard. It may require more conscious effort for city dwellers to imagine such a scenario, but it's likely to be an easy problem to deal with. If you have friends or relatives whom you would normally expect to call to offer a Happy New Year's greeting, be aware that either your phone or their phone might not be working.[10] If your office hasn't bothered upgrading its PBX system, be aware that you may be without telephones on Monday, January 3. If you have a cellular phone whose service is provided by a different vendor than your land-based phone, you may find that it comes in very handy during these brief outages; in case there are also intermittent electrical outages, you should ensure that you have spare batteries and that they're fully charged before you become too giddy from champagne on New Year's Eve.

Fallback Advice—One-Month Disruptions

At this point, things become fairly serious: A month without telephone service or mail service is enough to shut down most of today's business operations. Indeed, smaller companies with minimal cash reserves could find themselves bankrupted because they couldn't receive orders by phone, or payments by normal first-class mail. Larger organizations might be able to limp along, but there's a good chance that workers would be furloughed until the problem could be fixed. As for the ripple effect: A month-long telephone outage in the Wall Street area of New York, or the downtown centers of Chicago or Washington, would have devastating results.

As noted above, the major carriers and regional telephone operating companies are in the process of upgrading their technology now. While their business systems may not be completely Year-2000-compliant in time, we're reasonably confident that any problems in the network switches will be fixed in a matter of days. But, smaller telephone companies might have more difficulty—simply because of limited resources and technical expertise. The real problem, we believe, will be in the PBX systems. The June 1997 *Information Week* assessment of the PBX situation gave an interesting example that illustrates the point:

> *Siemens Business Communications Systems Inc. in Santa Clara, Calif., says systems and upgrades it delivered after Aug. 1, 1996, are compliant, and it estimates that through routine upgrades 90% of the company's installed base will be compliant by January 2000.*

From the vendor's perspective, 90% probably sounds like an acceptable percentage. But simple arithmetic tells us that Siemens expects that 10% of its customers will *not* have Year-2000-compliant PBX systems on January 1, 2000. If the same is true of the other PBX vendors, then 10% of the country's office telephone systems won't be working in early January—and that might include the telephone system in *your* company. It might also include the offices of your bank, or the electric power company, or the fire department.

The reason we're discussing the PBX problem again in this section of Chapter 13 is that the sudden discovery on Monday, January 3 that the phones don't work will lead to a panicked call (whoops! from whose phone?) to the company that installed the equipment. That company might be a local tele-communications service company rather than the manufac-turer of the PBX hardware/software unit; and since the PBX may have been installed several years earlier, the service com-pany may be unresponsive or even out of business. In any case, there are likely to be a flurry of such calls in the early days of January, 2000—and the backlog could easily lead to one-month delays before the PBX can be upgraded, replaced, or repaired.

What kind of planning should you do if you believe that one-month outages of your phone service or, in a similar fashion, your FedEx/UPS/USPS service are possible? To whatever extent is practical, make sure that you've got backup services available—e.g., a cellular phone if your normal house phone doesn't work, or an alternative carrier for your important business documents. Encourage your friends, relatives, and business associates to do the same; and be prepared to use the more primitive fallback mechanisms of ordinary first-class mail, if necessary.

Of course, this isn't going to help you if your office phone system is down for a month, or if you work for a mail-order shopping company (e.g., Land's End or the Sharper Image); the most likely consequence of a month-long corporate disruption in telecommunications is temporary unemployment, or a permanent loss of one's job. This involves the job-related issues we discussed in Chapter 2. So, our primary advice in this chapter too is to take stock of your situation now, while you still have the flexibility of changing jobs, to see if you're more dependent than you really want to be on telecommunications and mail-delivery services.

Fallback Advice—One-Year Disruptions

We fully expect to see a rash of two-day failures across the country, mostly associated with PBX problems and minor glitches in other parts of the telecommunications infrastructure. For reasons discussed above, we wouldn't be surprised to see a few month-long failures—not on a nationwide basis, and probably not even affecting an entire city, but nevertheless painful and disruptive for the individual neighborhoods or companies affected.

Is it even possible to contemplate a one-year telecommunications failure? The only plausible example we can imagine is a possible breakdown in international communications between the U.S. and certain other countries. England, western Europe, and most advanced countries will be grappling with virtually identical problems, and it wouldn't be surprising if there were some minor-to-moderate glitches in the overseas links. But, we expect that these would be fixed in a matter of weeks or months, if not sooner. The real problems are likely to occur in eastern Europe, Africa, parts of Asia, and parts of South America (many of which had not even begun to consider the Year-2000 problem as this book was being written). In several of these countries, bureaucratic government monopolies are still in charge of both the telecommunications and mail-delivery services; the equipment is old and service is miserable. It wouldn't surprise us, for example, to see a one-year telecommunications collapse in a country like Venezuela or in some of the former Soviet republics.

Should such a scenario come to pass, it could mean that all modern forms of communication with these countries are cut off. After all, the overall focus of business and government in the U.S. is likely to be on fixing its own problems and re-establishing contact with other advanced countries. Fixing the telecommunication problems with Venezuela and Uzbekhstan will probably not be a high priority. Of course, it *might* be a high priority for you, if a major part of your job or business activity involves these stranded countries—and it might also be an urgent matter if you have close friends or relatives in those countries.

We have no simple, easy answers for a problem of this magnitude; all we can do is ask you to think about the problem carefully now, while you still have time to make some alternative plans.

Fallback Advice—Ten-Year Disruptions

Especially within the U.S., the telecommunications industry is highly competitive—and has been so for well over a decade, ever since the U.S. government made the landmark decision to break up the AT&T monopoly and to foster a more deregulated environment. Thus, even if a Year-2000 problem completely destroyed an MCI or a Sprint or an AT&T, we're highly confident that the remaining vendors would take up the slack and rebuild any part of the telecommunications infrastructure that required it. This might take a couple years, but certainly not a decade.

Similarly, the competition between UPS, Federal Express, Airborne Express, DHL, and other carriers is intense; if one of those carriers should be bankrupted in a Year-2000 crisis, we're confident that the others would carry on, at least in the field of parcel post and overnight mail delivery. The UPS strike that took place while this chapter was being written did provide some convincing evidence that neither the U.S. Postal Service nor the smaller carriers could take over all of UPS's business instantaneously—but given a year or two, we assume they would be able to expand their resources and fill the vacuum left by even the largest of carriers.

The only component of the telecommunications/mail infrastructure for which a ten-year "disruption scenario" is plausible is the U.S. Postal Service. Our reasoning here is similar to what we've discussed in previous chapters. Though quasi-private in nature, the Post Office is still largely dependent on the federal government for its existence. Though it has improved substantially in recent years, the USPS is still large, inefficient, bureaucratic, and floundering under its own weight—even in today's pre-2000 "normal" times. Millions of Americans cheerfully spend $10-15 to send a package via Federal Express, DHL, Airborne, or UPS, rather than spending 32 cents for what the Post Office euphemistically refers to as "first-class" mail. In the aftermath of a serious Year-2000 failure, it's conceivable that the nation's leaders might decide to let the private sector deal with *all* mail delivery, and simply abandon the Post Office, to see if the private sector can survive on its own.

Obviously, a $15 FedEx package is too expensive for most middle-income and lower-income people who merely want to send a letter across town; but UPS has demonstrated that it can move large quantities of packages and documents across the country for a modest price, so it's not inconceivable that the private sector *could* take over mail delivery at an acceptable price. However, it's important to remember that the Post Office delivers much more than just first-class letters and express mail packages. It also delivers second-class magazines and newspapers, as well as staggering quantities of third-class and fourth-class materials that the public generally refers to as "junk mail." While many citizens would be deliriously happy if junk mail disappeared, the elimination of a subsidized bulk-rate mail delivery service could be devastating to many American businesses that depend on it for their marketing activities. Catalogs, brochures, and other forms of direct-mail solicitations would be prohibitively expensive if they had to be sent at the first-class postage rates currently charged by the Post Office, not to mention the even higher rates that might be charged by private mail delivery firms. The ripple effect consequences of such a change would be far-reaching indeed.

The notion of eliminating the USPS sounds so radical that most people probably won't give it serious consideration. Indeed, it really *is* unthinkable in countries where both the telephone system and mail system are operated by government monopolies. But in the U.S., there has been a steady movement toward deregulation and privatization (of which FedEx is a notable example); and there is an increasing awareness that there are many alternatives to "snail mail" in today's high-tech world. Thus, if a severe Year-2000 crisis provides the opportunity or the necessity (depending on whether you're an optimist or a pessimist) to start over with a clean slate, it's inevitable that serious, thoughtful, sincere people will ask, "Do we really *need* a Post Office any more?"

Endnotes

1. Siobhan Kennedy, "Phone firms hung up over millennium," *Computer Weekly,* Jul 17, 1997.
2. Mary E. Thyfault, "Call Center Crisis?—Outdated PBXs called vulnerable to date-field problems," *Information Week,* June 2, 1997. See also "Feds tackle telcom date problems," in the September 29, 1997 issue of *Federal Computing Weekly* (accessible at http://www.fcw.com/pubs/ fcw/1997/0929/fcw-newdate-9-29-1997.html), which says that approximately 25% of all government telecom switches need to be fixed because of Year-2000 problems.
3. Mary E. Thyfault, *op cit.*
4. Kim Girard and Robert L. Scheier, "Telcos lag on year 2000, analysts warn," *Computerworld,* Nov 11, 1996.
5. David Stout, "Shippers Scramble as Strike Hits U.P.S.," *The New York Times,* Aug 5, 1997, p. A12.
6. David Stout, *op cit.*
7. David Stout, *op cit.*
8. See http://www.usps.gov/news/press/97/97071new.html and http:// www.usps.gov/news/press/97/97019new.html for USPS press releases containing these figures.
9. Embedded systems, which we discussed in Chapter 11, are also involved here. It's now customary to attach to each package a shipping label with a "bar-code" that can be scanned by delivery personnel and by workers in the offices and dispatch stations; in addition, UPS delivery personnel carry hand-held computers

to log the pickup and delivery of packages. All of this greatly improves the operating efficiency of the shipping companies, and helps ensure that packages are not lost in transit; but if the embedded computers turn out to be Year-2000-sensitive, the faulty chips will have to be manually replaced or upgraded.

10. If your phone system isn't working, you will also have trouble connecting to the Internet. Many families have discovered in recent years that the Internet has made it possible for far-flung relatives and family members to stay in touch, communicating far more frequently and easily than was possible with telephone and "snail-mail." All of this could be seriously disrupted by a Year-2000 failure that brings down the Internet.

11. Mary E. Thyfault, *op cit.*

Conclusion

It isn't necessary to imagine the world ending in fire or ice—there are two other possibilities: one is paperwork, and the other is nostalgia.

Frank Zappa, The Real Frank Zappa Book, *Chapter 9 (1989).*

We are close to dead. There are faces and bodies like gorged maggots on the dance floor, on the highway, in the city, in the stadium; they are a host of chemical machines who swallow the product of chemical factories, aspirin, preservatives, stimulant, relaxant, and breathe out their chemical wastes into a polluted air. The sense of a long last night over civilization is back again.

Norman Mailer, Cannibals and Christians, *"Introducing Our Argument" (1966).*

Introduction

As we wrote the first two drafts of this book, we posted chapters on our Web site to solicit feedback and commentary from both technical and non-technical readers around the world. Among the many hundreds of comments and messages we received, this one (from a 50-year-old man who asked us to withhold his name) eloquently expresses the uncertainty, hesitation, and concern that all of us face after thinking carefully about the potential consequences of Year-2000:

As I plan my own fallback based on a one to ten year scenario, I am still searching for any hard evidence that those in denial will ultimately be correct. I am not anxious to go through all the changes. Instead, the more I look, the worse it gets.

I programmed for two years in the early 70's as I installed the first system for my parent's business on a DEC PDP-8. I also presided over a doomed attempt in 1979 to totally re-write the system and install it without running parallel. Yes, I know, very dumb! We pulled the plug after three disastrous days and threw away all that work and recovered to the old system. My promotion to president was permanently put on hold. Needless to say, I am wary of optimistic forecasts to replace 40 years of programming world-wide, most of it in less than three years.

Please tell me where you see the optimism, if you do... The problem is that no one in authority will tell the truth if they are not going to be ready, and they probably won't until after 2000. In the meantime, we all have to address continually the risks as we work on our own fallback plans.

We too would like to find some hard evidence that the Year-2000 problem has been solved, or that its impact on society will be minimal. We'd like to find a major bank, airline, automobile company, or government agency that can say it's fully Year-2000 compliant, and that all of its software professionals have been reassigned to normal maintenance work. However, we have to admit that we would be slightly skeptical if and when such assurances are made by major corporations, as we expect they will be in 1998 and 1999. What we *really* would like to see is the kind of independent testing that we've come to expect from *Consumer Reports* magazine and the *Underwriters Laboratory* for commercial products—i.e., an unbiased statement that says, "Yes, we've tested this product thoroughly, and it really *is* Year-2000-compliant."

As this book goes to press, we have not seen any such assurances; the more deeply we delve into the Year-2000 situation, the worse it looks. Meanwhile, the clock is ticking; if we're going to make fallback plans, especially those that involve time, money, and significant effort, we need to get started sooner rather than later.

And like our anonymous correspondent, we're not anxious to go through the kinds of changes that will be required if we take all of this seriously. We suspect that you feel the same way; and we suspect that there's an element of doubt in your mind, which says, "Does it really make sense to trust all of the gloom-and-doom conclusions in this book? Should I really begin making some unpleasant changes in my life, when nobody around me seems to be concerned about the Year-2000 problem?"

Ultimately, this is a decision you'll have to make, either alone, or in concert with your family, friends, and loved ones. You may find this to be a difficult, lonely decision—as did one woman who e-mailed us after reading the first draft of our book on the Internet:

> Y2K has been on my mind for some time now. My 72 year old father opened my eyes to it and directed me to these websites. I took him to buy his first computer two years ago. Today I drove to Wal-mart and started preparing for Y2K. Lanterns, flashlights, bottled water. On my way there I thought that I must be out of my mind and almost turned around and went home. It was a hard step to take. I know that I have a lot of work ahead of me yet, but I am going to be ready for at least 6 months of trouble. Something that I find to be hilarious as I write this. The TV is on in the background blathering about Marv Albert and his sex life. Almost makes a 2000 crash something to look forward to.

To help come to a decision—whether to accept or reject the possibility of serious Year-2000 problems—we suggest that you do your own "reality test" to follow up on what we've already discussed in this book. We also suggest that you carry out your own personal assessment of the impact of a Year-2000 disruption. And most of all, we strongly suggest that you spend the next two years paring down and simplifying your life, so that you can face the new millennium with as much flexibility as possible.

Do Your Own "Reality Test"

This book may have been your first exposure to the Year-2000 problem, but it certainly is not the only source of information. We've referred to several magazine articles and sources of information that were available to us during the writing process; there will undoubtedly be many more during 1998 and 1999, and you should be able to find them in your library, newsstand, or bookstore.

If you have access to the Internet and World Wide Web, you will find a wealth of up-to-date information about Year-2000. And if you have concerns about the Year-2000 status of specific companies, industries, or government agencies, a modest amount of investigation with Web search engines is likely to produce some relevant information. If you don't have access to the Internet, this is a good time to start; new information is being made available on almost a weekly basis now, and we expect it to intensify in the coming months. While the Year-2000 information is readily accessible on the 'Net, you probably won't find it in your local newspaper or general-interest magazines. This is particularly true when it comes to Congressional hearings and status reports from various government agencies; they may or may not get a superficial "sound-bite" mention on the evening TV news program, but you can find detailed coverage, if not the verbatim transcripts of testimony and presentations, on the Internet.

While we were writing the first draft of this book, Norman Kurland sent us an e-mail message with some excellent advice:

> *In this and other chapters, you do not say much about assessing the readiness status during 1999 in order to decide which level of fallback planning may be most reasonable.*
>
> *By early to mid 1999 we should have a good idea of what the impact of Y2K in various sectors is likely to be. That means that individuals and organizations should have a more solid basis for making their fallback plans. For example, if it is clear that there is likely to be serious disruptions in services during January, schools might plan to close for a month and to give study assignments so that students (and teachers) might be able to use the time productively.*
>
> *I anticipate that by early 1999 someone is going to give regular updates on Y2K readiness in various sectors. That should help reduce panic (assuming that the readiness reports are mostly positive) and help people prepare more intelligently for the BIG DAY.*

We also recommend that you talk to knowledgeable people about the technical and business ramifications of Year-2000. However, keep in mind that spokespeople, business leaders, and even computer professionals who have not had a direct involvement in Year-2000 efforts are likely to shrug it off. The e-mail message that we received from Brian Oates during the writing of this book is a good example:

> *Being a programmer myself I considered the y2000 compliance issue and basically blew it off. I use Windows 95 and 75% of our computers have been purchased in the last year. However since reading several chapters of yours I get the feeling I'm living in a Michael Crichton novel. I've asked two of my computer friends about it. One said he's stayed out of it, the other hasn't given it a passing thought. "They'll fix it", he said. "It's just changing their databases to hold a four digit year instead of two." (He's been programming for over five years, he should know it's never that easy...)*
>
> *If programmers who should know better aren't alarmed, how can we hope to lessen the ripple to anything less than a year?*

As you've seen from the discussions in this book, there *are* Senators, Congressmen, banking officials, and other business leaders who are grappling with the consequences of Year-2000; track down some of these people and ask them whether they're optimistic or pessimistic. There are also thousands of computer programmers and software managers working full-time on Year-2000 projects; it shouldn't be too much trouble to track down one of these people through your network of friends and acquaintances. In short, ask someone who is *involved* in Year-2000 what they think of the situation; it's conceivable that things will have improved by the time this bookreaches the bookstores, but we don't think so.

Also, try out the Year-2000 phenomenon on your own computer.[1] If you have a home PC, try setting the date to January 1, 2000 and see if everything works correctly; then try setting the date to 11:55 PM on December 31, 1999 and watch to see if it "rolls over" correctly after five minutes. If so, then power down the computer, power it back up again, and see if everything still works correctly. Try your favorite application programs to ensure that they handle four-digit dates correctly.

Finally, carry out your own Year-2000 compliance tests when you interact with computers in your day-to-day life. Whether it's an ATM machine, or a programmable VCR, or any other form of date-sensitive computerized equipment, see what happens if you enter a date beyond December 31, 1999. Ask your banker, ask the utility company, ask the manager in your favorite supermarket about their state of readiness; in other words, ask anyone whose ability to provide goods and services to you is dependent on computers. In the summer of 1997, when this book was being written, our own experience was that the most common response from such people was a blank stare and a question: "What's Year-2000?" This was understandable and perhaps forgivable, in 1997; but by 1998, it will be a dangerous answer.

If everyone you talk to can give you concrete, tangible evidence that the Year-2000 problem has been solved, then you're welcome to disregard everything you've read in this book. If the majority of people you talk to say, "Don't worry, they'll have it fixed in time," then you should start asking some specific questions. Who are "they"? How many of them are there, and when did they start working on the problem? What's their schedule for finishing the Year-2000 conversion efforts, and what evidence can they provide that will make you confident of their ability to finish on time?

The acid test—and one that we strongly urge you to use whenever you have any doubts about what you're hearing—is the ability to provide a written guarantee of Year-2000 compliance. Here, for example, is what the Federal Reserve said to its member banks about the revisions that it is currently making to the PC versions of its "Fedline" software:

> *Testing Fedline for year 2000 certification will span all business applications and many of the various hardware and software platforms that we support (e.g., 286 and up, and DOS 3.3 and higher). While it will be impossible to test with every make and model of PC used by our customers, we will identify all platforms on which testing has been successful. You also will want to take action to ensure that the equipment you have, or may be planning to purchase, will function correctly in the year 2000.*
>
> *Although we will rigorously test the Fedline software with date simulation tools, this software is furnished strictly on an "as-is" basis. We do not warrant that our software will meet the needs of a customer's applications or that it will be compatible with customer-owned equipment or that all software defects can be corrected. We will, however, provide reasonable assistance in resolving software problems.[2]*

In fairness, it should be noted that *most* software is sold on an "as-is" basis; check the first few pages of the user manual of your favorite PC software and you'll find a similar disclaimer. The reason is quite simple: Except for very simple computer programs that operate on a narrow range of well-known computer hardware/software "platforms," most software is too complex for today's software organizations to test completely. The Fed is being honest in its statement about the possible existence of "software defects" in its Year-2000 version of Fedline. And if you press any responsible corporate officer in any company or government agency around the world, you're almost certain to get a similar disclaimer with regard to the correctness of their Year-2000 efforts.

Obviously, that doesn't mean that the software *will* fail on January 1, 2000. It simply means that you have to take any bland, optimistic Year-2000 assurances with a grain of salt. Indeed, it's fairly difficult to avoid becoming distrustful and suspicious when you have a conversation along the following lines with a company official:

> *You*: "Is your company going to be fully Year-2000-compliant by December 1999?"
>
> *Official:* "Sure, don't worry about it. We're working on the problem, and we're confident that everything will be fine."
>
> *You:* "Well, that's great—but the ability of your company to provide products and services is really important to me and I have to be sure. Can you provide a written warranty, signed by an officer of your company, that you'll be Year-2000-compliant?"
>
> *Official:* "Well, no, we can't do that. But don't worry—we'll definitely be Year-2000-ready."

You: "Year-2000-ready? What does that mean?"

Official: "It means we're ready for Year-2000, and we stand by our commitment to provide superior quality and excellent service to our customers."

You: "But no warranty? No written guarantee?"

Official: "Ummm... er, ah, well ... no, we can't do that."

This could lead to another series of questions: If the company's products or services turn out *not* to be Year-2000, can you turn them in for a refund? Can you get a replacement product? If the answer to these questions is "No," then the company is effectively saying to you, "We don't *really* know if our product/service will function correctly on January 1, 2000—and we won't take responsibility if it doesn't. *You* take the risk."

Since this is likely to be the case with almost *all* products and services, the real question is: How much risk are you willing to take? What are the consequences if the products and services that you now take for granted stop working on January 1, 2000?

Make Your Own Assessment of Year-2000 Consequences

While attempting to explain the possible consequences of Year-2000 computer failures to one of our friends, we used the following metaphor: it's equivalent to the experience of being bitten by as many as a thousand gnats, a hundred mosquitoes, ten bumblebees, and one rattlesnake—possibly all at the same time. The gnats would be annoying and unpleasant; and the discomfort caused by a hundred mosquito bites would be sufficient that most of us would be willing to invest the time and money to buy mosquito repellent. Bee stings are *far* more unpleasant—and in some cases, a dozen bee stings could be fatal. As for rattlesnake bites, the prospect is sufficiently frightening that any sensible person would either take proactive steps to eliminate the possibility, or would ensure that he or she had an ample supply of the appropriate anti-venom.

The whole point of this book has been to suggest a wide range of Year-2000-related "What if?" questions for you to consider. But we don't know the specifics of your life, nor do we know what's important and what's not important to you. Now it's time for you to do some homework, quite possibly the most important homework of your adult life. For each aspect of the social infrastructure that we've discussed—jobs, telephones, banking, government, etc.—it's crucial for you to ask yourself, "What would happen to me if this part of society was disrupted by the Year-2000 bug?"

Some of the potential Year-2000 consequences are so unpleasant that the easiest course of action is to ignore them—on the theory that perhaps we'll be lucky enough that we won't have to deal with them. This is roughly akin to the reaction that teenagers have when informed of the dangers of smoking. Intellectually, they understand the medical warnings about smoking, but they'd like to think that they'll be one of the lucky ones who can avoid cancer and emphysema. And even if they do understand and accept the health risks on a personal level, the power of nicotine addiction makes it extremely difficult to change one's behavior. It's not much of an exaggeration to suggest that most of us are addicted to the comforts of our high-tech, computer-supported lives in today's world; breaking that addiction (if it turns out to be necessary to do so) will be one of the most painful things we've ever experienced.

The risk of denial is particularly high for many of today's American adults, simply because we're so busy coping with the demands of life. Many of us work 12-hour days and then spend the evenings and weekends raising a family and squeezing in shopping, laundry, and other personal errands. We're bombarded with news alerts, overwhelmed with e-mail and voice-mail, and utterly frazzled by the pressure and chaos of modern life. In the midst of all this, someone comes along and warns us that it might all collapse because of an obscure computer problem that most of us don't understand—and it's no surprise that most of us shrug and say, "They'll fix it somehow. Meanwhile, I've got more pressing problems to worry about." As Henry Kissinger once said, "There can't be a crisis next week. My schedule is already full."[3]

But ignoring the problem isn't going to make it go away—it simply changes the situation to one of Russian roulette, where we put our lives in the hands of companies and government agencies who may or may not be able to minimize the effects of Year-2000 disruptions.

As the Big Day approaches, it's conceivable that we may begin to see some concrete, tangible evidence that massive Year-2000 disruptions are unavoidable. And this may lead to another kind of denial on the part of some citizens: a gloomy denial that there is any way at all of surviving the Year-2000 crisis. As British novelist Iris Murdoch observed:

> *The notion that one will not survive a particular catastrophe is, in general terms, a comfort since it is equivalent to abolishing the catastrophe.*[4]

This kind of despair is more likely, we believe, if the bad news comes suddenly and unexpectedly. The "news" in this book may have been unexpected and gloomy, but at least you have a couple of years left to plan and prepare. If nothing else, you have time to prepare yourself psychologically for the likelihood that survival in post-Year-2000 society may not be as easy and automatic as it is today. As George Orwell put it in his recollections of the Spanish Civil War:

> *To survive it is often necessary to fight and to fight you have to dirty yourself.* [5]

Most Important: Maintain Flexibility

If it turns out that the overall impact of Year-2000 bugs is of the two-day or one-month variety, then it won't go down in the history books as a major disaster. Those who have planned for the disruptions by stockpiling a modest amount of cash, food, and other essentials will get through the disruptions with a modicum of inconvenience; and those who have not made such preparations will find it an extremely unpleasant experience—but then it will be over.

But if the Year-2000 problems disrupt society for a year— or, in some areas, as long as a decade—then many of us are going to find that it's a new ball game. In addition to finding that our savings and stock market portfolio has been wiped out, we may find that old rules, old skills, old careers, and old assumptions about cause-and-effect consequences in society are no longer true. The specific problems and disruptions could well turn out to be completely different than the scenarios we've painted in this book; we've used our knowledge of computer technology and economics to postulate what *might* happen, but we make no claims that our crystal ball can peer into the future with any precision.

Similarly, we would be extremely wary of anyone else's crystal ball if it purports to show a *specific* Year-2000-related scenario with great precision. A Year-2000-related crisis in banking and finance, for example, might lead to the familiar phenomenon of hyper-inflation; but one can also construct a plausible scenario in which massive deflation is the result. And if it turns out that the telecommunications system and the Internet remain intact after 2000, it's even possible that the collapse of traditional banking could lead to an entirely new scenario, in which economic transactions are conducted through Internet-mediated, gold-backed "digital cash." And there are probably a dozen other scenarios that are equally plausible; gambling all of one's current financial assets on any one of these scenarios is risky indeed, however.

Thus, if you're worried—as we are—about the possibility of severe Year-2000 disruptions in one or more aspects of the social infrastructure that we currently depend on, then flexibility, mobility, and liquidity are likely to be the most important criteria for survival. By analogy, if your house catches on fire in the middle of the night, your first priority is to get yourself and your family out of the building. You may not have time to save anything else; but ultimately, everything else can be replaced. And if you waste too many precious moments trying to save all of your clothes, all of your books, your stamp collection, and your high school yearbook, you may not survive at all.

A Final Thought

We are optimists at heart, and we agree with the late Mary McCarthy's assessment:

The happy ending is our national belief [6]

But we are also deeply concerned about the potential impact of Year-2000 software problems in every aspect of our lives. The more we've investigated the situation during the course of preparing this book, the more worried we have become. We would like to believe that the actions by computer technicians, business executives, and government leaders during 1998 and 1999 will give us cause for optimism—but we are reminded of Oscar Wilde's observation in *The Picture of Dorian Gray*:

> *The basis of optimism is sheer terror* [7]

In the final analysis, we believe that it's better to be terrified now and take appropriate actions, even if it turns out that the Year-2000 problems are no worse than a few mosquito bites. The alternative—being complacent now and facing the possibility of severe Year-2000 problems without any fallback plans—could turn out to be the equivalent of a fatal rattlesnake bite.

Consequently, we're making our fallback plans now—and we hope this book has convinced you to begin making yours.

Endnotes

1. We *strongly* recommend that you back up any important data on your computer before you try this—just in case the act of inducing a Year-2000 rollover creates some obscure problem that can't be easily remedied. Also, if you're operating a computer system in your office, make sure that you get the assistance of a professional computer person. Some of the commercial software packages in office environments have an expiration date, beyond which the software won't function. Thus, if you "fool" the package by resetting the hardware clock on the computer, you may create permanent damage.

2. This information was posted on the Internet at http://www.frbsf.org/fiservices/cdc/fedline.html, but by mid-August 1997, the Web link had been removed.

3. *New York Times Magazine*, June 1, 1969.

4. From *The Message to the Planet*, part 6 (1989).

5. "Looking Back on the Spanish War" (reprinted in *Collected Essays*, 1961).

6. Mary McCarthy, *On the Contrary*, part 1, "America the Beautiful: The Humanist in the Bathtub" (1962; first published Sept. 1947).

7. Oscar Wilde, from remarks by Lord Henry, in *The Picture of Dorian Gray*, Chapter 6 (1891).

What the Year-2000 Problem Is All About

He that will not apply new remedies, must expect new evils:
for Time is the greatest innovator: and if Time, of course, al-
ter things to the worse, and wisdom and counsel shall not al-
ter them to the better, what shall be the end?
Francis Bacon, Essays, *"Of Innovations" (1597–1625).*

Introduction

In a nutshell: The Year-2000 problem exists because most computer systems have been programmed to record and manipulate dates with only the least-significant two digits of the year; thus, "1999" is represented as "99" and "2000" is represented as "00". Once we reach January 1, 2000, most computer systems will produce incorrect results whenever "date arithmetic" is carried out. In some cases, the results will be amusing, but nonetheless will produce grossly incorrect behavior or output from the computer; in other cases, the results could have serious economic or life-threatening consequences.

Here's a simple example: you borrow $1,000 from your neighborhood bank on January 1, 1998, and repay it on January 1, 1999. The bank's computer system recorded the details of the loan transaction, and probably represented the date of the loan as "980101" (a compact shorthand notation for

"98th year, 1st month, 1st day") and the date of the repayment as "990101". To calculate the amount of interest that must be paid for the privilege of having borrowed the money, the computer system subtracts the loan creation date from the loan repayment date:

$$
\begin{array}{r}
990101 \\
\text{minus} \quad \underline{980101} \\
010000
\end{array}
$$

This is an oversimplification of the way computers actually work, but in essence, the result of the calculation above tells the computer that the duration of the bank loan was 1 year, 0 months, and 0 days—at which point the interest calculation can be carried out.

Now imagine what happens to a loan that was created on January 1, 1999 and repaid on January 1, 2000 (ignoring the fact that January 1, 2000 is a Saturday and that most of us will be too hung over to stagger down to the bank to repay a loan!). If the bank's computer tried to calculate the interest in the same manner shown earlier, it would attempt to carry out the following arithmetic:

$$
\begin{array}{r}
000101 \\
\text{minus} \quad \underline{990101} \\
-990000
\end{array}
$$

Thus, the computer would decide that the loan existed for a "negative" time period, i.e., a period of *minus* 99 years. In the real, physical world that all of us live in, this makes no sense at all; in the world of computer logic, it's clearly incorrect, and will almost certainly lead to an undesirable result. The actual behavior of the computer will depend on the technical details of the hardware, the operating system (e.g., software like Windows 95 for personal computers), the programming language used to write the banking software (e.g., COBOL, RPG,

Visual Basic, etc.), and whatever programming logic was created by the people who developed the banking system. Here are some, but by no means all, of the possibilities that could occur:

- The negative time period could be used, without any modification, to calculate a "negative interest"—i.e., the bank system could end up deciding that it owes you interest. This would be a pleasant surprise, but is certainly not what the bank intended!

- Because of the way numbers are stored internally in computer systems, the negative number could "wrap around" or "roll over" and appear to be an extremely large positive number—e.g., 990101. Thus, the computer could decide that you had borrowed the money for 99 years rather than one year, and the interest charges, with compound interest calculations, could be substantially larger than the principal of the loan.

- The computer system could decide that since dates were intended to be stored as positive numbers, it can replace any negative numbers with zero. Thus, the interest calculation decides that you borrowed the money for zero years, zero months, and zero days—and thus charges no interest at all. This is good for you, of course, but bad for the bank.

- The computer system might have been programmed in such a way that if a negative result ever occurred in an arithmetic operation that was intended to produce a positive result, it would abort all processing and halt. (This kind of behavior is relatively rare for arithmetic operations involving addition and subtraction, but it's very common when a computer attempts to divide a number by zero, because the results are mathematically undefined). Thus, the banking system screeches to a halt every time it processes a loan that extends across the Year-2000 boundary; you never receive any statement of the interest charges due, and the bank never collects any interest payments. Again, good for you, but bad for the bank.

- In a few rare cases, the banking system might have been programmed to ignore any unexpected negative values by computing the "absolute value" of a numerical calculation; in this case, the result of "-010000" shown above would actually be stored as "0100000", and everything would proceed normally.

It should also be noted that some banking systems would have no problems with any of this, because they were programmed from the beginning to be "Year-2000 compliant." It isn't a great surprise that the turn of the century is coming, after all, and some computer systems have been programmed with *four*-digit representations of the year. In this case, the date calculation shown above would look like this:

```
                    20000101
        minus       19990101
                    00010000
```

This example is admittedly simplistic, but it's enough to illustrate the fundamental nature of the Year-2000 problem. If it were as simple as this, we might have a chance of fixing the problem; but as we'll illustrate below, there are several more computer-oriented anomalies related to dates; and there are some *enormous* problems associated with finding all these quirks and fixing them within the computer systems of large organizations. Indeed, almost all of the computer professionals who are working on the Year-2000 problem today regard the technological aspects of the problem as relatively trivial; it's the management and logistics problems of finding and fixing *all* of the date calculations, all at once, that is proving to be so overwhelming.

Additional Anomalies and Quirks of the Year-2000 Problem

For a computer programmer reading through the hypothetical banking system example described above, it's fairly obvious that a date involving year, month, and day could cause problems if the year is represented with two digits. But sometimes dates are "hard-coded" and embedded within the computer program in a more subtle fashion; suppose, for example, that the programmer found the following piece of program logic within the banking system:

```
IF GEEZER > 65
        THEN INTEREST_RATE = 0.05
    ELSE
        INTEREST_RATE = 0.09
```

Here's the question: Is "65" a reference to the calendar year 1965, or is it intended to be the literal number 65? It's very difficult to answer this question without knowing the "context" in which this calculation is being carried out; in particular, we need to know what "GEEZER" really means. When programmers write computer programs, they use symbolic names to refer to an area of the computer's memory that will be used to store a piece of information. A good programmer will use a mnemonic name that helps other computer programmers understand what's going on. Unfortunately, smartass programmers use the names of their pets, their favorite foods, or their girlfriends/boyfriends. If the small piece of computer logic shown above had been written by a good programmer, it might have appeared thusly:

```
IF AGE_OF_BORROWER > 65
        THEN INTEREST_RATE = 0.05
ELSE
      INTEREST_RATE = 0.09
```

Or it might have looked like this:

```
IF YEAR_OF_LOAN_ORIGINATION > 65
        THEN INTEREST_RATE = 0.05
ELSE
      INTEREST_RATE = 0.09
```

In the first case, "65" is a literal constant and should *not* be changed to 1965 during a Year-2000 project; in the second case, the bank has apparently decided that any loan granted after 1965 should be given a preferential interest rate.

There are three things worth noting about this example:

- The person who has to examine the computer program to see if it requires changing is almost certainly *not* the person who wrote the program in the first place. Indeed, many of the computer programs that are associated with the Year-2000 problem were first written 25 years ago by people who have retired, died, or moved on to greener pastures at some other company. In the rare case where the same programmer is still working on software that he/she created, it's very difficult to remember the details of intricate program logic that was written years ago. By analogy, take a look at your checkbook from three years ago: Can you remember why you wrote that check to "cash" for $43.98?

- The details of a computer program are sometimes explained in separate documentation—memos, manuals, flowcharts, etc.—created while the program was first being developed. Thus, in the best of all cases, we might be able to find a document for our cryptic example above in which the original programmer wrote "I used the name 'GEEZER' to refer to the age of a person taking out a bank loan simply because my Dad always used to refer to people who had retired as 'geezers'." Unfortunately, in many computer projects, the documentation was never written at all; or it was lost; or it became obsolete because subsequent generations of maintenance programmers changed the program logic without updating the associated documentation. By analogy: Can you even find the checkbook for those checks you wrote three years ago? Did you even bother making an entry for that $43.98 check to "cash"? Was it perhaps a surprise birthday gift for your spouse, in which case you might have written an entirely misleading entry in the checkbook?

- While it's difficult to guess the underlying meaning of a cryptic name like GEEZER, sometimes it can be inferred by looking at other portions of the same program. In our banking example, for instance, a careful scrutiny might have uncovered another section of computer logic that read

  SUBTRACT BIRTHDATE_OF_BORROWER FROM TODAYS_DATE AND STORE RESULT IN GEEZER.

  This would obviously lead us to conclude that GEEZER was intended to be used as an "age" field, and so the literal reference to "65" should not be changed. While it's almost impossible for a human to scan through all of the complex interdependencies of a large program (some of which contains millions of computer instructions) to draw such conclusions, an automated analysis can be carried out by another computer program. An entire industry of software vendors has emerged in the past few years with automated tools to scan through programs like the hypothetical banking system and find both the obvious and not-so-obvious references to dates.

This example of "embedded" dates is just one of the problems; here are two more:

- Many computer programs were written in the 1960s, 1970s, or 1980s with the implicit assumption that they would be scrapped or replaced within 10 years; as a result, many computer programmers assumed that "99" and "00" would never represent legitimate values for a date-year. And because of this assumption, they would sometimes use these two values to assign a special status to a customer, or an invoice, or similar pieces of information.[1] A birth-year of 99, for example, might be used in a banking system to indicate that the account-holder has deceased, and therefore should not be sent any marketing literature. A birth-year of 00 might be used to indicate that an account-holder has declared personal bankruptcy, and is therefore ineligible for loans or certain other banking transactions. Note that this could lead to problems for the bank's computer systems before January 1, 2000; indeed, many organizations are bracing for problems on September 9, 1999 because of the tendency of programmers to use "9/9/99" as a special value in some of the older computer systems.

- 2000 is a leap year, but some computer systems fail to recognize this fact. Everyone knows that any year divisible by four is a leap year, and many computer programmers also know that there is an exception: a year divisible by 100 is not a leap year. But some programmers are unaware that there is an exception to the exception: If the year is also divisible by 400, then it *is* a leap year. Thus, 1900 was not a leap year, nor is 2100, but 2000 is. All of this is relevant for the computer programs that carry out a straightforward calculation to determine whether February 29 exists in the year 2000. Note that this is a problem that may not be recognized in some business organizations until two months after New Year's Eve at the turn of the millennium.

Consequences of the Problem

What happens when a computer system incorrectly interprets the date after December 31, 1999? Unfortunately, there's no single, simple answer to this question; we can't make a simple public announcement to the entire human race that says, "Whenever you have an encounter with a computer system that overcharges you by $3,141,592.65 after December 31, 1999, just ignore it. It's a minor problem, and it will be fixed as soon as the computer experts can get to it."

As we've seen, many of the common Year-2000 problems *do* involve incorrect calculations within business-oriented computer systems (e.g., computers associated with a bank, insurance company, phone company, etc.); but, here are a few more of the typical things that can go wrong:

- *Incorrect decisions resulting from erroneous date calculations*—There have already been reports of computer systems sending notices to 104-year-old grandmothers that they should report to kindergarten; and the British department store, Marks & Spencer, has reported that its inventory control systems have already begun rejecting incoming arrivals of perishable items whose expiration date is beyond January 1, 2000. As illustrated in the examples above, there will also probably be numerous cases in the early part of the next decade when a computer system incorrectly decides that a person is dead. If the bank's marketing department stops sending you junk mail based on that incorrect decision, you probably won't object; but if the electric company shuts off your electricity and the IRS fails to send your tax refund check, you'll be pretty annoyed. Stop for a moment and think about the situations you're likely to encounter with a computer-controlled bureaucracy that thinks you're dead...

- *Incorrect decisions, one step removed*—Suppose you open your monthly credit card statement on January 3, 2000 and find an interest charge of $3,141,592.65 for last month's unpaid balance. By itself, that's bad enough—but imagine what happens next. Your first reaction might be to ignore the bill on the basis that it's clearly incorrect; or you might decide to call the Customer Service department to complain about the bill. But if a million other customers also got an incorrect bill, then the phone line will be permanently busy (assuming it works at all), and you won't be able to rectify the situation. A month later, you'll get another bill; this time it's for $3,188,716.54 because the credit card company charges you an additional 1.5% per month for unpaid balances. You won't pay this bill either, of course, but the next thing that happens is that the credit card company cancels your card because of the large delinquent balance. Then it will send you a dunning notice threatening to sue you if you don't pay the entire amount ...

- *Corruption of internal databases*—Computers not only make decisions and generate bills and invoices "on the fly," they also store information for subsequent processing. Thus, if the credit card system sends you a monthly statement for $3,141,592.65, it also stores that information in a "record" or "file"—the electronic equivalent of a paper copy of that statement, which a nineteenth century clerk would have placed into a file folder and stuffed into a file cabinet. But the file storage area on many computer systems is often designed in a very rigid, constrained fashion, with an allowance of a specific number of characters, or digits, for each piece of information. The person who designed the credit card system, for example, may have decided that a storage area of only 20 characters would be assigned for the customer's name, and 30 characters for the customer's street address; that's why you sometimes find that your name or address has been truncated in a bizarre fashion in the computer-generated statements and invoices you receive. Suppose that the same programmer has decided (with or without approval and knowledge of his or her managers) that no customer will ever get a credit card statement involving an amount greater than $99,999.99—so he or she allocates enough space in the computer's file storage area to hold seven numerical digits. Now, because of the Year-2000 bug, the computer program tries to store a nine-digit number ($3,141,592.65) into that seven-digit space. What happens? Pos-

sibly the high-order two digits or the low-order
two digits will be truncated, which will lead to
further confusion if you ever do manage to talk
to a customer service representative to complain
about your bill; the representative will retrieve
the record from the computer file and assume
that you're complaining about a credit card bill
of $41,492.65. But here's a worse scenario: The
extra two digits of the invoice amount overwrite
the first two digits of whatever information was
stored "adjacent" to the invoice amount. For example, the computer programmer might have
decided that it would be a good idea to store
your home address in the file storage area immediately adjacent to the invoice amount. Because
of the Year-2000 bug, the first two digits of your
street address are now "65".

- *Aborts, abends, and halts*—In some cases, a computer system will make an incorrect decision, or
generate an incorrect output, or store some incorrect information in a file or database; and
then it will keep chugging along, carrying out a
similar (incorrect) activity for the next customer,
the next invoice, or the next "transaction" that
it's supposed to process. But, there will be numerous cases where a Year-2000 problem causes
the computer to stop all subsequent processing
and come to a halt; computer professionals
sometime refer to these situations as ABENDs
(particularly for older mainframe computer systems), or "aborts." For a business computer sys-

tem that's trying to send out thousands of
invoices or credit card statements, there won't be
any immediate consequences of an ABEND; it
may cause some middle-of-the-night phone calls
to the computer programmers, but it will take
awhile for the bank's customers to notice that
they haven't received their monthly statement.
The situation is far more serious, though, for the
vast number of "embedded" systems that perme-
ate society. As we suggested in the Preface, an aberrant computer may halt the fuel mixture
activity in your automobile while you're driving
home at 60 mph on New Year's Eve, 1999. On
a larger scale, "process control" computers are
used for refineries, nuclear reactors, air-traffic
control, traffic signals, and dozens of other systems in which a sudden halt could have life-
threatening consequences. We discussed these
consequences in Chapters 3 and 4.

How the Year-2000 Problem Came To Be

When your car malfunctions, what do you do? For most of
us, the answer is simple: yell at it, as if it were an unruly teen-
ager. When the word processor on your home computer or
office computer somehow deletes the document you were
working on, you're likely to snarl, "You stupid computer! How
could you do that to me?" We *anthropomorphize* complex
mechanical and computerized devices and treat them as if they
were living, sentient creatures; even veteran computer professionals have a tendency to behave in this fashion, and the
behavior has been popularized with examples like HAL in the
movie *2001.*

But there's an important point to remember in our discussion of the Year-2000 situation: *Computers* aren't responsible for all these problems, people are. Aside from transient hardware failures (e.g., from an overheated circuit, or the effect of a piece of dust in a disk drive), computers behave or misbehave in whatever fashion they were instructed by the computer programmer. In general, programmers try to design and implement a computer program to produce the behavior specified by their managers, or by the customers for whom the system is being developed. But in other cases, particularly when it comes to low-level technical details, programmers make their own decisions—because customers and managers trust the technicians to make the right decisions, because they're uninterested in the details, or because they're overwhelmed by the technical nature of the situation.

Thus, sometimes the managers of a computer department, and the business managers within the organization, were aware of the conscious decision to represent dates with a two-digit year, and sometimes they weren't. If this sounds sloppy and irresponsible, think about *yourself* as a "customer." When you bought your home, did you ask the architect whether the plumbing hardware and electrical wiring had been designed and implemented to last for any specific period of time? If this had resulted in a lengthy conversation with the plumber and the electrician, would you have understood the nuances of what they were telling you? Probably not.

Of course, you might have responded, "I don't have to worry about such details. I trust the architect because I know that he's/she's licensed. And I trust the plumber and electrician to do the right thing, because there's an independent building inspector who must certify that my new house has been constructed according to standard building codes."

Unfortunately, there's no such parallel in the software industry. Most computer programmers, systems analysts, software engineers, database designers, and other specialists have college degrees, but there's no such thing as a "license" in the field. And while the software systems in a few safety-critical industries *do* have to be "inspected" before they are allowed to operate, there's no equivalent of a "building code" regarding the proper way to represent a date—although the U.S. government has recently adopted a standard definition of what it means for a computer program to be "Year-2000-compliant." For the vast majority of business-oriented computer systems, though, and for a reasonable majority of embedded systems and control systems, there has been no oversight, review, or inspection at all.

If the legendary cartoon figure, Pogo, were a computer programmer, he might say, "We have met the Year-2000 enemy, and he is us ... and our managers." It's fair to say that, in most cases, the business managers—e.g., the Vice President of the credit card division of a bank—had no idea that the computer systems being developed for the bank had a Year-2000 time-bomb ticking away. But even if he or she did, he/she probably would have been susceptible to the same mistakes and weaknesses of the technical computer specialists.

But *why* did the technical specialists get us into this problem? After all, you don't have to be a rocket scientist to understand the potential problems we've outlined in this appendix. And most computer programmers *are* rocket scientists, in one fashion or another, so how could they have been so dumb? Here are the most common explanations:

- *Casual sloppiness*—Depending on how you count such things, four or five generations of people have been born in this century. The twentieth century is the only thing we've known, and that our parents and their parents have known. In our written and verbal communications, we naturally truncate the first two digits of the year: "Where were you back in '63 when Kennedy was shot? Were you in San Francisco during the '89 earthquake?" The assumption that only the low-order two digits are relevant permeates much of what we do; and though they're usually fairly careful about details, computer programmers suffer from this same casual assumption. It simply didn't occur to them, when they wrote their computer programs, that it would be a good idea to use all four digits of the year.

• *Computer hardware was expensive when most business computer systems were first developed*—As we pointed out earlier, many of the business computer systems that are most vulnerable to Year-2000 problems were designed 20 or 30 years ago. In those days, computers were several thousand times larger, and slower, and more expensive. Today, we casually buy a home computer with 32 megabytes (millions of characters) of memory and 2 gigabytes (billions of characters) of disk storage, and we expect to pay about $1,000. Thirty years ago, business organizations had to spend a million dollars to buy a computer with 32 kilobytes (thousands of characters) of memory and 2 megabytes of disk storage; instead of fitting on a desktop, the old computers filled an entire room. In the 1960s and 1970s, programmers were expected to use every trick they could think of to save a few precious characters of storage; if a bank had a million customers, and each customer's banking record had a dozen different dates (e.g., the customer's birthdate, the date the account was opened, the date of the last deposit, the date of each of the checks written during the past month, etc.), then eliminating the high-order two digits of the year could save a few dozen characters for each customer, and a few hundred million characters of aggregate storage requirements. Today, we would shrug our shoulders at the prospect of a few hundred million characters of storage; Microsoft's new Office97 software gobbles up 300 million characters when it's installed on our home computer. But in the 1960s or 1970s, numbers like those could represent the difference between success and failure. So the Year-2000 problem was, in a sense, created deliberately by well-intentioned programmers who were coping with the economics of the times.

- *Nobody thought computer systems would last so long*—Thirty years is a long, long time in the computer industry; the speed, power, storage capacity, and cost of computer hardware has improved by a factor of approximately one million. This is not just an academic notion. If you bought one of IBM's first PC computers in

1981, you've seen five subsequent generations of Intel-based PC hardware: the 286, 386, 486, Pentium, and Pentium II. In this kind of environment, the natural assumption is that software will be replaced quickly too; indeed, some of the computer systems designed in the 1960s and 1970s used a one-digit representation of the year, on the assumption that the software would almost certainly be replaced or rewritten before the end of the decade. The situation was sometimes exacerbated by business managers who yelled at the programmers, "Don't waste your time trying to design the system to last for 20 years—we only need to run the system once or twice to produce some reports for the government, and then we'll never need it again." True, some software does get used only once or twice; and some software does get rewritten and replaced after 4–5 years, in order to take advantage of more powerful hardware capabilities. But to everyone's surprise, many of the largest and most complex systems have survived (albeit with extensive modifications, enhancements, and repairs) for 20–30 years.

• *Nobody thought of the "system-level" consequences—* In the cases where computer programmers did think about the consequences of a Year-2000 problem, they typically thought about it only in the context of the particular system they were working on, e.g., "Uh oh, what's going to happen to the insurance billing system that I'm responsi-

ble for when we reach New Year's Eve, 1999?"
And in the rare cases where a higher-level computer manager contemplated the problem, the attention was focused only on that manager's
organization, e.g., "I sure hope I'm retired when it
comes time to fix all the Year-2000 problems in
our systems!" But until a year or two ago, it didn't
occur to anyone that every computer program in
every company in every industry in every country
was going to face the Year-2000 problem at the
same time. As we'll explain in Appendix B, it's the
"system dynamics" aspect of the Year-2000 problem that's most difficult to anticipate or control.

• *Nobody wanted to be the victim of "shoot the mes-
senger" politics*—Though it might appear that
computer professionals have been unbelievably
short-sighted with regard to the Year-2000 problem, a few individuals began thinking about the
problem in 1990. A new year, a new decade, the
last decade of the century… a few forward-
thinking computer managers began muttering
to themselves, "Uh, oh … it may be ten years
away, but it's pretty obvious that our systems
won't work at the beginning of the next decade."
And it became a little more obvious in 1995,
when a few companies began to notice that their
five-year financial forecasts were blowing up because of the Year-2000 problem. But the politics
of dealing with the situation are pretty difficult,
especially when: (a) most organizations have a
planning horizon of one year or less; (b) comput-

er budgets are being scrutinized more and more
carefully; and (c) a Year-2000 project provides
no new functionality or "business value." Imagine what it's like for the manager of a computer
department at the XYZ bank, who finds himself
saying to the Vice President of the credit card division: "You know that new credit card billing
system that we developed a couple years ago, for
a cost of $10 million? Well, I'm sorry to tell you
that we're going to have to spend another $3
million to make it Year-2000-compliant. You
won't get any additional benefit from that $3
million expense, except for the fact that, five
years from now, the software will still run correctly. Oh, and by the way, this project will require all of our best programmers, so we won't
be able to work on any new computer projects
for the next two years."

What To Do?

In the rare cases that senior business managers were made
aware of the Year-2000 problem in 1990 or 1995, they generally ignored it. The typical response was, "We'll worry about it
next year, when we have more time and more money in the
budget." Or, "I'm going to be transferred next year, and it's
crucial for me to achieve all of my revenue and profit and cost-
reduction objectives this year. I'll let my successor worry about
this problem." Indeed, this continues to be a common reaction: "Hey, we still have a couple years left—we can take care
of this sometime in 1999."

But, the widespread discussion and debate about the Year-
2000 problem within the computer industry has gradually

made it evident that it will be far too late to solve the problem in 1999; indeed, for many organizations, it was already too late when this book was written in the summer of 1997. Throughout the U.S., computer departments are gradually shifting more and more of their energies to Year-2000 projects, which usually involve one or more of the following strategies:

- *Retiring the systems that are no longer needed—* Even though some 30-year-old systems are still being used on a daily basis, and are considered "mission-critical," there are other business computer systems that have fallen into disuse. More importantly, there are computer systems that run daily, weekly, or monthly to produce reports that nobody bothers looking at anymore. Obviously, the best Year-2000 strategy here is euthanasia of the old systems; however, this requires a careful analysis and assessment of the organization's "portfolio" of software systems, as well as a consensus among the senior business managers as to which systems are mission-critical and which ones are irrelevant. The time required for this kind of analysis and consensus-building can take longer than the technical work to fix the programs—and there's not much time left to do it!

- *Replacing old systems with commercial "packages"—* Imagine the scenario of a medium-sized company that runs a weekly payroll system, which was developed 20 years ago by a programmer that has vanished. The software is not Year-2000-compliant, and nobody can figure out how it works because the documentation has disappeared.

Finding and fixing all the date occurrences will be time-consuming, tedious, expensive, and error-prone; an obvious alternative is to scrap the program and replace it with a commercial "package" or payroll service. The same is likely to be true for accounts payable, accounts receivable, general ledger, inventory control, and a wide variety of common business applications. However, for large Fortune 500 companies, it typically takes 2-3 years to customize, configure, and install a large, complex commercial package from vendors such as SAP, Peoplesoft, and Baan. It was often an attractive, practical alternative in 1995; by the beginning of 1998, it will be too late.

• *Changing two-digit year fields to four digits*—This is the "obvious" correction, of course, and it's one of the more common approaches taken by companies today. But it has two problems: first, the extra two digits take up additional space on printed reports and on computer display screens; and second, it requires updating and expanding of date fields on database records and files. The first problem is likely to be a minor one, though you would be surprised how many computer systems have used every conceivable piece of "real estate" on such reports and screens—in some cases, it's not possible to cram in an extra two digits without a major redesign of the report or screen layout.

The required modifications to the database are far more problematic. Again, there's the prob-

lem of "real estate." As mentioned earlier in this
appendix, some of the older computer systems
are designed so that the information in a database record takes up all of the available space
within the storage area of the hard disk or magnetic tape; adding two more digits (or, more
likely, several instances of double-digits, since a
typical business database record will have multiple instances of date fields) could mean redesign-
ing the entire database. And even without this
nuisance, there's the enormous logistics problem
of updating (and expanding) the database while
the organization attempts to continue running
its day-to-day business operations. Many large
organizations now have databases consisting of
several terabytes (trillions of bytes), and it would
require weeks or months of uninterrupted computer time to update the database.

• *Using a "windowing" approach*—Because of the
   database and report expansion problems mentioned above, many organizations have decided
   to use a programming approach known as "windowing" to deal with the Year-2000 problem.
   Essentially, this involves defining a century-wide
   "window" with which to interpret the real meaning of a two-digit year. For example, an organization might decide to define a window that
   extends from 1920 to 2019; this means that
   whenever computer programs encounter a two-
   digit year field of, say, "43," they will be interpreted as 1943; and a two-digit year field of "03"

will be interpreted as "2003," etc. Of course, if
such a computer program is dealing with birth-
dates of people, then it's going to make the
wrong decision if it encounters someone born
before 1920, and it's going to run into far more
serious problems if the same program is still being used in the year 2020. Thus, it's crucial for
companies to choose a window carefully, depending on the nature of their business applications; unfortunately, this is a concept that has
not been standardized, so if company A's computers send date-related information to company B's computers, there's going to be a lot of
confusion unless both companies have chosen
the same window, or have some way of translating between one window and another.

Year-2000: The Biggest Computer
Project of All Time

While we've over-simplified some of the technical details in
this appendix, the essence of the Year-2000 problem is not
very difficult to understand from a technical perspective, nor is
the solution. While the concept of a Year-2000 problem might
have taken you by surprise when you first picked up this book,
and while the whole thing might seem a bit overwhelming,
most computer professionals tend to downplay the problem
when they first hear about it. An eminent computer consultant, who is now *very* aware of the magnitude of the Year-2000
problem, commented to one of the authors in early 1996:

Who can believe we are about to be undone by such a noth-ing problem? The mighty software monolith brought to its knees by diddly squat. It's like reading through 900 pages of Gibbon only to be told that the decline and fall of the Roman empire was really due to a bad case of head lice.

Technologically, the Year-2000 problem *is* diddly squat—so why is everyone making such a big deal of it? The answer is simple: Industrialized society is now filled with millions of computers, which contain hundreds of *billions* of program instructions. All of these computers, and the "portfolios" of software systems they contain, must be examined and updated appropriately. And, with minor exceptions, they all need to be updated at the same time, with proper synchronization, to avoid what we'll describe in Appendix B as the "ripple effect" problem.

In 1996-97, several consulting and research organizations began "sizing" the Year-2000 problem; in addition to the rather crude approximations that have been widely publicized by the Gartner Group, more careful estimates have been prepared by Dr. Howard Rubin of Hunter College and by Capers Jones of Software Productivity Research. Of these, Jones has the most detailed figures, and the ones that appear to be the mostly widely accepted by other professionals and researchers in the field. Here are just a few snippets of data from his recently published book, *The Year-2000 Software Problem:*[2]

- The U.S. has a total, aggregate portfolio of ap-proximately 1.57 billion "function points" of software. A function point is a language-inde-pendent way of measuring the size of a computer program, and is approximately equal to 100 COBOL statements. Thus, if all of the comput-er software in the U.S. had been written in

COBOL (which was largely true for the business computer systems of the 1960s and 1970s, but is definitely not true as an overall characterization), we would have 157 billion program statements to deal with.[3]

- The effort to perform Year-2000 repairs on this software is estimated by Jones to involve approximately 9.3 million person-months, or slightly more than 750,000 person-years of work. The cost of this effort, given typical salaries and overhead, is approximately $74.6 billion.

- While the U.S. has more than twice as much software as the next largest country (which turns out to be Japan), the overall global figures for the 30 most significant industrialized countries are astounding: 7 billion function points (approximately equal to 700 billion program statements), 3.5 million person-years of effort, and approximately $297 billion in repair costs.

- None of these figures include the cost of likely lawsuits and post-Year-2000 repair efforts associated with software that was not fixed correctly.

All of these figures must be taken with a large grain of salt, for at least two reasons:

- The vast amount of software that companies run on their mainframe computers is gradually being dwarfed by the even vaster amount of software on millions of PCs. In addition to professional-

ly-developed software on the PCs (e.g., the copy
of Microsoft Word and Excel that you might
have on your own computer), there are millions
upon millions of hand-crafted spreadsheets and
database programs that have been developed by
amateurs over the past 15–20 years.

• While it's no surprise that the amateurs have
typically never documented anything they've
done, many large companies are discovering the
humiliating fact that the same can be said of
their professional programmers. A company
might have a payroll system, for example, that
was written 20 years ago, and is still running on
a weekly basis today. Unfortunately, the program that actually runs inside the computer is a
"binary" or "machine language" program that's
almost impossible for a human to read and understand. The original "source program," typically written in a language like COBOL, BASIC,
or FORTRAN (and from which the binary program was produced by "compiling" the source
program) has been lost; or it was compiled by an
ancient version of IBM's compiler, which no
longer exists. Or … well, the problems go on
and on here, but the bottom line is that many organizations are now discovering that their "legacy" programs are completely out of control.

So, in short, the Year-2000 problem is an enormous one, by
far the largest software project any company has ever undertaken. To complicate matters, *every* company will be working
on it at the same time, leading observers like Capers Jones to

suggest that "the costs of fixing the 'year 2000 problem' appear to constitute the most expensive single problem in human history."

Problems that are large, messy and expensive have a tendency to be postponed or avoided within many organizations—both from a governmental/political perspective, and also within the bureaucracy of business organizations. The situation is complicated further because, in most cases, there is no "added business value" associated with a Year-2000 repair effort. Computer departments in most organizations are routinely criticized for spending lavish sums of money on advanced computer systems that fail to provide a tangible "return on investment" (ROI); consequently, the political climate in many such organizations prevents anyone from even suggesting a multi-million dollar Year-2000 project, because the resulting software won't do anything bigger, better, faster, or sexier than the old system ... the only difference is that two years from now, it will continue to function correctly. For the Vice President who worries about *this* year's budget (and the personal bonus or stock options that may be associated with it), the temptation to postpone the Year-2000 effort for another year is powerful indeed.

The problem is compounded further in many government agencies, because once a computer project has been justified and approved, *then* the necessary tools and contractors have to be acquired—typically through a procurement process that can last months or years. The notion that some state and federal government agencies won't have their personnel and Year-2000 software tools in place until 2001 would be enormously amusing were it not for the fact that millions of citizens could be affected; we discuss this situation in more detail in Chapter 11.

As already noted, most organizations will need to overlap the Year-2000 conversion efforts with their ongoing day-to-day business affairs. This going to cause the following additional problems:

- Additional hardware resources will be required for all of the scanning and analysis of old legacy programs, conversion efforts, compiling, and testing of Year-2000 programs. Some of the work can be done on PCs and workstations, but additional mainframe resources will be required. This will not only add a large cost item, but introduces a logistics problem of its own: you can't order a mainframe from an overnight mail-order company the way you can with a PC.

- The personnel assigned to Year-2000 projects will, to some extent, have to be taken from other software development projects the company would normally be working on. By early 1997, a survey of U.S. organizations conducted by one of the authors indicated that approximately 15–20% of the software staff had already been thus diverted.

- Even if all the personnel could be obtained from outside the organization (from consulting firms, big vendors like IBM, or "outsourcing" firms in India, etc.), it would still represent a significant expense. If Capers Jones' worldwide Year-2000 cost of $297 billion is at all accurate, that money has to come from somewhere—and the first place it will come from is the "normal" software budget of the organization.

- The demand for Year-2000 personnel is going to exacerbate a shortage of software professionals estimated in early 1997 to be 300,000 professionals in the U.S. alone. It typically takes 5–10 years for universities and educational institutions to respond to marketplace shortages like this, which means that for the remainder of this decade, the shortage will probably get worse. One of the most obvious consequences of such a shortage is rising labor costs; many researchers are already predicting that the costs of Year-2000 conversion projects in 1998–99 will be 50–100% more expensive than they would have been in 1996–97.

- While all of this is going on, the business will have a demand for ongoing changes, corrections, and improvements of the business applications that are simultaneously being reviewed and corrected for Year-2000 compliance. The trivial solution to this problem is to "freeze" all existing computer programs in their current state, and to disallow any changes until the Year-2000 corrections have been made. For obvious reasons, this will turn out to be unpopular, expensive, impractical, and in some cases, downright impossible. Thus, the organization will have the added burden of coordinating the following entirely different categories of "maintenance" projects: a

massive Year-2000 effort with a bare-minimum
of "ordinary" enhancements.

- The same problem exists with the database, as
  noted earlier in this appendix. Indeed, even if the
  programs could be "frozen" for the duration of
  the Year-2000 projects, the databases would
  continue to change on a daily, hourly, or even
  continuous basis—reflecting the orders, invoices, payments, and other business transactions
  that are the very heartbeat of the business organization. For a medium-sized organization with
  a modest-sized database, the solution is to halt
  normal business operations early on a Friday afternoon, and tell the Year-2000 project team to
  work around the clock through the weekend, in
  order to have an updated, Year-2000-compliant
  database ready to resume normal operations on
  Monday morning. This sort of thing has happened before, and it's always stressful and problematic; for large organizations, it's simply
  impossible to accomplish all of the database conversion within a limited time-frame of 48 hours.

As you can see, the logistics and project management
aspects of the Year-2000 project are daunting, to say the least.
There's one last discouraging item: The software industry, as a
whole, has *never* been very good at completing projects on
time, within budget. The situation varies by industry, by programming language, and by size of project—but in general,
only 15–20% of software projects are finished within the budget and timeframe originally allocated. About 15–20% of
projects are canceled, and the most common scenario is a

project that exceeds both its budget *and* its schedule by 50-100%. Whether a budget overrun is acceptable depends on the specific circumstances, of course; but the obvious constraint of a Year-2000 project is that it *cannot* overrun the deadline of December 31, 1999.

When software project schedule delays first began to be noticed 30 years ago, there was a common tendency to add more programmers to a project, in the optimistic hope that the additional personnel could help speed things up. But in a classic software engineering book, first published in 1975, Dr. Fred Brooks articulated what has come to be known as "Brooks' Law": Adding more people to a late software project just makes it later.[4] Like trying to produce a baby in one month by assigning nine women to the task, there are some things you just can't speed up.

Producing software isn't quite like producing babies, of course, and you *can* produce software somewhat more quickly by adding more people to the project team, asking everyone to work double overtime, etc.; but the law of diminishing returns sets in very quickly, and the *negative* effect of Brooks' Law occurs much sooner than the layperson would think. Every professional programmer and project manager is well aware of this fact, but it probably won't prevent senior management in large organizations from attempting to refute Brooks' Law by throwing large numbers of programmers at the project as the December 31, 1999 deadline looms nearer and nearer.

The likelihood of any software project finishing on time is dependent on many different variables, including such obvious things as the competence of the programmers working on the project. But if all other factors are fixed (because of the shortage of programmers, the finite amount of dollars, and other resources that can be allocated to Year-2000 projects, etc.), it's likely to turn out that the biggest single determinant of Year-2000 success will be *how much calendar time is available for the project.* Imagine, for example, that an organization developed a "rational" estimate, devoid of any political bias, of its Year-2000 software efforts and determined that it would require three years of calendar time to finish the job properly (an estimate which usually includes the need to spend most of calendar year 1999 on testing all of the modified software to ensure that it runs correctly). Now assume that because of politics and bureaucracy, the Year-2000 project doesn't actually begin its efforts until January 1, 1998; not only will the costs escalate, but the odds of finishing the project successfully by the (non-negotiable) deadline drop sharply. If additional politics and bureaucracy prevent the project from beginning until January 1, 1999, the odds of successful completion are perilously low. As Capers Jones argues, "Roughly October of 1997 is the last time at which even specialists with automated search engines have a high probability of finding, fixing, and testing the year 2000 problem in a typical 500,000 function point corporate portfolio and finishing prior to midnight on December 31, 1999."[5]

Summary

During the summer and fall of 1997, when this book was being written, various surveys and estimates suggested that approximately 35-50% of computer organizations had not yet begun their Year-2000 projects, and that 15–35% would *not* be finished before the December 31, 1999 deadline. As Jones puts it, "data as of early 1997 indicates that at least 15% of software applications will not be repaired in time. For some enterprises, the unrepaired applications may be 100%."

As you can imagine, the problem could be annoying—or worse—if the non-compliant computer systems happen to be associated with *your* bank, or *your* telephone company, or *your* employer. But as we'll demonstrate in Appendix B, the problem is likely to be magnified by the "ripple effect" caused by interdependencies between organizations. If 15% of the banks fail to convert their software in time, for example, the simplest scenario we could imagine is that *only* those banks would fail—that would be a problem you could ignore with a sympathetic shrug of your shoulders, unless your bank was one of the unlucky 15%. But the problem is that some of the non-Year-2000-compliant banks won't cease operations as of midnight on December 31, 1999; they'll start spewing out incorrect inter-bank transactions to other banks, the Federal Reserve, and the U.S. Treasury. And if the non-compliant banks *do* fail, they not only consume the deposits and savings of their immediate customers, but also the deposits and loans of other Year-2000-compliant banks. What happens then?

One last item: Many business organizations and government agencies that have finally begun to pay attention to the Year-2000 problem in 1996 and 1997 have already concluded that they simply *cannot* fix all of their software in time; if the October 1997 deadline suggested by Capers Jones is accurate, then it's a virtual certainty that any organization beginning its Year-2000 efforts after January 1, 1998 will be forced to admit that complete success is no longer possible. That doesn't mean that the organization will give up and declare bankruptcy right away, though one of the authors has heard an apocryphal story of a company whose owners concluded in 1996 that successful Year-2000 conversion was no longer financially and logistically possible—so the owners sold the business. What most organizations will do, if and when they face up to the impossibility of complete Year-2000 conversion, is simple and obvious: *triage*. A careful assessment of their software portfolio will reveal that there are some systems and application that are so critical that the business will halt immediately if they're not fixed; there are other systems for which a Year-2000 failure would be painful and expensive, but which would not put the company out of business (or at least, not right away). And finally, there are some systems that are already "dead," in the sense that they're not being used, or nobody cares about them; those systems can be ignored, and precious Year-2000 resources can be diverted elsewhere.

Year-2000 guru Peter de Jager offers an intriguing example of the triage decision: If you're an airline, and you only have enough time and/or Year-2000 technical personnel to fix *either* your airline reservation system *or* your aircraft maintenance/repair system, which one should you choose? The manager in charge of airline reservations (which might be a marketing function, or perhaps something reporting directly to the finance/accounting department, depending on the airline) would obviously argue that reservations are critical to the success of the airline: no reservations, such a manager might argue, means no tickets, and thus no revenue, and thus a very quick death of the business. But "shuttle" airlines like Delta, US Airways, and Southwest Airlines have demonstrated that customers *will* show up at the airport, pay their money, and get on the flight even if they don't have a reservation or ticket. On the other hand, a failure in the maintenance/repair system means that engines will fail, tires will blow out, and airplanes will fall out of the sky. *That* would be terminal.

Unfortunately, the fact that most organizations will find a way to limp along by sacrificing some of their non-critical systems does *not* mean that individuals like you and me will be shielded from the problem. To offer one trivial example, consider the ticket agents and airline reservation clerks who work for the hypothetical airline mentioned above. Given the scope of its problems, the airline could easily decide that it will take six months to repair the airline reservation system, and furlough the appropriate employees without pay for that period. For the airline's customers, the lack of a reservation system is an annoying nuisance; for the airline reservation clerks, it's a much more serious problem.

And while this is only a small—and admittedly hypothetical—example, it illustrates the perspective that you'll see throughout this book. We don't expect large, responsible organizations to ignore the Year-2000 repairs on their most critical systems; consequently, we don't expect airplanes to fall out of the sky, nor do we think that Western civilization will come to a halt. But we do think that there will be serious, visible, widespread problems not only at the corporate level (as in the case of our hypothetical airline, which will presumably lose some revenue because of the faulty reservation system), but also at the personal level.

Endnotes

1. Computer consultants Joe Celko and Jackie Celko have reported on the situation in a prison system where the "prisoner release date" field was coded in such a way that "999999" was used for prisoners on death row and "888888" was used for those with a life sentence. See "Double Zero," *Byte*, July 1997.

2. Capers Jones, *The Year 2000 Software Problem: Quantifying the Costs and Assessing the Consequences* (Addison-Wesley, 1997).

3. It should be emphasized that these figures vary dramatically depending on the programming language involved—which is the main reason that Jones and others prefer to express the Year-2000 economic data in terms of neutral function points. While older business applications are typically programmed in COBOL, newer applications are programmed in a variety of so-called "fourth-generation" languages such as PowerBuilder, Visual Basic, and Delphi. But of more concern is the category of embedded systems and military systems that

have been programmed in "low-level" languages, such as assembler. Jones estimates that approximately one-third of the Year-2000-sensitive software in the U.S. is written in COBOL, but there are actually several hundred specialized, obscure, and proprietary programming languages that have been used for software applications over the past 50 years.

4. Frederick P. Brooks, Jr., *The Mythical Man-Month,* revised 20th anniversary edition (Addison-Wesley, 1995).
5. Capers Jones, *The Year 2000 Software Problem,* p. 22.

The Ripple Effect of the Year-2000 Phenomenon

No man is an island entire of itself; every man is a piece of the Continent, a part of the main.... Any man's death diminishes me because I am involved in Mankind; and therefore never send to know for whom the bell tolls; it tolls for thee.

John Donne, Devotions Upon Emergent Occasions, *Meditation 17 (1624).*

Six Degrees of Separation, a popular off-Broadway play written by Thomas Guare, makes an intriguing assertion: If you communicate a message to all of the people you know, and each of these people passes on the same message to all of the people they know, and each of those people does the same thing—then after six levels, or "degrees," of communication, you will have reached everyone in the world.[1]

When it comes to the Year-2000 problem, the same principle applies. No person stands alone; no computer system stands alone; no company stands alone; no industry stands alone. *Everything,* as computer expert Tom DeMarco humorously puts it, is deeply intertwingled. Thus, even if you feel that you've fixed or avoided *your* Year-2000 problems, you may be at the mercy of others who have not done so.

Here's a visual representation of the situation. Suppose, notwithstanding John Donne's observations, that you were an "island," independent of everything else in society. As we discussed in Appendix A, you probably have a dishwasher, VCR, microwave oven, and a few other appliances that might be affected by the rollover from 1999 to 2000; perhaps you have a home computer too, which is also likely to be vulnerable to the Year-2000 phenomenon. We've represented these items as small circles within the larger circle shown in Figure B.1.

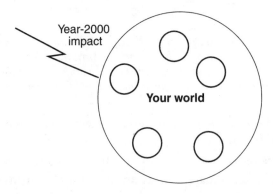

Figure B.1   The impact of Year-2000 on an individual person.

If this is your perspective, the Year-2000 problem is like a lightning bolt; it threatens to disrupt or destroy a number of important items in your world. Interestingly, this is the same perspective that most companies have too—except that the little circles in their world are not simple household appliances, but large computer systems they use to run their day-to-day operations. Nevertheless, the typical corporate reaction is likely to be the same as your personal reaction: Get rid of the Year-2000-sensitive items that you're not using anymore, fix or replace the ones that are important to you, and figure out how to survive without the other ones.

Unfortunately, it's not as simple as that. Unless you're a hermit, or marooned on a desert island, your personal world is interconnected with a number of other "worlds." We're not talking about your family members (all of whom could conceivably be *inside* the circle shown in Figure B.1), but rather the Year-2000-sensitive systems that exist outside your world. If you consider only the first-level interactions, it might look something like Figure B.2:

Figure B.2 The interactions between your world and other worlds.

Note that we've drawn arrows that point in both directions between your world and the various other worlds that you interact with. You interact with your employer, for example, and your employer interacts with you; if the Year-2000 problem prevents interactions in either direction, it could cause a problem. Note also that we've shown the Year-2000 problem impacting *each* of the various worlds, including your own; it's unlikely that anyone will go unscathed. Furthermore, the Year-2000 impact hits everyone at the same time, aside from the minor issue of time zone differences around the world; within 24 hours after the first part of the world celebrates New Year's Eve in 1999, everyone else will too. And so will their computers.

Although the situation in Figure B.2 looks fairly complicated, it omits an obvious point: In addition to the various worlds interacting with your world, they interact with each other. Thus, a more realistic scenario is shown in Figure B.3.

Some simple examples will illustrate the point. If the electrical generators fail and the lights go out because of the Year-2000 problems discussed in Chapter 3, it will be pretty difficult for your employer to conduct business; as a result, you're out of work. If the phone lines don't work (for reasons we discuss in Chapter 13), most of Wall Street will be unable to conduct business. If schools are closed because of Year-2000 problems (a possibility we discuss in Chapter 12), a lot of parents will find that they've lost a surrogate babysitter; they'll have to stay home to keep track of their kids.

Now let's make the situation even more realistic: Each of the "worlds" that we've shown in Figure B.3 depends on a complex network of suppliers, vendors, subcontractors, customers, employees, and others. Some of these are already represented in the two-way interactions shown in Figure B.3, but there's much more involved. If a newspaper company doesn't receive its regu-

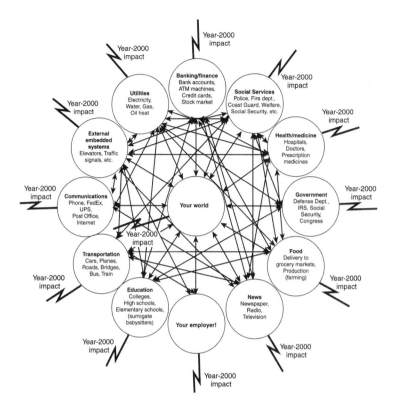

Figure B.3   Interactions between the various worlds.

lar supply of paper and ink, it can't produce newspapers even if the lights are on, the phones are working, and the employees show up for work. Similarly, if the feed stores and fertilizer suppliers are closed, farmers can't feed their animals or plant their crops. We've represented all of this in Figure B.4.

All of these secondary worlds are potentially impacted by the Year-2000 phenomenon; and they not only have interactions with the primary worlds, but also with each other. We haven't drawn the appropriate arrows to represent this in Figure B.4, for it would result in a completely unreadable spider's web.

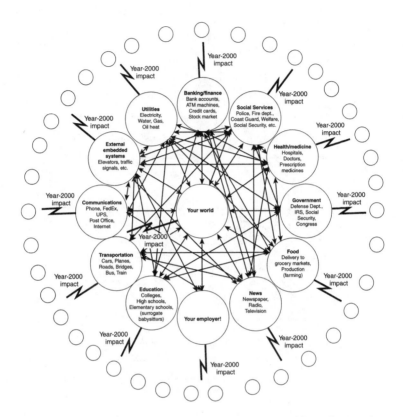

Figure B.4 The interactions between primary worlds and secondary worlds.

In some cases, these secondary worlds might consist of individual people; thus, they might view their world in the same way you do—i.e., as a small circle in the middle of a complex universe. But when you consider the secondary worlds that "feed" General Motors or Citibank or the U.S. government, it's more likely that you're dealing with medium-sized companies—which have their own network of suppliers, subcontrac-

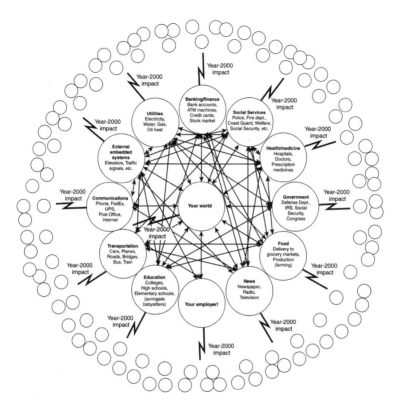

Figure B.5   Interactions involving secondary worlds and tertiary worlds.

tors, vendors, etc. Thus, we're likely to find that the Year-2000 interactions involve a situation like that shown in Figure B.5.

You can tell what's coming next: The tertiary worlds have their own network of suppliers, vendors, and subcontractors. And those fourth-level worlds have their own network, and so forth; and if we extend this notion to the level where each "world" consists of a person or an individual computer system, we may indeed be dealing with "six degrees of separation."

While we firmly believe that the fundamental concept illustrated in Figure B.5 is correct, we have no way of knowing whether the Year-2000 problem will have a noticeable impact on three, four, five, or six levels. But the precise number hardly matters. The point is that your day-to-day life in today's society depends on the smooth operation of at least a dozen other "primary worlds," and that those worlds depend, in turn, on the proper functioning of each other, as well as proper interactions with one or more additional levels of worlds.

Some of these interactions might not involve computers. They could consist of person-to-person conversations, or hand-delivered pieces of written correspondence. You might leave a handwritten note for the manager of the neighborhood liquor store, asking him/her to have a case of beer delivered later in the day; and you might then walk down to the neighborhood branch of your bank and complain to the branch manager that you think the bank's mortgage interest rates are outrageous, and that you're considering moving your account elsewhere. Those interactions don't involve computers, and they'll function just as well after January 1, 2000 as before.

But for business-to-business interactions, the situation is quite different. As far back as the early 1980s, studies indicated that 50–75% of the interactions between company A and company B consisted of "transactions" (purchase orders, payments, inquiries, etc.) generated by a computer system in A and processed by a computer system in B. Many, if not most, of those transactions involve Year-2000-sensitive dates: the date of the transaction itself, the date of a purchase order, the date that the ordered items are expected to be shipped, the date that payment is due, etc.

Note that this situation already exists today; it has nothing to do with the Year-2000 phenomenon per se. Amazingly, this "system of systems" works, and it manages to maintain a fairly steady equilibrium. Economists and politicians have argued for centuries whether a complex socio-economic system like the one illustrated in Figure B.5 can operate with an "invisible hand," or whether it requires a Soviet-style centralized planning mechanism to keep it from getting out of whack. We're not trying to argue in favor of socialism, capitalism, or communism here, but we do want to emphasize that if this system receives a sudden jolt—e.g., a stock market crash, a hurricane, an earthquake, an oil embargo, or an epidemic—it can cause a massive set of ripple effect interactions before everything settles down to a new equilibrium. The Year-2000 phenomenon is clearly such a jolt, and we believe that it will be much more pervasive and serious than most of the jolts we've experienced in modern history.

Year 2000 and the Concept of System Dynamics

Back in the 1960s, MIT Professor Jay Forrester began developing the field of *system dynamics*, based on earlier work in the field of operations research and cybernetics. Forrester's work led to a "world model"[2] that attempted to extrapolate the current trends in energy consumption, population growth, food production, etc. to see what conditions would be like twenty or thirty years in the future. Though the model was probably overly ambitious, and while it was severely criticized by economists and systems researchers for both political and theoretical reasons, it nevertheless set into motion the development of a number of "micro-world" models that have proven to be enormously useful in various companies and government agencies around the world. The field is too elaborate and too technical to discuss here, but we highly recommend Peter Senge's wonderful book, *The Fifth Discipline*,[3] as a very readable and entertaining discussion of what system dynamics is all about.

There are two key system dynamics concepts that are relevant when thinking about the Year-2000 problem: feedback loops and time delays. They can be explained simply, and we'll use a non-computer metaphor to get the point across. Suppose you wake up tomorrow morning in a foul mood, and you happen to encounter your next-door neighbor as you leave home for the office. Having no one else to vent your bad feelings upon, you shout at this innocent soul, "You're the most pig-headed idiot of a neighbor I've ever known. I don't know how I got stuck living next door to you!"

What happens at that point? Probably nothing. Your neighbor is too stunned by the outburst to do or say anything. Both of you then get in your cars and drive off to work; having reached the office and having had a cup of coffee, you find yourself in a better mood and you forgot the entire episode.

Unfortunately, your neighbor also happens to be your spouse's supervisor—and he/she has *not* forgotten the insult. Six months later, when it comes time for your spouse's annual review, the neighbor/supervisor unexpectedly yells at your spouse, "You're the most pig-headed idiot of an employee I've ever seen in my entire career! I don't know how they hired you in the first place, and you're certainly not getting a raise this year!"

Stunned and shaken, your spouse stews about this all afternoon, becoming ever more frustrated and angry. You're not aware of this, of course, because you work in a different company; but when you get home from work that evening, you're flabbergasted when your spouse shouts at you, "You're the most pig-headed idiot of a spouse I could ever imagine! I don't know how I could have married you in the first place—I want a divorce!"

Obviously, this is a bit melodramatic, but you get the point. To paraphrase one of Newton's laws, every action has a reaction—but in situations like the one described above, it may not be an "equal and opposite reaction." And more importantly, the reaction isn't necessarily immediate, nor is it necessarily aimed back at the source of the original action. Your neighbor doesn't yell back at you when you insult him/her, and he/she doesn't take *any* immediate action.

If we were to pursue our metaphor a little further, we would encounter what the system dynamics experts call a *causal loop*, one version of which is known in popular terms as a "vicious circle." Because your spouse has asked for a divorce, you're in an unbelievably bad mood the next morning when you encounter your neighbor on the way to work; of course, it never occurs to you that the entire situation was caused by your insulting remark six months earlier. All you know is that you're in such a bad mood that you can't stand the sly, mischievous grin that your neighbor is aiming in your direction. Enraged, you punch your neighbor in the nose; and a week later, your neighbor retaliates by firing your spouse. Your spouse is both furious and frightened at the prospect of being unemployed, and thus decides to accelerate the divorce process, suing you for all your worldly possessions.

What's this got to do with the Year-2000 crisis? In a nutshell: The problems won't all occur at the stroke of midnight on December 31, 1999; and the problems won't consist of direct, "one-time-only" interactions between the "source" of the Year-2000 problem and the "victim" of the Year-2000 problem. In some cases, the consequences of the Year-2000 problem will be delayed by a week or a month or a year; and in some cases, the consequences will "ripple" from the source to victim A, who then causes problems for B, which creates larger problems for C, which then "feeds back" an even larger problem to the original source. Here are a few examples:

- Some of the problems will occur before January
  1, 2000 because of its anticipated effects. If you
  thought that there was a good chance your
  bank's ATM machines wouldn't work for the
  entire month of January 2000, you would probably withdraw a few hundred dollars of spare
  cash; you might even close your account and
  withdraw all of your money. What if all of the
  bank's customers did the same thing? Here's a
  better example: If you thought there was a good
  chance the IRS would shut down in January
  2000, would you bother making your estimated
  tax payments in the last quarter of 1999?

- Some of the problems will occur on January 31,
  2000, when computer systems generate invoices,
  statements, and other monthly reports for the
  month of January. Other problems will occur at
  the end of February, because a few computer systems will mistakenly decide that 2000 is *not* a leap
  year. Other problems will occur at the end of the
  first quarter, or at the end of the calendar year.

- Some of the problems will occur at random intervals during the first year or two after the rollover date because of subtle, insidious computer
  errors that corrupt the organization's database.
  Imagine, for example, a billing system associated
  with your credit card company: In January
  2000, it calculates the interest on your unpaid
  credit card balance, and because of a Year-2000
  bug, it does so incorrectly. As we illustrated in
  Appendix A, this might not only involve sending

you an outrageously high invoice, but it might also "clobber" another database record—e.g., the database record of another customer of the credit card company, Mr. Jones. Suppose Mr. Jones has no unpaid balance in December 1999 or in January 2000, but he buys a new television set in February, and has an unpaid balance in March. When the monthly billing system runs in March, it retrieves Mr. Jones' record, computes the interest payment, and sends him a statement. Even if the Year-2000 bug was fixed, it might not be evident that the *address* in Mr. Jones's record was clobbered. Thus, Mr. Jones' statement is sent to the wrong address, and a complete stranger throws the statement away after muttering about "those damn computers." After three months of non-payment and increasingly nasty warning letters sent to the wrong address, Mr. Jones' credit card is canceled.

• The feedback loops are potentially the most serious aspect of the Year-2000 problem because of the vast numbers of people that may be involved. If Mr. Jones has problems with his credit card, as in the example above, society won't notice or care. But suppose the credit card company has the same problem with a *million* of its customers; what happens then? It's reasonable to assume that a substantial percentage of those people will get on the phone (assuming it works) and call the toll-free customer service number. A few people may get through, and may receive a plau-

sible reassurance that everything will be fixed;
but, the majority won't. What happens to the
disgruntled customers who couldn't get
through? Chances are that a lot of them will cancel their credit card (before or after the credit
card company does the same thing!) and take
their business elsewhere (assuming they can find
another credit card company whose computers
work). Along the way, they tell all of their neighbors and friends to avoid their original credit
card company because of its lousy computer systems. Conclusion: The original card company
loses a substantial number of customers, and
thereby loses a substantial amount of revenue
(from the interest charges it would have collected), and could conceivably go bankrupt.

- If you want to think about some *serious* feedback
  loops, try these scenarios: The Social Security
  System (which, by the way, is further along in its
  Year-2000 conversion efforts than most other
  federal government agencies) fails to send out its
  monthly retirement checks to a few million retired citizens. And the state welfare agencies and
  unemployment agencies fail to send out their
  monthly welfare and unemployment checks. Or
  food stamps get lost because of a Year-2000
  computer bug. When electric power failed in the
  eastern U.S. for a couple days in 1977, riots
  broke out. What happens if the problems extend
  for a month? Or a year?

One of the reasons we're particularly concerned about all of this is because of the "triage" strategy discussed in Appendix A. In the case of a telephone company, for example, it's obviously critical to produce a dial tone when customers pick up the phone; and all of the other computer systems that effectuate a phone call from person A to person B are critical. Without these systems, there is effectively no phone company; and for what it's worth, the major telephone companies swear categorically that these systems *will be* Year-2000-compliant, if they're not already.

What about the telephone company's billing systems? Arguably, the phone company won't shut down if it can't generate bills on January 2; however, the volume of billing is so high that most phone companies have to distribute the billing for all of their customers across the entire month in order to finish an entire "cycle" by the end of the month. But let's assume, for the sake of argument, that all of the bills are generated on the last day of the month; and let's assume that a Year-2000 bug made it impossible for the phone company to generate those bills on January 31, 2000. Would the company declare bankruptcy on February 1? Not likely—but if the billing systems failed again in February and March, the company's cash flow situation would become rather precarious. So, the billing systems are extremely important, or "mission-critical," even if they don't cause a total collapse at the stroke of midnight on December 31, 1999.

What systems are *not* critical? Perhaps some of the *internal* systems used by the phone company to manage its affairs. Any large organization typically has dozens of internal management and reporting systems to keep track of what it's doing; these include scheduling, inventory, human resources, financial accounting systems, and on and on. All of these are typically considered "important," but in a severe emergency, the business could probably continue to function without them, at least for awhile.

Whether the phone system keeps track of its internal affairs may or may not be of interest to you; but what about the important-but-not-critical *external* systems? One possibility is the computer systems that generate all of the marketing and promotional literature that seems to be stuffed into every piece of junk mail that comes to your house. Think about this for a moment: You would probably be delighted if you didn't receive that kind of junk mail, but what about the advertising agencies, graphic artists, printers, paper supply companies and delivery organizations that carry out the marketing/promotional activities? Many of these are likely to be small organizations for whom the phone company is their largest (and perhaps *only*) customer. Thus, when the phone company casually announces, "We won't be sending out the usual 10 million pieces of junk mail per month in 2000 because it's one of the non-critical systems that we didn't have time to fix," the result could be that half a dozen small companies eke out an existence for a few months, but then go bankrupt.

While this particular example involving the phone company may or may not actually occur, we hope that you see the point: what one company deems a non-critical system may well turn out to be a *very* critical system to one of its suppliers, subcontractors, vendors, or customers. And the corollary point is that some of these company-to-company interactions are going to be terminated deliberately and consciously on January 1 (quite possibly without any advance warning) as a matter of expediency.

As we discussed in Appendix A, vintage-1997 estimates by software metrics experts indicate that roughly 15% of the computer systems in the U.S. will *not* be Year-2000-compliant by January 1, 2000. Some of those non-converted systems will be the "dead" or "dormant" ones that are of interest only to the most moribund of bureaucrats within the organization; but it's inevitable that there will be many non-converted systems that fall into the category of the phone company's marketing system discussed above. And this doesn't count the critical systems that didn't get converted because the organization simply ran out of time, or the critical systems that were *incorrectly* fixed (i.e., additional bugs were innocently and unconsciously injected into the systems as the programmers frantically tried to fix the Year-2000 problems), or those that were *incompletely* fixed (i.e., the programmers overlooked some subtle occurrences of date-related activities within some of the programs).

Bottom line: The interactions shown in Figure B.5 are virtually certain to receive a series of "jolts," ranging in size from moderate to massive. The initial series of jolts will occur on or about January 1, 2000, and there will be a series of aftershocks that last for at least a full year, if not longer. Though it's stretching a point, the situation could be compared to the meteor impact that occurred in the midst of the dinosaur age. Some scientists argue that within a matter of days, the entire earth was covered by a dense cloud of ash and dust that effectively blocked all sunlight for a period of time. Debates continue as to whether this was indeed the "jolt" that killed off the dinosaurs, either directly (through short-term loss of plant life) or indirectly (though long-term changes in the weather and climate), but one thing is indeed clear—it was sudden, massive, and pervasive.

Scientists don't really know, with absolute certainty, what happened when the meteorite hit, and whether it really killed off the dinosaurs. Similarly, we don't really know what the impact of the Year-2000 meteorite will be, nor can anyone else predict the outcome with certainty. The feedback loop, time delay, and ripple effect consequences of a pervasive series of Year-2000 jolts upon the complex socio-economic system shown in Figure B.5 is beyond anyone's ability to predict in a precise, mathematical fashion.

By the way, at least one species *did* survive the age of dinosaurs—the cockroach. Hopefully, we'll do better!

Endnotes

1. Actually, this depends heavily on the size of each person's circle of friends. If each person knows 40 other people, with no overlaps (e.g., you and I have no friends in common), then after six levels of communication, a total of 4,201,025,641 people will have received the same message.

2. See *The Limits to Growth* by Donella H. Meadows, Dennis L. Meadows, Jorgen Randers, and William W. Behrens III (1972).

3. Peter M. Senge, *The Fifth Discipline: The Art and Practice of the Learning Organization* (Doubleday, 1990).

Index